CW00525918

OUR VILLAGE ANCESTORS

OUR VILLAGE ANCESTORS

A Genealogist's Guide to Understanding the English Rural Past

Helen Osborn

ROBERT HALE

First published in 2021 by Robert Hale,
an imprint of
The Crowood Press Ltd,
Ramsbury, Marlborough,
Wiltshire SN8 2HR

enquiries@crowood.com

www.crowood.com

British Library Cataloguing-in-Publication Data
A catalogue record for this book is available from the British Library.

ISBN 978 0 7198 1416 7

Typeset by:
Catherine Williams, Chapter One Book Production

Cover design by:
Catherine Williams, Chapter One Book Production

Printed and bound in India by Parksons Graphics

Contents

1
The Rural Past

This book is aimed at those who have discovered a love for filling in the details about the lives of their ancestors as they build trees; even the novice family historian should be able to take something away from it, although it is not a 'how to' guide in starting genealogy research. There are many books and resources that show how to start researching a family tree, and it is expected that the reader will have already progressed beyond the stage of simple name gathering, and will be ready to discover increasing amounts of local and historical context and how to open up the records to gain the maximum from them.

The subject is a wide one: English village life from the middle of the sixteenth century up to the nineteenth century, viewed through the lens of documents that genealogists commonly use. This 400-year sweep of time resulted in the creation of almost all the local records we use to build the pedigree of a family, whether that family is rooted in landed gentry and the lords of the manor, or came from the ranks of the humble farm servant.

The period begins with the setting up of parish registers in England and Wales in 1538 during the reign of Tudor king Henry VIII, and ends with the nineteenth-century census and the administrative reforms that centralized administration and records, making them less useful at the local level. Along the way we will meet some of the most important records that give information for genealogical tree building and evidence of relationships, as well as illustrating how life was lived in the countryside, through the stories they tell.

Notwithstanding the blood kinship links that DNA investigations have brought to the study of genealogy, genealogists remain overwhelmingly reliant on written sources – and luckily there are a huge number of sources for England. From the Middle Ages onwards the growth in those sources allows an increasing amount of light to be shed on our ancestors' lives. As the centuries unfold, the documentary sources for both village history and family history simply within a rural parish multiply, and do not stop being of use until the late nineteenth and early twentieth centuries when the parish lost many of its administrative functions.

As well as the parish registers, there are other records of the parish, such as surveys and tithes, accounts and records of the poor law, and records of local charities. Outside the parish system there were the records of the manor, concerning themselves not only with tenancies and cultivation of land, but also with the misdemeanours of villagers.

This book doesn't describe all the possible records in which people can be found for the whole of a 400-year period, but tries to put some of the most common and usable local records into a useful context. The emphasis throughout is on thinking about geographic and historic context, and the records that are created and held locally.

I do not deal with records created by the Victorian national administrations, such as civil registration, which started in 1837, although we will meet the Victorian census because it gives us so much useful information about a place. Nor do I describe many records created at the local but wider levels of diocese or county, except where they are particularly important to showing how life was lived, such as with probate inventories and the records of quarter sessions. Many of these records are of equal importance to the history of towns and cities: they are certainly not all unique to the village.

The family historian who desires to get 'under the skin' of their ancestors and understand their way of life, as well as to interpret the records correctly, needs to switch their focus away from names and on to geographical places. In that respect, this book is an antidote to the myriad online data websites, which encourage quick searching for names. I am convinced that research into the people of a place – research that unfolds in a more leisurely fashion, allowing the family historian to truly understand both the records and the location – is ultimately the most rewarding.

The Importance of Place

The sixteenth century witnessed a huge rise in record creation, documentary sources and writing of all kinds useful to both the genealogist and the historian. It is possible to combine information from these sources so that pictures of even ordinary individuals can be built up. The survival of all these records varies a great deal from parish to parish and village to village, yet it is still true that most English parishes have extensive sets of records from the sixteenth century up to the present. Even if records from the nineteenth century appear different from the earlier types, they were still created for the same purpose: to deal with the same kinds of problem that a community needs to deal with day to day. The good news for the genealogist is that they record individuals, sometimes in detail.

The way we should approach these records and interpret them is the same, whether the local system varies from north to south or east to west, although it is necessary to keep a firm sense of place and to understand that the interpretation and practice of the law in one area might differ from another.

As I showed in my book *Genealogy: Essential Research Methods*, genealogists often need to analyse documents in a very exacting way. This gives us special needs, which differ from the needs of local historians, because genealogists are always concerned with small personal details and minutiae. Historians choose topics and themes, and thereby select which sources to study; however, genealogists do not get to choose their sources: they are forced to use all available sources to prove a pedigree. Questions about individuals appearing or not appearing in records are of vital importance to the genealogist, while the local historian is quite rightly more concerned with whole communities rather than single families or individuals.

Yet there is much cross-over between local history and genealogy, because in order to gather truly the evidence that we need to reconstruct families into genealogical trees, we should understand both the historical and local context as well as have a good understanding of the documents used. Thus, local history and family history come together over questions of place and community, and the melding of family history and local history is nowhere more apparent than when a locality has given rise to a particular surname.

As we get further involved with the history of our families, and in the wider context of surname history and the development of surnames, we find that many English surnames come from place names, some of them recognizable places today, others generic, still others so small or local as to be all but lost, others with subtle spelling changes: Attlee, Bainbridge, Bakewell, Eccleston, Greenwood, Heath are just a few examples from hundreds. Many of us still carry information about an original village, hamlet or farmstead around as our surname, like a long invisible thread tying us to a specific place.

The genealogist tends to look at his or her ancestors with backward glances, travelling in time backwards, starting in the crowded cities and moving backwards through parishes of lesser and lesser population, and sparser and sparser records. In a way it is the opposite of the traditional historian's view of the forward march of history, with expanding populations, new places created, and social progress. As the genealogist progresses backwards up the tree, the broader world increasingly gives way to the smaller and smaller place, even while at the same time the whole ancestral tree increases! We move from the base of a pyramid up to the tip.

Adding a deep sense of geographic place to the analysis of records, as is the practice of good genealogists, takes family history into a whole new realm. It is often slow research, with an emphasis on acquiring knowledge through a deep understanding of place and context, yet it is deeply satisfying as mysteries and problems are solved or at the very least made a whole lot clearer.

Life has never been straightforward. Laws may be enacted and records created, and administrations can be messy, and it helps us to untangle whether the community in which our ancestor appears was interpreting the law as it was written, or whether it was widely ignored. Local situations can be just as complex as individual relationships, so any local or family historian must be aware that while a broad-brush approach can start you off on a voyage of discovery, the true prize is likely to be in bringing to life the real, messy human situation.

It has become a cliché to talk about putting the flesh on the bones of the family-history skeleton, but even when all the facts about someone's life and family are discovered, the full story of the place your ancestors lived in, and the community that surrounded them, is often ignored. The distillation of my theme therefore is that whenever we genealogists research a person or family, we should really be thinking not just of the name or of the individual, but of the place. It is the place that adds the needed context: it is the cloth that clothes our ancestors, cut here by the wealth or poverty of the land, darted there by the climate, embroidered here by the local customs, and trimmed and seamed by local officialdom.

The English Village

So much has already been written about the English village that it almost consists of a genre in its own right. Local histories of specific villages are available in their hundreds; books specifically about records, such as John West's *Village Records*[1] and Peter Edwards *Rural Life*[2], have pointed out interesting trails for the local historian to follow. However, there has not been a great deal of work putting together the study of the local community with an analysis of local documents from a genealogical point of view, nor from the point of view of genealogical problem solving, with most books aimed at family historians simply being a description of different types of record. The late historian David Hey has trodden this path with his books on family history and his interest in the communities of Yorkshire and Derbyshire, particularly *Family History and Local History in England* (1987), *Journeys in Family History* (2003), and within his editorship of the very useful *Oxford Companion to Family and Local History* (1996 and 2008) – yet there is certainly room for more to be done in this area.

Almost everybody with English roots will have an ancestor who lived in a village; some of us have ancestors who lived, were married and died in the same village for generations. We often first pick up the trail of our ancestors through finding them in the census in the big cities, usually in the nineteenth century. We follow them backwards for only a few generations, and then find that the family's origins are in the countryside. The cities took in so much immigration during the nineteenth century, firstly and partly due to better transport links, the coming of industry and the factories, and the economic pull, the promise of a better life in town, but also due to the push of agricultural depression and land reforms. However, the transport and industry that drove so many to an urban life is a relatively recent phenomenon, and it is in the countryside where our collective history began.

If your own starting point has been the census, and the discovery that your nineteenth-century town-living ancestor was born in a country parish, then, other than the county and the parish name, this may be all you know. If you have a parish name, a very good piece of advice is to look up the parish, village or hamlet in a good nineteenth-century gazetteer such as Samuel Lewis, *A Topographical Dictionary*[3], to discover more. Lewis is available in a number of editions online, and also at some of the genealogical websites such as *Ancestry*. His entries will give you a brief description of that place at the date of publication. But however useful that may be, it won't even begin to really inform you about the sort of community your ancestor lived in.

The village and the parish are, of course, not necessarily the same thing. A parish often contains several villages, with hamlets and scattered farmsteads as well, or it might have just one main settlement. In the north of England, parishes can be very large, and then they may contain many different settlements, commonly known as townships, but of village size. Looking at a modern map may not prove very enlightening, although it is certainly better than not looking at any kind of map, and will at least enable you to have some idea of the topography and the main features, although many of them are likely to be modern.

As population has risen, and as industry has grown and maybe collapsed again, it has left a very different landscape from the one our ancestors knew. Nevertheless, in the absence of other information about a place, a modern map is a starting point. The Ordnance Survey Land Ranger series allows you to see individual plots and fields clearly, although it is better to get hold of a map from the Ordnance Survey County Series (1840s–1890s), which is drawn at a large scale. *See* the section on Starting Points for the Researcher at the end of this chapter for more information.

There is, or was, no such a thing as an average village over such a long period of time as 400 years over the whole of the country. Villages are all alike, up to a point, and then they diverge according to soil, to region, to local culture and historical happenstance. We all think we know what a village consists of. It sits in the mind's eye as a small, but not too small, settlement around an ancient church, a venerable public house or two, maybe a shop, sometimes a village green. Green fields and farms lie round about it, and it has its own distinct identity developed over hundreds of years.

I was born in a Hertfordshire village, went to the village school, and was christened and married in the parish church, so I can certainly claim acquaintance with what a village means to me personally, and I don't find it so very difficult to imagine the same place 100 years ago, or even 500 years ago. Un-tarmac the roads, shrink the field sizes, increase the woodland, of course lose just about all the houses, and put dozens of people to work in the fields, and there you have it.

Not everyone who lived in a village was working on the land. Apart from the farmers and their many labourers, village residents often included the parson or rector of the parish, some gentry folk in the bigger houses, shopkeepers, innkeepers or beer-house keepers. There were blacksmiths, wheelwrights, carpenters and other tradesmen as well, and waggoners and carriers too. Sometimes there were grander folk, with some villages being owned and part of large estates. There were people who took the crops from the farmers and turned them into food and drink, such as millers and brewers. And there may have been some industry: mining, quarrying and clothworking all took place largely in rural areas.

For our ancestors, the village was both a place in which to live and work, and a place to retire to, a place to be born in, marry in and die in, a place where everybody knew you, and you knew your place – but it was also a place to escape from.

Historical Background

Before we can jump in at our starting point of the English Reformation and the first parish registers, it is useful to survey the scene from even further back and discover some of the remnants of the culture of medieval life that were still very much clinging on in the mid-sixteenth century. Historians like to divide up the periods of time into nice neat packages, and the mid-sixteenth century is often referred to as being within the 'early modern period'.

This time-span takes in 400 years, roughly 1400 to 1800 – but even so, Tudor people with their odd customs and costumes, Henry VIII and England in the 1540s, seem very far from modern to the ordinary reader. It is 'early modern' to the historian because it is no longer medieval, and both state and country were changing. Indeed, the whole of Europe was changing. But to the non-historian it is certainly not 'modern'. In fact, it is almost as if we must learn about a totally different country, largely because the medieval world was still very much around.

To ensure the broadest possible overview we should travel even further back than 1400, to be sure of the full context for all the records we are going to use. There is such a history of continuity in rural English life that even if we start at the year 1000, there would still be even more ancient customs that we could discover underlying the history of the parish, the manor and affecting village life.

By the late Saxon and early medieval period, the village as a recognizable entity was starting to come into being. The word 'village' is derived from the word 'vill', but the two are rather different. The 'vill' of the Domesday Book in 1086 was a unit of land that did not have to include a settlement, or it could include several hamlets – whereas any village is a single settlement. The location of any village settlement was dependent on soil, on climate and on the availability of water, as well as population and the carrying capacity of the land.

It was also dependent on, and intertwined with, a feudal system of lordship, specific jurisdictions in the locality, and any local customs.[4] Three structures were at the heart of the early medieval village community: land ownership, social hierarchy and the Church. All three resonated down the ages and were still impacting on people throughout our much later period. First, land was paramount for feeding people, both rich and poor. Food was not imported as it is today, and it didn't even move very much from its own locality. The early village story is therefore one of self-sufficiency. The organization of land holdings (land being the purest representation of wealth) was of prime legal importance, both at the time of the Domesday Book in 1086 and into the future as generation succeeded generation.

Already established before the Norman invasion of 1066 was feudalism or service to the local lord. This service was bound up with land holding, farming and tenancies known as the 'manorial system', all of which continued to affect the lives of villagers (and indeed townsfolk) right into the nineteenth century, and even today can still have a residual effect on land and property ownership. We meet some of the records created by the manorial system in Chapter 3.

Ownership of land changed slowly over our period. In general, large landowners such as the Church or the aristocracy tended to remain large landowners. In some areas land became ever more concentrated in a small group of hands. However, what mattered to our rural ancestors, over and above whether they were part of a huge estate or not, and what enables us to trace them, are the dealings they had with their landlord and their communities through the manorial courts.

Local customs sometimes had extremely ancient roots, often pre-Norman, and are important because they can affect inheritance in ways that are strange to modern people. We tend to think that the system of the eldest son getting the property was fixed and immutable, but it was dependent on local custom. These inheritance customs can extend a very long way back in time – to the Saxons, or the Angles for example. Customs were written down in manorial records, which therefore provide the local historian with a wealth of information about differences between manors and localities.

These differences extended to dialect and language. It can be worthwhile considering the very oldest history of any area: customs and language that developed in the north and east under the Vikings or Norse invaders differ very much from those of the southern counties, which differ in turn from those of the West Country.

Yet while many places were slow to change, change did, of course, happen. Rural life was disrupted by changes in agricultural practice, by the growth and then decline of the wool trade, by new laws enacted by parliament, by the coming of the industrial age, by the growth of transport systems across the country, particularly the coming of the railways in the first half of the nineteenth century, and by changes in society itself as Britain grew an empire and forged trade links abroad. Some villages grew and prospered, others were poorer, and differences in location as well as landlords played a vital part in differing fortunes.

The locality of a person's birth, as well as their status and circumstances, must have affected them for the remainder of their lives. Many of them stayed put in the same region or area, if not the same parish. About one in ten migrated to London, but there isn't thought to have been much trans-regional movement, except where the pull of new industries in the eighteenth and nineteenth centuries sucked in people from far and wide. Anyone who did move a long way out of their own area would be marked out as a stranger by their accent, even their choice of words, and would no doubt have been made to feel like a fish out of water, unless of course they were within a migrant community of other folk like themselves.

Twentieth-century historians argued that it was the Tudors who 'united' the country. They brought Welsh blood into England and forged a sense of identity and community. Yet they weren't quite like us. There were no Scots or Irish in any numbers in Tudor England, and even the gentry and aristocrats were largely homogeneous. The Tudor period was a time when people, particularly in rural areas, were ultimately descended from the local tribes, even if they could not trace their ancestry back there using documents.

Things began to get more mixed during the seventeenth century, as the Scottish, who moved south under the further uniting force of James I of England and VI of Scotland in 1603, added their genetic heritage. The sixteenth century also saw increasing immigration from the continent, but if you were living in Tudor England in a village, then your blood undoubtedly went back for hundreds of years into a purely indigenous population. What this means is that any provincial characteristics must have been very much more marked than they are today. A thick accent might be almost impenetrable anywhere except on its own territory, and dialects were commonly used, being a hangover from the very earliest settlements.[5]

Genetic research may yet overturn this view, or at least allow it to become more nuanced; however, for our purposes we need to recognize that the individual ancestor might be taken out of the community and studied in isolation, but ultimately we can't remove the community from the individual. People in the past carried their original communities with them in a way that simply does not happen today.

Population and Economic Growth

At the time when parish registers started in the mid-sixteenth century there are estimated to have been about 2.8 million people in England, a severe decline on the numbers before the Black Death 200 years earlier. Of these 2.8 million, only around 25 per cent, or 750,000, lived in the cities and towns. England was very sparsely populated compared to today. More or less everybody, even those in the towns and cities, lived very close to the countryside, within a short walk away. Vast tracts of countryside might be traversed without perhaps meeting anyone, and many marshy areas of the landscape were undrained and essentially wild, such as most of the fens, the Somerset levels and other marshlands.

Between 1541 and 1801, the population of England grew from 2.8 million to 8.6 million, with rapid growth between 1560 and the 1650s. Decline in the second half of the seventeenth century was followed once again by growth in the early eighteenth century, and then by more rapid growth from the 1740s onwards. By 1781, the population was 7.2 million, and then very rapid growth saw rises in the nineteenth century from 8.6 million in 1801 to 21.5 million by 1871.[6]

The implication of this for the genealogist is that most of us will have family trees that explode with collateral lines in the eighteenth and nineteenth centuries, but once we get back into the seventeenth century and further back, the brothers and sisters of our direct ancestors are much less likely to have survived. Our direct ancestors were the survivors: we are all descended from the strongest or the luckiest. Nevertheless, the high death rates mean that burial registers can be very useful for pinpointing any family within a parish.

Up until the nineteenth century the majority of people lived a rural existence. However, by 1801 one-third of England's population was already urban. But all was soon to alter dramatically, as the pace of change in both population growth and migration to towns and cities accelerated throughout the nineteenth century. By 1851 a majority of English people lived in towns and cities.

Right at the end of our period, the countryside was depopulated of the agricultural labourer. Between 1850 and 1914, an agricultural workforce of just over 1 million collapsed to just 225,000, as child labourers were brought out of the workforce, and people migrated to urban areas. Machinery and changes in agricultural practice of course helped push this vast migration along, just as much as rising employment opportunities in towns and cities pulled people in. The population in England in 1901 was 30.8 million.

Our whole period is thus a time of increasing population, at first slowly and sporadically and with great differences according to area, but then with increasing pace. Eventually, towns and cities grew so fast that whole villages were swallowed within them.

The implication of all this expansion should be self-evident. As research proceeds backwards in time there are simply fewer people to find. If we were able to find all our possible Tudor ancestors – perhaps our tenth through to our thirteenth great-grandparents – then some of them would be related to others of them with many cross linkages, leaving us with fewer actual ancestors than we would have in theory. This is called pedigree collapse. From a numbers point of view it makes it easier to reconstruct families further back into the past as there are fewer of them to search for; however, the records also get sparser around the same time to frustrate us.

Family size varies, too. Greater numbers of death due to disease meant Tudor families were smaller than might be imagined since so many babies died soon after birth. Property could therefore become concentrated in only a few hands. As population rose, and particularly if a place and family were generally healthy, in the eighteenth century more members of a family might be surviving, thus in turn leaving many more descendants. However, this also allowed some people born into previously comfortably off families to fall down the social scale.

In his wonderful study of Kibworth in Leicestershire, Michael Wood found that soon after the Black Death in the mid-fourteenth century people were marrying later than previously as well as having fewer children. This tended to mean that family property became concentrated in just one branch of a family. The consequence of this was that by the time of the sixteenth century, there was a marked change between the extended families of peasants in the village of the Middle Ages, to just one nuclear family branch, as people had died and families had split and migrated.[7] This development obviously has implications for any genealogist who is researching in the sixteenth century. It is a pattern that is familiar to me from various families researched in the seventeenth century as well.

Historians believe that agrarian reforms helped the rising population feed themselves, as new land was reclaimed from waste, marsh drained and so on during this period. The Tudor period was characterized by a young population, with about a third of the population under fifteen in 1541. An expanding population led to price rises and the expansion of existing villages, rather than new villages being founded. With this sixteenth- and seventeenth-century expansion came a great rebuilding in England, as newly prosperous villagers built bigger houses. This was the time that the stone houses of the Cotswolds and the timber-framed houses in southern counties – such as Sussex, Essex, but also Warwickshire and Cheshire – were erected. Many stone farm-houses in the Yorkshire Dales and other northern areas also date from the seventeenth century.

In the sixteenth and seventeenth centuries there was also a fashion for the wealthier to erect family monuments and tombs in the parish church; this was coupled with an interest in genealogy and heraldry among the newly emerging middle and professional classes[8], and is extremely helpful for the family historian who is descended from such families. Many of the most interesting records used to trace the history of a family also come from this period of expansion; for example, probate inventories from the sixteenth and seventeenth centuries, and surviving parish registers, are relatively complete as compared with the eighteenth century.

Among other changes, in areas that grew arable crops there was a trend over time for farms to get larger, and to employ wage-earning labourers from outside the family or immediate circle of neighbours. Aside from the men working on the land, some of these workers were women who worked in the dairies, at brewing and in domestic service. A newly prosperous merchant class also needed domestic servants, and adolescent girls and boys who moved from home into the local towns and to the bigger farms became part of everyday life. It is thought that labourers and servants added together made up the biggest section of early modern English society, making up to 60 per cent of the population.[9]

The Church and the Parish

The Christian church, one of the three great pillars at the heart of medieval society and village life, was already well established in England at the time of the Norman Conquest in 1066. The church kept its power over, and its effect upon, the village and parish right through the medieval period and into the early modern period. While the Crown and the landholder had relaxed some of their grip, in the 1540s the church was still the predominant force in any villager's life. No one of modest means could escape, as the church acted not only as the registrar of births and deaths, and as the local administrator, but also as moral judge and jury.

The church and monasteries were also large landowners; individual monasteries prior to the Reformation farmed large estates of land. However, at the start of our period the church had only recently become the Church of England, a reformed church with an English bible and English services, not Latin ones, and churches were newly deprived of painted decorations and carved rood screens and the colourful gaiety of the medieval world.

The monasteries may have been swept away and their land redistributed, much of it ending up in private hands, but the old intertwined Christian and folkloric or superstitious belief system was far too strong to disappear, although it was more pervasive at the start of our period than at the end. Far from being swept away, the influence of some of the older systems held on: for example, church courts, originally created in 1072, were still very much there to judge both clergy and the layperson, as well as to administer probate after death. Throughout the medieval period the church had been enlarging its role and jurisdiction so that by 1540, a large amount of law was covered by the church court as the church sought to have jurisdiction over moral behaviour.

For the average villager who had no goods to leave and did not transgress, it was the parish priest himself who was all-important. Genealogists and local historians need to know not only about the parish registers that record people – they also need to know the way the parish priest was supported by a community. Priests' income did not come directly from the church as in a modern salary, but from special plots of land granted to them, known as glebe lands, from offerings from the congregation, and from tithes. The parish and the tithe were closely interlinked, and have, of course, created a large number of records.

Parish registers were not the only documents created by the parish, and the village researcher will want to study more or less all records that survive. These records tend to be known as 'parish chest records', because they were originally kept in a big wooden chest in the church. The parish was the local administration, much like a local council. It was concerned with supporting the poor, supporting the priest, keeping out beggars, the upkeep of roads and perhaps waterways, as well as maintaining the fabric of the church. This was all done against a background of the overall authority of the local bishop, who periodically sent out visitations around the diocese to check on things, mainly record keeping. Each parish had to send a representative to these visitations with copies of documents.

As the centuries rolled by, the Crown spotted various opportunities to raise money, by taxing entries in registers, or supporting the woollen industry by decreeing that all burial shrouds be made of wool. This created a pattern of ecclesiastical records, with additional records created for civil purposes. It is possible to see this as state interference in local matters. At the start of our period, back in 1538, the balance was tipped more towards the ecclesiastical authorities, but by the end of the nineteenth century their powers had declined by a very large extent, and civil matters had more prominence.

The Great Poor Law Act of 1601 is probably the real start of what became known as the civil parish, as opposed to the ecclesiastical parish. This Act, and its many further amendments, needed the creation of a number of new records, ostensibly concerned with accounting, but which provide wonderful material for genealogists. They include records of apprenticeship, settlement papers, and removal orders and payments to the poor.

How to deal with the poor and those who could not work, and their strain upon parish resources, is a constant theme in both rural and urban areas throughout our period. Records from the parish that provide evidence as to measures taken to support the deserving, or to inhibit those likely to become a burden on a local community, are extremely useful to the family historian. Many families are recorded in such records, and they often provide the best evidence of migration from place to place, and evidence of relationships for the very poorest, who are not so well recorded in other records. Generally people were supported by their villages and parishes, and tales of outright starvation did not happen as much as might be imagined, although they did occur – we meet a notorious case later on in Chapter 5.

The civil authorities therefore started interfering in local administration, which had hitherto been left up to the church. In a sense it can be said that the civil authorities – that is, the government of the day – were using the parish as an instrument by which to rule and organize. The parish was given a large range of responsibilities, and ended up touching on almost every aspect of everyday life. It had to collect local rates, and was also used to gather up any national taxes. The parish constable was meant to report to the local quarter-sessions courts on a variety of public nuisances. This work of the parish provides a parallel to the manor, which is discussed in Chapter 3.

The church had its own concerns. Any parish was not just an area of pastoral care, but also a self-supporting area that had to provide for its priest and the maintenance of the church buildings. Thus there is an emphasis in parish records on amounts paid for this support, and the boundaries of the area. The payment of tithes was a part of this – namely, who paid what, and the local customs surrounding these payments.

Boundaries and Administrations

For the genealogist, boundaries, jurisdictions and administrations loom large because they tend to dictate where the records we seek were created and end up. For example, our family history societies are organized by county, and so are many of our local records. However, for our ancestors it may have been irrelevant whether they were in Hertfordshire or Bedfordshire, or whether they lived in Kent and came to market in Sussex: what was important for them were physical barriers to travel, such as hills and rivers, the state of the roads, whether they could travel by boat – in other words, the utter practicality of moving around.

The parish, too, may not always be the best way to understand a local area. The parish did create and hold a number of useful records for genealogists, which is why we tend to emphasize it over all else; however, in many places the researcher is going to be just as interested in the manor, the township, or perhaps the tithing.

Tithings originated in Anglo Saxon England as ten householders who acted as a group responsible for keeping law and order and for collecting payments. The tithing answered to the hundred, which had its own court. During the medieval period, the tithing lasted in southern England as a peace-keeping force. It was headed by the tithing man, or 'headborough', who was equivalent to the constable of the township. The tithing and the township became the basic small districts for the keeping of law and order. The township, strictly speaking, was defined as having its own constable, but the word 'town' is misleading, as townships could be very small hamlets. In northern England overseers of the poor were appointed at this level.

In the North, a quarter is the name for an administrative area that is a division of a parish just for the collection of rates. Other divisions, which may or may not be important to your research, are the hundreds, known as 'rapes' in Sussex, 'lathes' in Kent, 'wapentakes' in Danelaw counties, 'wards' in the north-west and 'leets' in East Anglia. These are ancient divisions of shires, consisting of a group of parishes.

In some southern and eastern counties of England parishes were very small, and it was possible to reach a dozen other parishes within an hour's walk from one village. In northern counties, parishes were very large indeed, and townships may or may not have had their own chapel. Whether the villagers could physically attend a service or bring a child to be baptised might depend on floods or snowfall and other natural barriers. In large parishes, chapels of ease were set up to serve a more local population. In some cases they had the right to baptise and bury, and more occasionally to marry, those who lived in their bounds. Thus in a parish with both parochial records and chapelry records, it always makes sense to look for both.

Rural market networks were also extremely important. In an age without shops, being able to hold a market was of vital importance for a community. Towns that were positioned on boundaries between different farming regions could encourage trade between two regions, and attract people from both. Links for trade crossed boundaries, and this means that the researcher often needs to spend time studying a whole region in order to work out where a migrant ancestor might have come from.

Starting Points for the Researcher

There are some well-established and invaluable guides, or jumping-off points, to help you discover more about historical geographic context in England. I have already mentioned Samuel Lewis and his series of topographical dictionaries of England, first published in 1831 before county and parish boundary changes. The second and greatest in its ambition is the *Victoria County Histories* series; and third is historical mapping. If you use all these together, you will be able to locate places and to understand something about their administration and boundaries, and their relationship to their locality.

It is also useful to know who the big landowners were, what crops were grown in the region, where the rivers were, and find the nearest market town. Any printed or online history of a village, or history of its church, can also provide a starting point. Armed with the basic background knowledge that all of this brings, some preliminary searches of the local archives catalogue can then be started.

The *Victoria County History* was originally founded in 1899, and is a long run of printed volumes organized by county; although sadly incomplete, its aim is to provide each county with its history. Where they exist, volumes can give detailed information about manors, parishes, towns, boroughs and other settlements to provide essential background reference. Often the local landowners will be mentioned by name, and sometimes memorial inscriptions in the local church are listed.

The project is organized by the Institute of Historical Research at the University of London, and is still ongoing, with the modern volumes usually the most useful. Major libraries and the local county record office should have the volumes for their county, and a full set is held at The National Archives on the open shelves on the second-floor reading room. They have an online presence at http://www.victoriacountyhistory.ac.uk/ and the volumes can also be searched online at British History Online (http://www.british-history.ac.uk).

Samuel Lewis was the publisher and editor of topographical dictionaries of England, Wales, Scotland and Ireland, with the aim of providing a description of every place. *A Topographical Dictionary of England* lists every place in alphabetical order, showing exactly where a particular settlement, village, parish or place was located in relation to the nearest town or towns; this includes any relevant barony, hundred, county or province, the saint's dedication of the church, the Poor Law union, and the tithes and living of the church. The 7th edition (1848) of Lewis's dictionary can be found online at British History Online (http://www.british-history.ac.uk/) where it can be searched and read for free.

Three different and contrasting entries from Lewis are given here as examples, from Kent, Hertfordshire and North Yorkshire:

> BREDHURST (St. Peter), a parish, in the union of Hollingbourn, hundred of Eyhorne, lathe of Aylesford, W. division of Kent, 5 miles (S.S.E.) from Chatham; containing 131 inhabitants. It comprises 600 acres, of which 274 are in wood. The ancient village is said to have stood at a short distance, near a wood, where several wells are still visible. The living is a perpetual curacy, in the patronage of the Rector of Hollingbourn,

and endowed with the tithes, which have been commuted for £130: there are 9 acres of glebe. The church is a small edifice, consisting only of one aisle and a chancel, with a tower surmounted by a low spire: adjoining it is a small ruinous chapel in the early English style, formerly the burial-place of the family of Kemsley. There is a small dissenters' place of worship.[10]

DATCHWORTH (*All Saints*), a parish, in the hundred of Broadwater, union and county of Hertford, 2½ miles (N.E. by E.) from Welwyn; containing 581 inhabitants. It is situated on the great road from London to York, and comprises 1922*a.* 3*r.* 35*p.*, of which 1491 acres are arable, 230 pasture, 97 woodland, and 60 common or waste; the soil is chiefly gravel, in some parts alternated with clay. The living is a rectory, valued in the king's books at £14. 13. 4., and in the patronage of Clare Hall, Cambridge: the tithes have been commuted for £475, and the glebe comprises nearly 24 acres, with a glebe-house. The church has been enlarged by the addition of 150 free sittings.[11]

ABBOT-SIDE, HIGH, a township, in the parish of Aysgarth, wapentake of Hang-West, N. riding of York, 1¼ mile (N.W. by W.) from Hawes; containing, with the chapelries of Hardraw and Helbeck-Lunds, and the hamlets of Cotterdale, Fosdale, Litherskew, Sedbusk, Shaw, and Simonstone, 574 inhabitants. The two townships of Abbot-Side received their names from the monks of Jervaulx Abbey, who had considerable property in the district. This township, which comprises by computation 13,000 acres, is altogether wild and mountainous, and consists of moors, dales, and ravines; it is rich in springs, waterfalls, rocks, and caves, and a variety of interesting natural curiosities. The magnificent cataract Hardraw Scarr, 102 feet in height, with its stupendous rocks and romantic caverns, and the elevation of Shunner Fell, 2329 feet above the level of the sea, and commanding views of several counties, are both situated in the township. The River Ure, on which are several beautiful waterfalls, rises at the head of the valley. A rent charge of £163 has been awarded to Trinity College, Cambridge, in lieu of the appropriate tithes.[12]

I have chosen these three entries for a purpose, firstly because they show us how widely any village or settlement can differ, and how different administrations have played a part in the language used. Thus for Hertfordshire, a hundred is used, for Yorkshire, a wapentake, for Kent a lathe. These areas of land are very ancient. The unit of land called 'a hundred' existed until relatively recently, and certainly for all the period that is discussed here. It was originally an area consisting of one hundred 'hides', but more latterly is a collection of parishes used for administrative purposes, such as tax collection. The hide was the amount of land, depending on soil, that a team of eight oxen could plough in one year: around 120 acres.

The two southern entries refer to villages that are also parishes, one very small, while Abbotside is a township. Abbotside is within the much larger parish of Aysgarth, and contains several little hamlets strung out along the hillside above Wensleydale. Both Abbotside and Datchworth are connected to Cambridge colleges, Clare Hall and Trinity respectively, thus demonstrating how widespread the landholdings of the early universities could be.

In addition to using the above resources, the researcher should always arm themselves with plenty of maps; a modern one is useful, but the first and second series Ordnance Survey are invaluable. The first series for all the counties in England and Wales was published from 1842 at 6in to the mile, although the second series, starting in 1854, gives greater detail, being mapped at 1:2500 and known as the 25in maps. The National Library of Scotland now allows online access to the full range of Ordnance Survey maps, including for England. Those most commonly found online are from the 6in to the mile, but if you can get hold of the sheet from the 25in series for a place you are interested in, then that is to be preferred because of the amount of detail shown, even down to individual trees.

Once you have located some good large-scale maps, learned something of the local history and found an entry in Lewis and/or the *Victoria County History*, you will be properly equipped for some serious study of the records via the relevant archives catalogues.

2

Parish and Family

Parish Registers in Context

We start our journey into the records with a birth. It is Sunday 1 December in the year of our Lord, 1577. Queen Elizabeth has been on the throne for nineteen years, and in less than two weeks' time Francis Drake will set out from Plymouth, with 164 men and five ships, on a mission to raid Spanish holdings on the Pacific coasts, which three years later ends as a circumnavigation of the globe.

Meanwhile, far from any matters of state and world-wide exploration, rural life in England continues much as it has for centuries. In the village of Bredhurst in north-west Kent, a new little soul is brought to the font for baptism at the parish church of St Peter's. This tiny place, high on the North Downs, is in the middle of a sparsely populated area in a triangle of land between Chatham, Sittingbourne and Maidstone. The village and parish consist of only 602 acres, heavily wooded with poor soil. There were just seventy adults in 1640, so numbers in 1577 were probably less. The topographer of Kent, Edward Hasted wrote in 1798:

> The parish is surrounded by an extensive range of woods, in it and the different adjoining parishes, the north-east part of this parish being almost covered with them. It is situated in so unfrequented a part of this county, that it is hardly known to any one, it lies mostly on high ground, and very cold and bleak. The hills here are very frequent and steep, the lands very poor and hungry, and the flint stones very numerous. The village is built round a green, with the church at a small distance eastward from it.[13]

Thomas Berd, the son of Richard and Agnes, our Elizabethan newborn, is brought to be baptised a few days after birth, as was the normal custom. It would be most terrible if a child were to die unbaptised, and unreceived by the church, so every effort was made to get babies baptised as soon as possible. In effect, the church expected and required that children would be baptised within the first seven days of life, and this continued until 1650 when it was lengthened to fourteen days.

The Elizabethan villagers of England in general, and Bredhurst in particular, are very much ruled by both religion and superstition, as well as the farming year and the customs of their time and place. Many of them started life as Catholics, and the oldest saw the destruction and turmoil of the Reformation, but nineteen years into Elizabeth's reign there is now more stability in religious matters, and the Protestants are firmly in control. It would be years yet before the old Catholic loyalties would totally fade, and some people did still cling to the earlier faith, albeit in secret for fear of persecution. The more remote areas of country were the most resistant to change.

Many children of this period died in their first year, but once baptised they could enter the Kingdom of Heaven. How much comfort this knowledge of heaven was to those who lost their children is hard to know. By 1577, Thomas's parents had been married for some time and had already lost several children. It is possible that Thomas's mother would not have attended the baptism.

Women who had recently given birth had a period of time before they were 'churched' – a form of purification when they were brought into church again about a month after the baby was born. Churching as purification was abandoned theologically in 1552, but in practice, a period when a woman who had just given birth was taken away from society remained a part of local life. Her husband was supposed to spend the month after the birth of a child attending to his wife's normal domestic duties, this being known as the 'gander month'.[14] Churching as a welcoming ceremony into the church was still performed in some parishes up to the eighteenth century, with some keeping records of fees for this.

Childbirth itself, although dangerous, was attended entirely by women. The local midwife may have had some social standing, and the church issued midwives' licences so they could privately baptise a child if it were in imminent danger of death. Later on, in the eighteenth century, it became fashionable for children to be baptised privately, in which case you may come across a P for 'Private' in the church baptism register against a child's name.

Chrisome children were technically those buried before their mother had been churched, the chrisome being a white linen cloth that was laid on the child and worn after baptism until the mother was churched. A child that died beforehand was buried in this cloth. However, it is not uncommon to come across mentions of chrisome children well into the eighteenth century, and the use of a special cloth continued. It would also seem that chrisome was used as a term for 'unbaptised'.

Forty years earlier, before Thomas's parents were born, on 5 September 1538, Thomas Cromwell issued a mandate that all the parishes in England would from then on have to keep an official register of the christenings, marriages and burials in their parish with the names of the relevant people. The parish also had to provide a coffer or chest in which to keep the registers, and this had two locks: the parson or vicar had the keys to one lock, and the churchwardens had the keys to the second lock. Cromwell was taking no chances.

Although there was much suspicion at first that such records would be the prelude to some kind of taxation, it was also increasingly apparent that more often people needed to prove their age, or their parentage. England was not unique in this. A similar system had been in force in Spain since 1497, and had spread to the rest of Western Europe. Some priests had actually kept records before 1538 in England, but it was by no means widespread. Cromwell's order referred to the parish priest having to write up every baptism, burial or marriage in the presence of the wardens, or one of them, every Sunday. Thus began the single most useful genealogical source that we have.

The keen genealogist immediately spots a potential problem: what if the memory of the priest is deficient, or the churchwardens are lax, or what if the rule is not kept to? It is obvious that the system was not rigorously adhered to in its early years, as several subsequent orders had to be made; the priests were writing events on scraps of paper and then transcribing those into registers, or keeping their records in a variety of not very satisfactory ways. Eventually a further order of 1598 under Elizabeth I required that these scraps and paper books be copied on to parchment in order that the records be better preserved.

Bredhurst, like many other parishes, was a little slow to get this 1538 innovation implemented, and the very first register book, made up of all the baptisms, marriages and burials occurring in the parish, appears to have been started in 1545. By the time of Thomas Berd's birth in 1577, the recording process for the vicar would have been familiar: each Sunday after service, he settles down to write up all the events of the past week into a register. He writes in Latin, which is still the language of the law and the church.

Unfortunately we don't know the name of the vicar of Bredhurst at this time, and there are very few entries in the registers in the 1570s. Nevertheless, Thomas Berd *is* duly recorded as having been brought into the church. If he lives longer than a year or so, his chance of survival into adulthood is high, and before he dies, he is likely to be recorded a few more times in the registers of Bredhurst, or the neighbouring parishes, and perhaps also in a scant few other documents. But in contrast to a modern baby, his life in the main will go unrecorded. No photographs, no school registers, no census, no street directories will capture him. Even his grave marker, if there ever was one, after a short period of time will no longer exist, so the small amount of written words in the parish records are all that survives of him, and of millions of others like him. The information on the parish register is very spare: just the date, the child's name and his father's name. Nothing more was necessary.

> Primo die decembris baptizat[us] fuit Tho: Berd filius Richardus Berde.[15]

Spelling at this date was not fixed as it is now, and a name could be spelled in many different ways within the same document. It is known that Shakespeare himself used several different spellings for his own name, and in any official document, the clerk or parish priest would not necessarily be consistent either.

The spelling of surnames gives the genealogist many headaches. The trouble is that before universal education, and at a time when spelling was very fluid even among the educated, the genealogist needs to keep an open mind about spelling and not dismiss families as being unrelated due to spelling of the name. Berd/e is a slightly more uncommon spelling of the more modern Bird. Byrd and Byrde are also found in Kent parish registers at this date, so the name was a local one, yet with variations on spelling depending on the parish priest or churchwarden's choice, and probably the place as well.

Most of the early parish registers in England are in Latin, because Latin was still the language of both the church and the law. The villager standing in the parish church each Sunday during the reign of Elizabeth heard the lessons in English, but the documents that recorded him and his family were all in Latin – and might as well have been in Martian. This point probably needs emphasizing. All the written records concerning him, his family, any court cases that he might be involved in, the manorial court – all of this was in a foreign language. How alienating this must have been, and how much reliance had to be placed on the priest, or a clerk of the court, unless one was lucky enough to have a scholar in the family who could read a little Latin.

Furthermore the clergy at this time were of mixed ability, some not very educated, others very well educated. It would not be surprising to find that the most erudite of them were able to secure the best livings in the richest parishes, and that the smaller benefices would end up with the least literate and educated.

This original Bredhurst register book has been lost or destroyed along with almost all the original English parish register books of baptism, marriage and burial following Elizabeth's decree in 1598 that all records were to be recorded on parchment. Because the decree said that all existing entries should be copied on to the parchment, not only from the beginning of the paper registers, but particularly from the start of her majesty's reign in 1558, it is thought that all surviving early parish registers from that date are the 1598 copies of the older entries.[16]

For the family historian this means that even if something has been re-copied into the 1598 register, almost certainly any notes or extra information about the family was discarded by the priest or clerk who had to copy everything out. Parchment has very good keeping qualities because it is made from animal skin, normally sheepskin, goatskin or, most expensively, calfskin. It is tough and can take some rough handling.

The structure of rural parish registers is very consistent from 1598 up to the mid-eighteenth century. Most rural parish priests had one register into which was written all the baptisms, marriages and burials. These are known as 'composite' registers, and combine christenings, marriages and burials in varying degrees of order; sometimes all events in a year are displayed on one page, more often a range of christenings is followed by a range of marriages, and then a range of burials, then the book will dart back to christenings or marriages, depending on whether enough space has been left in the register. Sometimes the order is very erratic, and the researcher must take great care with navigation and the recording of results. It is also a very good idea to check all pages to make sure that no entries have been inserted completely out of order, or that baptisms are not in the burials section, and vice versa.

In 1754, the books change and marriages are found in separate volumes, with a printed format for the entries. Baptisms and burials remained in a combined volume until 1813, when separate volumes for each event start to be used, and the use of printed forms to record information became proscribed. After 1813 the research process thus becomes easier, although there could still be problems of poor record-keeping and gaps in the records.

Thomas Berd's entry is in the 1598 parchment register, on the front of which it says in English:

> A Register booke of all the chryseneinges weddeinges and burialles whiche have ben in the parish of bredhurste in the countye of kente from the yeare of our Lorde one thousande fyve hundredth fortie and fyve as followeth made and copied and written out the Tenth daye of October Anno domini millesimo quinguentissimo nonaguessimo octavo 1598

Will our little Thomas make it through the next few years? The burial part of the Bredhurst register notes a number of Berd children being buried, starting with an elder sister Joanna in 1567 – and then in 1583, the burial of Agatha Berd, wife of Richard, is recorded – but Thomas himself is not there. It seems, therefore, that Thomas is motherless at six years old. His situation is all too common in an age when many children did not see their first birthday, and parents often died in their thirties. The death of a parent often meant that families were split, and could be the trigger for older children to leave the household, and for many of the younger ones to be brought up by step-parents. Where possible, people tended to remarry quite quickly because children needed looking after, and widows needed the income from a husband.

Historians are now clear that most English families in the sixteenth and later centuries were small and nuclear, consisting of just mother and father and children, or mother and stepfather, father and stepmother, depending on the circumstances. The extended family, all living together, did not exist in England. Although many children were born, many also died, so it would not be uncommon for a couple to have only two surviving out of six or seven births. This very high death rate accounts for the slow growth in population at this time, even though most couples had multiple births.

Just as the parish registers and the events being recorded within them were familiar to the villagers and parishioners of the time, so these, the first set of locally created and locally held records, tend to be the first local records the family historian becomes familiar with. We are familiar with the church being in charge of baptisms, marriages and burials, and the process seems a simple step away from the more modern civil registration process, whereby exact dates and more details of people are now recorded. It is therefore easy to see them like a mirror on a familiar society, when in fact things were very different to the modern world.

The family historian's first journey into parish registers tends to be in the nineteenth and eighteenth centuries, when we are still on the overall hunt just for names and have not started to build a detailed knowledge of place. It is easy to miss the little nuances that can made such a difference to successful searching – whether or not a church has any chapelries, how far a family might have had to travel to church, the idiosyncracy of individual registers.

In some cases, these records of baptisms, marriages and burials recorded by the minister and the churchwardens have been kept more or less continuously since 1538, although it is more common for registers to start in the seventeenth century, and many of them have gaps and missing register books. The researcher often has to do some detailed detective work into precisely what survives, so that any gaps in the records can be taken into account.

Parish registers are of prime importance to the genealogist for the evidence they give as to parentage and identity. For hundreds of families, as with the Berds in the 1570s and 1580s, there may be no other way of reconstructing the family if there are no probate documents, or land transfers. No other records will allow information about a whole family to be put together. Parish registers are also one of the easiest sets of records to find and to understand, and are very much the meat and bread of the English genealogist, as well as being the basis of many a regional population study.

Much has been written about how to find the parish register for any particular parish, as well as how to use them in genealogical research. Open any genealogy magazine and information about parish registers will be there. They have also been extensively used by historical demographers and historians in their attempts to answer questions about population changes over the centuries, and were used by the 'Annales' School of History in their then pioneering work on whole family reconstruction.

Population studies might appear to be quite a dry, quantitative subject of little interest to the genealogist. However, the work that has been done in this field can be of great interest to us, telling as it does of the rise and fall of birth or death rates, and giving us useful information about age at marriage, and the likely gaps between birth and baptism – all questions of which can shed light on a family. Was the family 'normal' for this area at this time? If all infants were baptised within two weeks of birth, and I cannot find a baptism within that two-week period, should I look further? What might any atypical events tell us?

One of the most comprehensive general introductions to interpreting parish registers from a genealogical point of view is the work of Don Steel,[17] building on the work of J.C. Cox.[18] Steel takes care to point out the differences in registers over time and from place to place. There are many pitfalls in their use, and the researcher must always be aware of the inaccuracies and gaps. Registers suffer from various insufficiencies and often have under-registration, simply because the clergyman was not a good record keeper or recorder of information.

The reason is probably due to the practice of writing events in rough notebooks and then copying them up later, something that happened in some parishes right from the very start. Later on, it has been found that under-registration of burials happened in at least some registers due to the non-payment of burial fees.[19] A conclusion of one study on rural parishes was that both baptisms and burials suffered between 20 and 34 per cent under-registration. This is a big blow to the genealogist, as inevitably it means that a large proportion of vital events is not going to be found in parish registers.[20]

Under-registration is a particular problem for the late seventeenth century and throughout the eighteenth century, not only due to the clergyman's carelessness but because of the growth of non-conformism, and the use of irregular marriages, until those were brought to a halt by Hardwicke's Marriage Act of 1753. During the period of the English Civil War and Commonwealth, 1649–1660, there are also well-known gaps in parish records. In other words, many registers simply do not record everybody who was baptised, buried or married in a parish, and the Acts of Parliament and orders to try to get the situation improved are testament to this. Further, there was often a great deal of moving around, so people disappear from one register, only to pop up in another.

The problem for the genealogist as well as the population historian is that one needs a whole region of parish registers in order to take account of short-distance migrations from one parish to another nearby. Those who stayed put are annoyingly never the people we want to research the most, and it is the travellers who provide us with the most problems. *See* Chapter 8 for more on migrations.

Because parish registers can differ so much, research in one parish doesn't fully prepare you for research in the next parish, and this means that in order to become fully proficient in all the possible pitfalls, you need to read through many different registers.

Bishops' Transcripts

The researcher should also seek out records known as 'bishops' transcripts', which, being contemporary copies, supplement the parish register entries. Thus within a year of his baptism, the entry for Thomas Berd had been copied out and sent to Canterbury for keeping with other records in the Consistory Court of Canterbury.[21] There is therefore a record of him and his family, and all the other parishioners mentioned in the registers, in two places.

Little is known about the uniformity of sending copies back to the bishop from before 1598 as so little survives, but it seems it may well have been a widespread practice. Certainly there are surviving records from Canterbury and Lincoln from the early years of Elizabeth's reign.[22] However, and as many family history books tell us, from 1598, following yet another decree, the churchwardens of each parish would be obliged to make a transcript of all the entries from the previous twelve-month period to send to the bishop's diocesan registry, where duplicate records were to be held, so the bishop was better able to keep on top of events in the diocese. This was to happen a month after Easter every year, and in Bredhurst it duly does, when copies of Bredhurst register entries are made, so that all entries supposedly appear in two places: the original register, and the copy held in Canterbury.

Because of the insufficiencies of the parish registers, genealogists should try as much as possible to use both the parish register entries and the bishop's transcripts when building family trees. Often information in one is missed, or is different from the other. Usually only by using them together is it possible to fully reconstruct a family. When using online indexes, it can be very difficult to tell whether one is looking at the index to a bishop's transcript or an index to the parish register.

This also explains how you may get anomalies between one set of indexes and another: the first may be from the original register, the second from the bishop's transcript. However, the careful genealogist will be certain what they are looking at. Because of the way the International Genealogical Index (IGI) (and other indexes available on familysearch.org) was originally constructed, it contains many records taken from the diocese, rather than the parish.

Because the bishop's transcript copy is a copy, usually the more interesting detail is left out. For example, a burial entry may leave out the occupation of the deceased, or their age, while the original parish register entry could have this useful information. However, there are also plenty of instances when the bishop's transcript gives more detail than that held in the original register, or contains an event completely left out of the parish register, due again to poor recording practices. This is thought to be due to the practice of copying to both the parish registers and the transcripts from a day-book.

Mortality and Ages

There is much confusion over the life expectancy of our ancestors. You may have seen statements such as the average age of death in Liverpool was thirty. But this does not mean that most people were dying before the age of forty, because these broad-brush figures include a huge number of child deaths. If a man had reached the age of thirty, then the likelihood was that he would get to sixty. However, to reach the age of eighty was rare, although certainly not unheard of, particularly in a healthy country district. The real killers were the filthy infested towns. Women, of course, had a high chance of dying in childbirth in their twenties and thirties, but having survived that, then they usually outlived the men.

The historian Peter Laslett has argued that infant mortality was not in a uniform gradual decline as our period unfolds, but instead the rate of mortality among infants dropped slightly in the early seventeenth century, rose in the second half of the seventeenth century, and then rose steeply throughout the eighteenth century.[23] There were therefore fewer children surviving to age ten in the first half of the eighteenth century than in any previous period, but still around 70 per cent of children throughout the whole of our period did survive to the age of ten. Thus any family historian would expect to find that in a family where there had been six or seven births, it was likely there would have been one or two deaths before the age of ten, depending of course on the time, the locality and the wealth of the family.

Because researchers often need to infer the exact age or date of birth of someone from a baptism date, it becomes important to know the likely age at baptism in any given period of time. This is problematical, as most parish registers do not show the date of birth (although some do), only the date of baptism, and practice differs from the strict letter of canon law. In the sixteenth century it is thought that we can be almost certain that baptism was soon after birth, but the situation after that is far more confused. Where baptism registers do show dates of birth, such as at Pevensey in Sussex, from 1761 to 1802 it can be shown that as the eighteenth century progressed, the length of time between birth and baptism lengthened from 75 per cent of children being baptised within twenty-nine days of birth in 1761, to 75 per cent of children being baptised within 154 days for the four years 1791–95, reducing to 119 days for the next four years.[24]

Other researchers have found that registers that show both baptism and birth dates together tended to fall into four periods: during the Commonwealth, 1653–60; the aftermath and introduction of the Marriage Duty Act 1695–1705; and then again in 1771–80 and 1791–1812. However, unless you are researching in a register where both dates are shown, only in the very early periods can you be sure that a child is going to appear in the parish register soon after birth. That certainty increasingly disappears, and varies widely from parish to parish until, by the end of the eighteenth century, nothing is certain.[25]

At what age did our villagers first marry? The answer to this question helps us to identify likely baptisms. There used to be a widespread belief among family historians that people in the past married younger than in our own times. For the English countryside the reverse tends to be true. Often marriage could not take place until the groom was earning an independent income – this might even mean that his own father had died and he had inherited land. The average age of marriage was thus high, but of course individuals all vary, and probably every family historian can find examples of people who married late or very early.

The registers also tell us that a lot of people did not marry at all, remaining single all their lives. Perhaps one-quarter of those in the sixteenth century fell into this category. Those family twigs that hold the brothers and sisters of our ancestors may never have turned into branches. This lack of marriage kept the population growing only slowly at the beginning of our period.

Most people chose their own marriage partners and paid no heed to their parents. However, second marriages may have been more often contracted for reasons of mutual economic support, rather than because of love. Of course, by the time they got married many people had no parent to offer any advice at all, as both their parents had died. Servants were released from their annual contracts around May Day, Michaelmas (25 September) and 11 November, and these became peak times for marriages to take place. After harvest was another popular time.

The age of bride and groom at marriage has been studied by demographers, because a later age at marriage naturally means that fewer children will be born, particularly in an era where women died younger and reached the end of their child-bearing years earlier than in the present day. Male age at first marriage was steady throughout our period, slightly higher in the seventeenth century, and becoming slightly younger during the eighteenth century, but even so varying only from twenty-seven up to twenty-eight and then down to twenty-six. Women have more of a jump, rising from twenty-four in the last half of the sixteenth century, to twenty-six and a half in the first half of the eighteenth, and declining more steeply to just over twenty-three in the last half of the eighteenth century.

Thus, when looking for people in the parish registers, it may help the research to bear in mind that generally men were about twenty-six to twenty-eight at marriage, and their first wives somewhere between twenty-three and twenty-seven. (Second marriages may be with a younger wife.) If it can be shown that your own ancestors do not fit this pattern, then it would be interesting to find out why: in what way, and why, were they different?

Unpicking Register Entries: What They Say and Don't Say

The Thomas Berd entry from the registers of Bredhurst illustrates some of the common problems faced by the researcher. The baptism entry tells us that on the first day of December Tho:

Berd son of Richard [Richardus] Berde was baptised. It does not tell us what spelling to use for this family, or the mother's name. In a more populated parish with more than one family of Berd, having no mother's name might make it difficult to distinguish between one or more Richard Be(i)rd(e)s in the parish. Thus using a single entry or several entries for children baptised to one couple, although useful, comes with a certain number of potential pitfalls.

A little further down the same register book, the following entry gives us no clues as to whether these Joanna and Maria daughters of Henry Wright are twins, or simply being baptised on the same day:

> Quarto die Maij Johanna et Maria Wright filie Henrici Wrighte.[26]

Although baptisms of siblings who were not twins often took place on the same day in later centuries, in the sixteenth and seventeenth centuries it was more common to baptise within a few days of birth. So it would be valid to take an educated guess that these are indeed twins. But it is still just an educated guess.

Parish registers allow families to be put together in a somewhat complete fashion: that is, a set of parents can be identified, and their children's baptisms and burial dates discovered. It is always necessary to use both baptism and burial registers, plus of course marriages as well. Even though the Bredhurst registers are far from complete for the Tudor period, if you make a complete survey of the composite register by reading through all the entries over a long period of time, it is possible to put together information from them on the family to show the following about the Berd family:

Richard Berd was married to a woman called Agnes. She was buried on 26 March 1583. Between the death of a daughter of Richard's, buried on 6 March 1567, and Agnes's own burial in 1583, six other children were baptised, and of them, at least three died as babies or toddlers. Also recorded is the burial of a Mary Mansell 'filia fratris' (niece) of Richard Berd, thus adding another dimension to the Bredhurst family.

Further speculations can be made about the family. If Agnes is Richard's only wife, then she was having children from 1567 to

1582, a span of fifteen years, which suggests that Richard and Agnes may have married in 1566 or 1567. However, research has shown that the average number of children at this period for a marriage was only four[27], so it is also entirely possible that Richard's children were by two wives, although there is no burial noted for the first.

It is considerations such as this that make unpicking the early parish registers a tangled mess of supposition and speculation. All that the parish register tells us for absolute certainty is that all the children were the sons and daughters of Richard, and that his wife died in 1583, assuming we trust that the vicar has not made mistakes with names and dates. However, when we do add in our educated guesses and then go on to test them out, such as 'was there one wife or two?' this can also lead to important genealogical breakthroughs.

Here is a list of the relevant entries from the registers, used to build a basic family tree for the Berd family, with my comments in square brackets:

Joanna, buried 6 March 1567 [first child found, baptism missing, death of first child]

Joanna, baptised 1570 [second child]

Robert, baptised 1571 [third child]

Robert, buried 25 March 1572 [death of third child]

Ann, baptised 5 July 1573 [fourth child]

Mary Mansell, buried 15 Jan 1575 [might she have been living with them?]. She is unmarried or would not have been noted as Thomas Berd's niece

Thomas, baptised 7 October 1576 [fifth child] [burial missing from register]

Thomas, baptised 1 December 1577 [sixth child] [the only entry to appear on the IGI, even though this register is *supposedly* covered by the IGI]

William, baptised 16 July 1581 [seventh child]

William, buried 6 November 1582 [death of seventh child, age fifteen months]

Agnes, wife of Richard, buried 26 March 1583

Elizabethan families were usually nuclear, which is to say only parents and children lived in one household, with no grandparents or extended family. However, the better off did have live-in servants, for both domestic and farming purposes, who were often relatives. The reporting of the death of this niece of Richard's may be a clue as to the status of the Berd family. It would also make sense to suggest that Mary/Maria is the blood relative of Agnes, and that this makes Agnes' surname possibly Mansell, although of course this is not proven on this evidence alone. She could also be the daughter of a half-brother of Richard. The Berds appear therefore to have been typical of the middling type of yeoman farmer.

We should note that all these events are being written up into the 1598 register years after the actual events: they are not the original entries, and the scraps of paper or the previous registers have been destroyed. It would not be possible to completely reconstruct the family as they were in life – gaps are obvious.

One thing that is strange to the eyes of a modern person is the reusing of names for the children. There are two Joannas, two Roberts, two Thomases and two Williams, a total of seven children, and possibly three of them living beyond babyhood. Again, the Berds are absolutely typical of families in this period in doing this, and the re-use of these particular names may be an indication of a family naming pattern, with the children being named after grandparents.

Agnes's burial entry in March 1583 is the last we hear of Richard Berd and his diminished family in the Bredhurst parish registers; no further mention of them occurs, so it seems likely that those who survived moved to better parishes, where life was perhaps a little easier.

Would there be memorial inscriptions for this family? Steel says that all burials were without coffins until the eighteenth century, unless the person was wealthy. The gentry were buried in the church itself, and if they were aristocratic the burial would be arranged by the College of Arms until the eighteenth century; however, the ordinary parishioners went to their rest in the churchyard. Wooden markers were almost certainly used, and would have rotted away within seventy-five years or so. Gravestones themselves are eaten away by acid rain, particularly in towns, and in practice many from before the nineteenth century are now unreadable. For the ordinary village family, even ones with some slight status, the grave places from the sixteenth century up to the eighteenth century are now mainly lost to time.

Unfortunately, entries for burials in the parish registers themselves are also frequently deficient. Thus, as we can see from the Berd entries, there are burials that are not noted, and most family historians are going to find baptisms for children with the same name in the same family where the burial is missing.

Registers in the Commonwealth Gap

Genealogists call the period of the English Civil War and Commonwealth in the seventeenth century the 'Commonwealth Gap'. Many parishes lost their incumbent priest during this period, there was local upheaval, and children were not baptised. In some cases the clergyman refused to baptise according to the new *Directory for Public Worship*, which had been produced by parliament in 1645. It was supposed to replace the *Book of Common Prayer* but was very widely disliked, and secretly ignored by many clergymen. Some of those not baptised in the 1640s and 1650s were subsequently baptised as adults after the Restoration in 1660. However, the gap in registers is real, and a long-standing problem for genealogists.

After the Restoration, parish registers become more reliable again, but not for long. Quite quickly thereafter the number of people dissenting from the Church of England's teachings began to grow. The baptism of everyone, or nearly everyone, in their home parish church then began a long and slow decline, from which it has never recovered.

Bredhurst Registers in the Eighteenth Century

From 1706, the *Register Book of Bredhurst* is a composite register containing entries in what looks to be a chronological order. The book is headed up:

The Register Book of all Christenings, Marriages & Burials

> Which have happened in Bredhurst in Kent since the twenty fifth day of December 1706.[28]

The very first page of the book relates to us the following events, here transcribed exactly, with the year added in brackets. Due to the old-style year-end being 25 March – it was not 31 December until 1752 – the year 1706 continues into January.

> Nicholas Wood of Bredgar was married to Margaret Peirce of the same Parish Jan 12 [1706]
>
> Moses Long of Bredhurst and Mary Rose of Gillingham were married Jan 13 [1706]
>
> Elisabeth daughter of Soloman Allen and Elisabeth his wife was baptized May 25 1707
>
> John the son of Mr James Andrews and Judith his wife was baptized Aug 2d [1707]
>
> Mr William Long of Sharsted in Chatham was buried Aug 30
>
> Robert Swan of Gillingham Houshold[er] was buried Sept 4th

Clearly, by 1707 and on the evidence of these entries, something had changed in Bredhurst. The insularity of the little village high on the hill in the woods seems to have vanished, and from this date, and increasingly from 1711 onwards, this register contains many events concerning people outside the village and parish, as the couple from Bredgar above show. There are several other Bredgar couples in the next few years, and also people from Boxley, Chatham and Hartlip, all nearby parishes. There are also several illegitimate babies baptised with fathers said to be of a number of different parishes, and burials of people outside the parish, too. The impression given is quite different from the carefully written up and insular register of the 1570s.

The handwriting in the register now varies, with some crossings out, and in places it has obviously been written up long after the event. It seems that the vicar of Bredhurst may have been trying to make extra money from what are known as 'clandestine' marriages, although they were perfectly legal at the time. It is important to note that these marriages may not have complied with the canon law, but they were legal marriages nonetheless. Why else would so many couples come to Bredhurst – such an out-of-the-way place – to marry, except that it was cheaper, or a blind eye was being turned to irregularities? Bredhurst was certainly not alone in this, if it were true. Many town and country parishes at this date have a larger proportion of outsiders in their register.

The most famous clandestine marriages occurred in London in the Fleet Prison and other London chapels. Yet clandestine marriages did occur in the countryside, and there are many examples of marriage registers that show increased numbers from outside a parish marrying in a particular place. Steel says that each county had its marriage mongers – those who would disregard the rules and marry under-age couples without banns outside either parish, and/or without a licence.

It is simple to spot those churches where this took place if you have access to a run of parish marriages prior to the law on marriage being changed in 1754. For example, Richard Cardin and Ann Nokes were both from the county town of Lewes in Sussex, yet they married in December 1726 in the tiny village of East Blatchington, some 11½ miles away.[29] It appears that practicalities may have come into play in their choice: it was near enough to get there in a couple of hours' ride by horseback or even by foot, yet far enough away from nosey neighbours – and given that Ann was only eighteen, the marriage may well have been without her father's consent.

It is for reasons such as this, where marriages don't take place in the parishes that you expect, that comprehensive surname indexes to all parish registers within a county are invaluable. Happily, most county family history societies do have such indexes, or are in the process of preparing them.

The record keeping of parish registers continued in more or less the same way in Bredhurst, as in all the other parishes in England, until the authorities in the eighteenth century started to get very concerned about the under-recording of baptisms due to the rise of non-conformity, and about the many anomalies concerning marriages. An Act of 1753 known as Hardwicke's Marriage Act sought to assert more control over marriages by requiring that they took place in a Church of England parish church, with the exception only of ceremonies for Jews and Quakers. Marriages performed anywhere else were now illegal.

Furthermore, marriages now either had to be announced in advance by banns being called, and banns registers kept, or a licence needed to be sought, and these were to take place in one of the parishes where the bride or groom normally resided. Banns and licences were of course used before 1754, but were now required to be formally recorded, instead of the previous 'hit or miss' system, whereby the minister might write against a marriage entry 'by banns' or 'by licence', or may or may not have kept a separate banns register.

For the average villager who worshipped at the parish church, the changes made little difference. Their marriages had always been announced in church in advance by the reading of banns. For the genealogist, however, the changes mark the first time a printed register was used for marriages and banns, and thus a new set of books. For the marriage, more was to be recorded, including signatures or marks for bride and groom, and the same for witnesses, and whether the happy couple were bachelor, spinster or widowed. Also now added as a matter of course was the place of residence of the bride and groom, and the name of the minister marrying them.

All this provides the researcher with many more clues to follow up. The recording of banns means that a useful secondary set of records was created, although the calling of banns did not mean that a marriage actually took place, nor did the issuing of a licence. While the marriage entry itself would only be recorded in the parish where it took place (often the bride's home parish), the banns were (and continue to be) held in the parish of both parties, and therefore can be useful for discovering a marriage if the parish is unknown or where the original marriage register is missing.

Starting Points for the Researcher

Parish registers and other records in the parish chest are held by the relevant county record office, and bishop's transcripts by the diocesan record office (which is usually the same as the county record office, but not in all places). There are now increasing numbers of filmed original parish registers online on the paid-for data websites such as Ancestry.co.uk and Findmypast.co.uk, and via Family Search at the select libraries designated, such as the resources held by the London Family History Centre, which is now within The National Archives at Kew. The Society of Genealogists also has a very large collection of parish registers, both on film and transcriptions.

There are also some notable free-to-use online projects such as the Medway City Ark project where you can fully read and search the registers of Bredhurst and other Medway parishes for yourself. Working out which parish registers appear online, and whether there are gaps in what is available, can be very complex. Websites that help with this are Dusty Docs (www.dustydocs.com) and Archer, which can help you to locate and understand how films are organized by Family Search (http://www.archersoftware.co.uk/igi/) as well as the genealogy portal Genuki.org.uk.

It is vital to work out exactly which church or chapelry your ancestors would have been most likely to visit, and for this you need to understand parish and township boundaries. The Family Search website has a wonderful set of maps called the England Jurisdictions, 1851 (www.familysearch.org/mapp/). Alternatively a comprehensive printed volume is Tim C.H. Cockin, *The Parish Atlas of England* (Malthouse Press, 2017). This is a monumental work of boundary mapping, seven years in the making. *The Phillimore Atlas and Index of Parish Registers* edited by Cecil Humphrey Smith (3rd edition, 2002) is also a vital reference tool for the bookshelf.

Finding Parish Registers and Bishops' Transcripts

Knowing which parish to look in is one of the very first vital steps to research success in English records. Locating the parish helps unlock that vital 'place' information, without which the research grinds to a halt. There is still no comprehensive national surname index to all known parish registers, although great inroads have been made by the indexes held by the Church of the Latter-Day Saints on their website Familysearch.org, supplemented by the family history society indexes available on the commercial website, findmypast.co.uk, and held by the family history societies themselves.

Family Search contains a variety of country-wide indexes, including indexes to some or most parishes in every county, but not all, and with a variation in county coverage. They also have a collection of original images of parish registers that can be searched frame by frame, as if using microfilm, but usually with better contrast and so easier to read, now online. There is access to most of the parish register material from a handful of counties, and to some registers from individual cities.

If all that you know is that your ancestor came from a particular county, trying to determine the parish of origin can be a very longwinded task without a complete surname index to help. Normally the first task would be to use whatever indexes can be searched first, and then cross them off your potential list and physically look in any remaining original parish registers. *The Phillimore's Atlas and Index of Parish Registers* will help you to determine what survives and where it is held. It can be used simply as a listing of all the parishes in a county, as well as a finding aid to the original records, and where duplicates are held.

For those who need more detailed information, or find themselves very often with research questions about parish registers for a particular county, the volumes from the *National Index of Parish Registers*, published by the Society of Genealogists, can be consulted. Many counties are covered, and each volume is an invaluable research tool.

Genealogists have to take great care that they understand the difference between an index to a parish register, and the actual parish register itself. Most websites commonly used for family history research provide indexes, or indexes to brief transcriptions, and sometimes they also provide images of the originals, which is much better – but they then omit to tell you that not all the possible entries will appear in their indexes. This is a particular fault of commercial websites. So if you don't find an event, you would not be aware of whether this was because the indexes are deficient, or the records themselves have gaps, or because you are simply looking in the wrong place – or because the event in fact never happened in the first place.

Another potential pitfall is that very few online resources make a distinction between an index to the original register and an index to the bishop's transcript. This can matter because it is necessary to use information from both together in order to build up the most complete picture of a family. A good researcher will want to make sure what has been looked at, and what has not.

Finding the original registers and bishops' transcripts is less complex if you are prepared to make a physical visit to the relevant county record office. Bishops' transcripts will also be held there if they are a place of deposit for the diocesan records. This is easy to check by enquiry at the record office or using online resources.

Understanding Detailed Catalogue Entries

When on the hunt for parish registers, it makes a great deal of sense to use the county record office catalogue, if you can, to search and check how the original registers are structured, and what gaps there may be in a run of registers.

Paying close attention to the catalogue entry should help. For example, the catalogue entry given below comes from the Medway City Ark project for Kent parish registers and shows the full information for the Bredhurst register I have been describing, which is helpful to understand before diving into the images from this register (available online). The detail given by the Medway archivists in describing the parish registers under their care is excellent. The main heading in bold tells you what to quote if you were ordering the register in the physical archive. This is the reference. The parish is given a number – 44, and this entry is for the first volume in the first series. The main part of the entry gives the content of this single volume, which runs from 1546 to 1701, giving clues to the layout.

Title: Composite register
Reference: P44/1/1
Date: 1546–1701[1789]
Level of description: file
Extent: 1 volume

Scope and content: Baptisms 1547–1699, with entries for 1701–1707 at 1701 marriages, and cross-reference to 'alium librum [another book]' for 1706–1707 entries (mixed) following; marriages 1546–1705; burials 1547–1704; 1705 plus one of 1789 are in the 'alium librum' entries; several burials in Bredhurst church noted, 1659, 1664. Births only, 1655; two civil marriages, 1655. No marriages, 1644; no burials 1598, 1672. At end reversed, note of appointment of Jeffrey Oldfield MA, late fellow of Brasenose College, Oxford, as 'Registrar of Bread-hurst [i.e. Bredhurst]' signed by John Osborne [JP; see 1655 marriages], and his having been 'comended' to the parish by the rector of Hollingbourne, 1655.

Existence and location of copies: Microfilm Number 003

Digitised version: P044-01-01.pdf[30]

The first thing to note about the entry above is that this register is one volume, and the date range within the volume is 1546 or 1547; there then seems to be a bit of confusion up to 1701, with a few stray entries in the register beyond 1701, including one for 1789. The baptism and marriage entries have been intermixed with baptisms appearing in the marriages from 1701. It shows that for the Commonwealth Gap there are only births from 1655 and two marriages.

Finally, for good introductions to using parish registers for family history, Don Steel remains invaluable for his sheer detail, and there are many other worthwhile guides aimed at the family historian.

Rebecca Probert's books on marriage law are also interesting and invaluable for understanding more about the law: *Marriage Law for Genealogists* (Takeaway, revised edition 2016) and *Divorce, Bigamist, Bereaved?* (Takeaway, 2015).

3

The Land and the Farmer

Different Soils, Different Folk

It has become a cliché that there is a north–south divide in England. It has even been said that the northern half of England is as different from the southern half as is chalk from cheese. That very saying 'chalk and cheese' derives from the regional differences between farming on the chalk and limestone uplands (all sheep) and the dairy lowlands (all cheese). However, it is not just north and south that differ: east and west do as well, and whether an area is arable or pastureland gives a different character to a place. The geology and therefore the soil was all-important in the development of the historical character of an area or region: thus upland limestone may be used for sheep, but not for growing wheat, while thick clay is good for brickmaking, flat peaty soil for potatoes, and dry sandy heathland not much use for anything. These simple geographical facts were of profound importance to our ancestors, so they should be of equal importance to us as family historians.

Soil types may even have had some influence on how long the medieval system of manors and their administration lasted in a district as well as the later process of enclosure, with the clay soil 'champion lands' of the Midlands being the place where the manorial system in general lasted the longest. The Midlands just so happened to be the least resistant to early enclosure, with soils that are naturally suited to mixed arable farming, with sheep, cattle, pigs and arable crops all together. The strength of the manorial system, as well as the individual customs on the manor and the character of an area, are therefore linked by soil and geology. Of course, regions haven't stayed static; whole areas that were once mainly pasture, such as Norfolk and Suffolk, are now arable 'prairie' lands, and areas that were arable in the past are now improved and enclosed pasture for cattle and sheep.

The tendency of genealogy textbooks to rely on generalizations about commonly used records (because describing all the possible local variations of creation and use of records is difficult and complex) means that the unsmooth is smoothed out, and the individuality of areas and people blurred, if not erased. To counter this smoothing, and however well you think you know the records, it is always a good idea to examine them in tandem with the local situation. Were your ancestors from a village on chalk or a village on clay, a village near marshland or a village on moorland, somewhere lowland or upland? Did they farm or work with sheep or cattle? The physical setting, the topography and the soil has had a profound effect on the shape of the village, the types of work, the sort of agriculture that is possible, and even the character of country folk inhabiting it.

David Hey and George Redmonds in their local history and genealogy books, as well as other local historians, have both pointed out that for our ancestors, England was a country of wide regional differences. What was 'their country' for rural folk was their own region with its own characteristics, its own landscapes and soils and its own dialect. Regions were not neatly delineated, and they certainly did not abide by county boundaries. It may be helpful to the genealogist to place their ancestors into more than just a backdrop of parish, and county, but to think more widely; whether that is the Forest of Dean, the Forest of Arden, the Black Country, the Kent and Sussex Weald, the Lincolnshire Wolds, the Yorkshire Dales, and so on. [31]

This idea of thinking in regions may also help in working out where families and individuals might have migrated from, because the county boundary probably meant next to nothing to the labourer moving within the same region to find work. What might have been important to them were physical barriers such as hills, rivers, marshland or heathland frequented by robbers, as well as where their 'own country' folk might be found. Thus having located the county, parish and village of your ancestor, don't forget to consider the region, because those regional characteristics that bind folks together are so much more meaningful than lines drawn on a map.

An understanding of the way the population of a village or place is actually distributed over a landscape is also surprisingly useful for the genealogist. Is the village long and strung out, compact and nucleated, or does it have no exact centre but consist of isolated hamlets and farmsteads? This analysis of landscape is difficult to make with only documents and records such as parish registers, or census returns to work from. It requires maps and some background reading about the region.

In the past, some counties were overwhelmingly rural and empty of people. It is understandable that Cumberland and Westmorland might have been underpopulated due to their mountainous terrain, but it is less obvious that a southern county not far from London would also have been very empty of people. The modern county of East Sussex is an example. By 1801 about a third of the population of England was already living in a town; however, in 1801 only five towns in East Sussex had over 2,000 people: Battle, Brighton, Hastings, Lewes and Rye. Overall, the county of Sussex had just 113 people per square mile, far fewer than its immediate neighbours.

Today we would think two thousand people in one place a 'village', so these simple figures give us a good impression of the rural scene away from cities and larger centres of population, and how truly sparsely populated many places in England were. Sussex had a notorious reputation for the state of its roads, the sticky clay was impassable unless in a period of drought, and this may have played a part in its relative lack of larger urban settlements. Hertfordshire, on the other hand, is geographically smaller than Sussex, yet had nine towns with over 2,000 people, and a total of 165 people per square mile in 1801. Hertfordshire's location just to the north of London, with better drained and more easily farmed soil, contributed to making it far more populated than East Sussex in 1801.

The Manor and the Village

The medieval village and its people were almost completely occupied in agriculture, and the situation was one of self-sufficiency in many things, not least food. It had to be. The food brought to table was monotonous – there was often not enough of it, and daily life and work was hard. Under the medieval manorial system, the land was farmed collectively by the landlord or landlady on his demesne land (the land kept for his own food requirements), and by the villagers both collectively on strips of common land, and by working for the lord on his land.

Naturally, the common land and the way it was farmed in strips, with all the rules and customs that were necessary to keep people from committing 'nuisance' to each other or to the lord, played a major part in the life of villagers. This was the feudal system of manors and service to the lord, and in turn the lord's military service to the king, which makes up the feudal pyramid that many of us were taught about in school history lessons, parts of which lasted until 1660.

At the bottom of the pyramid, the social status of the village labourer depended on the type of work he had to do. He was subjected to a huge number of personal restrictions, and might have little say on what he did from day to day. He was in all senses tied to the land, even to the extent that if he ran away, in theory he could be brought back in chains.

Not every part of the country was divided up into manorial units, and the village and township continued unchanged before and after the Normans introduced their feudalism. Northumbria, for example, was not under the manorial system in the same way as the Midlands and South. The South West also refused to conform. In fact, local variations are so great as to preclude any generalizations at all. The manor was a large part of life in England, but only a part. Where the manorial system existed, the land in a manorial unit was held for the king by a lord of the manor. Very large estates, called an honour, could contain a hundred of these units, while a manor could be a whole village, or a village could be subdivided into several manors. The villagers themselves could hold sub-tenancies, but paid their rent not necessarily in money, but often by their labour or with crops. The system was very complex and also fluid over time.

A village was therefore not the same as a manor, and did not have the same boundaries; just as a parish could contain more than one village or settlement, so could a manor. A manor was a unit of property and always a place under one lord's jurisdiction, while a village was a block of territory with a definite boundary, and which might be divided up among many owners. It would have been possible for manorial tenants to have felt more community with the other manorial tenants than they did to their respective villages.

One example of geographical variations comes from Kent, where farmers on some manors held land in two quite separate, non-contiguous places. The low-lying Weald was good for cattle, and there were separate holdings on the wooded downs, some miles away, useful for keeping pigs and stores of timber. One can see the essential fairness of such a system where the land can be farmed in common, with everyone getting something of everything.

The village, parish and manor of Bredhurst, Kent, is an interesting example of the relationship between these low-lying areas and downland areas. The village of Bredhurst is believed to have begun its life as a detached part of Hollingbourne manor, being an upland swine pasture (pigs were often run on wooded land, providing them with the habitat that they love, and helping to clear the wood of thickets and brambles) of the otherwise lowland manor. This relationship was also reflected in the ecclesiastical history, as Hollingbourne had a chapel at Bredhurst that predated the church of St Peter.

If you consult a map showing parish boundaries in Kent you will see that Bredhurst is actually a little way removed from Hollingbourne, with other parishes lying in between. It may well be that the people of Bredhurst moved back and forth, to and from Hollingbourne after the medieval period, which of course has implications for parish register research. Thus it can be useful to tease out these old relationships between places for the clues they give for migration between one place and another.

The village was also a unit of royal administration: when personal taxation was introduced, the collectors did not go to the manors, but they *did* go to the villages.[32] Therefore, any researcher must not assume that village, parish and manor were interchangeable geographically, because while this is true in a minority of places (mainly in the south of England), more often they covered different areas.

As well as being a method of collectively farming the land, the manor also acted as the local, civil administration in the medieval period. From the sixteenth century onwards the secular part of that administration was taken over by the parish; this consisted of poor relief, highway maintenance and so on. Thus during our period, the parish came to replace the manor as the lowest rung on the ladder of local government.

Landlords and Their Tenants

Yet another reason that researchers need to be attuned to the type of land and land ownership is to do with record keeping and survival. Landholdings in all periods of time are important to genealogists, because land tends to pass down the generations of a family. This is not just relevant to those families who owned large estates, but applies also to their tenants, whether that tenancy was on a manor or another type of estate. When records that are rich in people's names are deficient, it may become important to trace people by linking them to plots of land.

Helpfully, many plots remained the same size over many generations, and it is possible to identify them in different sets of records when they are described using measurement and by relation to their neighbours and local landmarks. However, records were made and kept by the larger landowners, rather than the national or local government. They are essentially private records, and this has implications for whether or not they have survived and where they are found.

By the time of Elizabeth I's reign (1558–1603) the existing complex and murky law regarding property ownership was becoming clearer. On the manor, no longer was there a feudal system of labour service in exchange for land to farm, except in a few odd instances. Any labour service had been turned into monetary payments, usually known as 'fines'. The last remnants of feudalism (paying rent by the giving of labour) were removed finally by statute in 1660. Nevertheless, throughout our period the lord of the manor continued to sit at the top of a pyramid of tenancy and landholdings. Below the lord of the manor at the top of this pyramid there were freeholders, and below them, two main types of tenant known as 'copyhold' and 'customary' tenant.

The terms 'copyhold' and 'customary' derive from the 'copy' entry that was entered into the manorial court rolls, and the customs of the manor, at the will of the lord. These two types of tenant were those who held their land by inheritance – in other words, it passed down through the family, and those who only held it for 'life', which was a predetermined period of time, usually twenty-one years. This twenty-one-year period represented the three lives of the tenant, his wife and his heir.

Any manorial land held by customary holders of inheritance descended to an heir, depending on the custom of the manor, which is why it is important to understand the customs of the manor. This was usually the eldest son (known as primogeniture), but in some localities, mainly in the South East, the inheritance of copyhold and unfree manorial land went to the youngest son or daughter (known as Borough English[33]), or, as in Kent, to several people (called 'gavelkind' in Kent).

By the mid-sixteenth century it was also possible for the copyholder to choose another heir by enrolling a copy of their will in the records of the court. Land would then be surrendered 'to the use of the will'. If manorial records survive, and the relevant probate court has records missing, it might be possible to find a missing will within the manorial records, if it has been used in this way.

Being a copyholder was not the same as freeholding, and to become a copyholder there were entry fines (sums of money to be paid to the lord) and an ancient payment known as a heriot. 'Heriot' originally meant the 'payment of a best beast', but by our period was normally monetized. These payments made copy-holding precarious, because the tenant had to be able to afford them. Thus there are cases where land was left vacant on the death of a tenant because the heirs could not afford the money payments to have their holdings copied to the court roll.

Because customs varied greatly between different manors, a successful husbandman or farmer who was building up his farm might well hold land in two manors and find himself subject to two different sets of customs. This must have presented difficulties, as he would have to present himself at each manor court as well, if the landlord was different for each manor.

To further complicate matters, both freeholders and copyholders could also lease land. This leasehold tenure was originally used for the 'demesne' land, which was originally farmed specifically for the landlord's use. Over time, and as the general wealth of the country grew, the landlord no longer always needed this land for his own food, and often rented it out. Demesne land was always outside the restrictions of the manorial customs, and thus the lord could set his or her own terms. Rents could be set at market value, and rent reviews built in. For some landlords, this became a way to make increasing money out of their manors.

At the start of our period, land in England was still being brought into cultivation for the first time, and brought back into cultivation after the population declines of the Black Death. Fields were hacked out of scrub and woodland, marshes were drained and poorer land was improved. Increasingly things such as mills, quarries and other buildings appeared, and could then also be let out by the lord in order to provide extra income. These other types of lease were extended by the sixteenth century to cover twenty-one years, or three lives (as with customary tenants).

Renting out his land using a leasehold arrangement became more and more popular with the landlord because he could set a market rent and review it upwards regularly. A clever lord therefore persuaded more and more of his tenants to give up copyhold status and take up leasehold land. Copyhold land that was not taken up by heirs could also be turned into leasehold land. Therefore slowly but surely the make-up of tenancies changed over time.

The very poorest people could neither afford to take up a copyhold (if they were entitled to one), nor in fact make much rental payment at all. People like this were reduced to squatting on waste land, or on the fringes of the common in hovels and little shelters. They became known as 'tenants at will', because it was only at the will of the lord that they were allowed to stay. The lord might collect a small rent from them, but they held no rights over the common land. If they cultivated a small plot of land, then they might contribute to the economy, and they may also have been used as labour by other tenants and by the lord himself – so they were often granted permission to have these little plots, until they failed to pay a rent or possibly caused a nuisance. They will only be found in any surviving records if they paid a rent.

Manorial tenants were also allowed to sub-let, subject to the approval of the manor. Provided the rent was paid and the sub-tenant did not infringe any of the customs or local laws, the sub-tenant may not be recorded in any surviving records and will therefore be invisible to researchers.

Some farmers owned freehold land, held other land as a customary tenant, and had yet other plots as a leaseholder, all at the same time. The manor itself could contain only copyhold land, or be a mixture of freehold and copyhold and leasehold, or perhaps have mainly free land. By the sixteenth century there was no stigma attached to being a copyhold tenant, and freeholders could, and did, take on copyhold land. This means the researcher has to be quite careful in interpreting any social status from any one landholding. No wonder that manorial records have a reputation for being intimidating!

The landlords themselves were not all the same, neither were they necessarily aristocratic. They were not all men, and did include women. They were largely businessmen made good, minor gentry families, institutions such as the Cambridge and Oxford colleges, and of course the church, as well as the aristocracy, including some unmarried women. Increasingly during our period London merchants were using their money to purchase manors as investment vehicles, and to become 'gentlemen'. So the lords were not an amorphous blob, any more than the agricultural labourers at the base of the pyramid.

There were plenty of distinctions between the very wealthy and the local gentry landholder, although inter-marriages between the two abound. They all derived their income from their landholdings, but there was a great difference in the amount of wealth whether or not they were aristocratic. The very wealthy became members of parliament and county lieutenants, and could be huge landowners and absentee landlords. The more middling sort filled the other sorts of local office. Across our period, from the Tudors onwards, land gradually became more and more concentrated into the hands of this gentry class.

The example of Bredhurst manor illustrates a variety of lords. The landholder at the beginning of our period was Sir Thomas Cheney, treasurer in the household of Edward VI. His son, Henry

Cheney, sold it in 1570 to Richard Thornhill, a grocer of London. The Thornhills held it for around 100 years, when it was sold to Sir John Banks. When Banks died in 1699, the property passed to his son-in-law the Hon. Heneage Finch, who became Earl of Aylesford, and it was still with that family in 1805.[34]

Datchworth in Hertfordshire is one of those villages that was divided between two manors: Hawkins Hall and Datchworthbury, with a good survival of a variety of documents. Both manors appear to have still been active into the nineteenth century. Landowners in Datchworth during our period were not aristocratic, and at one time Datchworth manor was divided so that two halves were in the ownership of different people. However, those halves came together again and passed through many hands, finally settling from the early nineteenth century to the owner of local country house Woodall Park, Samuel Smith, and then his heirs. Hawkins Hall also ended up with the owners of Woodall Park, thus providing an example of the consolidation of land into the hands of fewer people.

High Abbotside, that sprawling township in Wensleydale, North Yorkshire, that we met briefly in Chapter 1, has no manorial records surviving for any manor of that name, according to the Manorial Documents Register (*see* section below on Starting Points on p.81). However, it is part of the very large parish of Aysgarth, and the manor of Aysgarth does have manorial documents surviving. The most important factor for the manorial tenants of Abbotside would originally have been the power of the local abbey – Jervaulx.

Jervaulx Abbey was a Cistercian abbey situated at the entrance to Wensleydale, now a ruin. It was founded in 1146 by Peter Quintain, a Cistercian monk, on land granted to him by Earl Alan, the Earl of Richmond, and was called the Abbey of Fors, on the edge of Askrigg. It was then moved from there to its current position, as the original land was too wild and inhospitable. The Abbey came to own half of Wensleydale, and was also famous for its horse breeding. However, at the dissolution of the monasteries, the land was taken from the monks, their abbott Simon Sedburgh was hung at Tyburn in June 1537 for resistance and refusing to forsake the Catholic faith, and the lands of Jervaulx were made forfeit and granted by Henry VIII to Matthew Stuart, 4th Earl of Lennox, and his wife Margaret, who was a niece of the king.

Thus the three examples from Kent, Hertfordshire and North Yorkshire show some differences in ownership and also survival of records, with Datchworth having both less aristocratic owners and more surviving records. Normally if one large landholding family has owned a manor for centuries, then the records are more likely to survive, than if a manor has been broken up and sold on many times.

As the manorial system broke down, from the Tudor period onwards, so rose a new class of landless labourer in the villages and hamlets, the man who had no means of subsistence apart from his labour. In the manorial system, the very poorest would always have had some common land they could use for their animals; however, by 1850, the old medieval system of collective farming, together with 'common rights' – such as the right to take your own pig into the local woods for pannage, or to put your single cow out to graze in a common field – was gone. By the mid-nineteenth century almost all land was privately held, with no access rights to the commons.

Manorial Records

The manorial system left its own unique set of records, but it was not consistent across the country, and the survival of records is even more inconsistent because they started life as private documents belonging to the lord of the manor. They are perhaps the least used of records by the family historian, because of their odd language, the difficulties in finding them and their scattered survival. Furthermore it doesn't help their general popularity that they are usually in Latin prior to 1733. Those that survive can be very informative about the pattern of life, and once the customs of the manor are understood, then with luck they can be used to follow inheritance and families over several generations.

The key to using these records is to understand the basic formula of the way certain documents are laid out, and by always trying to ascertain the particular customs of the manor concerned. The manor was run as a business to make money for the landlord, so there are records reflecting that business use, but it was also run via a system of courts known as the court leet and the court baron, and these courts created many records.

The court baron was held for the transfer of lands, debts and disputes between tenants. The court leet was for petty crimes against the community, such as breaking down fences and selling poor quality ale and bread. The free tenants had to attend the courts, and in many manors act as jurors. They appear in the records even if they did not attend, as they would be fined and thus recorded for non-attendance. The main sets of records of the court leet and the court baron are known as court rolls, as they were quite literally kept tightly rolled up.

The main officer for the manor was the steward, appointed by the lord or lady of the manor to be their agent to represent them at the manor courts, and to make sure that money was collected from the tenants. In many ways he acted in a similar manner to a modern letting agent. Subordinate to the steward were other officials such as a bailiff who acted as the day-to-day administrator, and the reeve or grave who was mainly responsible for cultivation and was elected from the copyhold tenants. His job was to oversee the farming activities and the use of the commons. Other officials could be the pindar, or pinder, who was responsible for impounding stray livestock, and the hayward who was originally in charge of boundaries and hedges, as well as in some places meadows and hay making.

From the point of view of locating people within the records, it is fortunate for the researcher that manorial tenants were supposed to attend at each manorial court, and those who did not were fined. Where court records survive you may be lucky enough to find all the tenants listed together with their land holdings, and also to trace inheritance of land. Procedure in a manorial court derived from local custom and practice, not from law. It was also overseen by the steward, who by our period had legal training of some kind, and who by the eighteenth and nineteenth centuries might also be a local attorney or solicitor. Many of the records were prepared in advance of the proceedings, and use of these records is helped by knowledge of their context, and the formulae they use.

The court meeting itself was held in a public place, often in a prominent public house or inn; the place varies from manor to manor. The meeting would start with the steward calling the tenants to order, and he would then read out the title of the manor and the name of the official presiding. These details were recorded at the top of the court minutes. Then the tenants who had not attended were noted down. Those who formally opted out of appearing paid a small fee called an essoin. Persistent offenders were punished by the steward setting a more substantial fine. Those who failed to appear and did not send a suitable reason would also be fined, and listed. Manorial court fines are known as amercements, and the sums involved could be quite large. These details are normally very formulaic and can be quite easily picked up at the start of each set of court minutes, even when they are in Latin.

The names of the jurors appear next. The number of jurors at the court leet was normally twelve, but at the court baron this might vary. The tenants who attended the court were called the homage, because they paid homage and service to the lord; therefore homage is one of the words that you can look out for to help you navigate in the records. Jurors were current tenants of the manor in good standing, and are evidence of a certain local status. Widows might be included, but not married women.

Depending upon the period, there might be two separate lists of jurors, one for the court leet and one for the court baron. The two courts were usually held one after the other on the same day, although two separate homages were called, often the same names appearing. Or, both the courts were combined into one. For some manors all the different sections of the court roll may potentially be found as separate documents, and probably were expected to be copied later in a fair hand on to a roll or, for the eighteenth century, into a book.

After the homage listing of names there came a list of matters to be dealt with by the court, known as presentments. This list was sometimes very long, and was probably prepared in advance of the actual court session. The presentments tended to be minor offences against the customs of the manor – for example letting an animal stray, or cultivating more than one's fair share. For those tenants found guilty, the steward levied yet another fine or amercement.

The presentments were sometimes written separately from the main minutes, in which case they were probably written in English, but over time it was more usual for them to be recorded together with the main record of the court.

Special tenants known as affeerers were also chosen at court to oversee the setting of fines. Their job was to ensure that fines were fair, with the power to reduce a fine if appropriate.

During the court, any officials were also appointed on an annual basis, and the manor customs might be read out to remind all tenants of their duties and rights, together with the penalties. These customs may be termed ordinances or pains, bylaws or orders. The manorial customs are worth looking for, and are most often to be found at the first court after a new lord takes over. In fact, if you do find a reading of ordinances, it can be a useful indication that the lordship has changed hands.

After all, or some, of the set formulae of the above, the court baron continued by listing all new tenants and out-going tenants since the last court. These were known as admissions and surrenders. In other words, the outgoing tenant surrendered his holding to the lord of the manor, and the new tenant was admitted to the holding. The names of one or both people involved in the transaction were usually written in the margin, which helps identify specific entries. Admissions and surrenders are extremely useful to the researcher because often a date of death of the previous tenant is given, as well as family relationships. New tenants could only take legal possession of land using this process. The use of the phrase 'to the use and behoof of' also helps locate these admissions, the same phrase in Latin being *ad opus et usum*.

As part of the admission process to a tenancy, there was often an eccentric ceremony recorded in the minutes using the term 'by the rod'. This was an ancient custom of physically handing over a piece of turf or stick of wood to the lord of the manor, who then passed it over to the new tenant, representing the transfer of the land. Over time it became a symbolic gesture, and a physical pole or rod took the place of an actual sod of earth. In some manors it was 'by the verge', 'by the straw' or even 'by the glove'.

After the symbolic transfer took place, an account of the surrender and admission was written into the court roll and a copy given to the tenant. Court rolls and their copies were important legal documents to be kept safe, and could, and often were, used in a court of law to prove ownership. The equity law courts of the time, such as the Court of Chancery, are full of cases where these documents have been lost or stolen or perhaps deliberately hidden.

If a tenant needed a loan, it was possible to conditionally surrender his copyhold property to someone else in exchange for the loan money. The loan had to be repaid in full with interest by a set date. In other words this was a type of mortgage, known as a conditional surrender. If the tenant failed to make the repayment, then the person making the loan could keep the property, subject of course to the will of the lord.

The jury at a court baron also had to present the death of any tenant to the court so that the lord could collect his heriot. The death was announced at the court, and heirs would be called for to come and claim the tenancy. These are known as proclamations. Three proclamations were made, and the process could take up to three years if the court only met annually, after which time the holding could revert to the lord for re-letting. Because there would often be yet another fine or heriot to pay to be admitted to a tenancy, it quite often happened that the non-appearance of heirs did not mean that they were not there, but simply that they did not have enough money to pay for the admission.

In such a case, if the land reverted to the lord, this was a good thing for the lord, as he would then be able to change it to leasehold and get a higher rent for it. The researcher needs to be alive to such a situation so that no assumptions are made as to whether there were surviving heirs after a copyholder's death.

A transcribed example of an extract from an eighteenth-century manor court from Kendal in Westmorland is shown below. This bound book is in English in an untidy hand:[35]

> Court Baron and customary of the right hono[u]rable Henry Lord Viscount Lonsdale Lord of this manour holden in the Moot Hall in Kirby in Kendall the second day of July in 13th year of [th]e reigne of George [th]e 2[n]d King of Great Britain Etc. & in the year of our L[or]d 1739 before Walter Chambers Deputy Steward of same Court.

[There then follows a very long list of customary tenants organized by settlement, with their rents, not shown here]

Names of customary Tenantes impanelled & Sworne to inquire for this Manour

William Shepherd	Thomas Jackson	Thomas Lowes
John Mattison	John Wilkinson	William Kennet
John Beck	Francis Burton	Waltar Beck
John Atkinson	Henry Rowlandson	Martin Fell

who p[re]sent upon their oaths as ensueth

1. We find & p[re]sent that James Germann of Hakering side in Hutton in the Hay ought to be admitted Tenant of a messuage & tenement called Hakering side by deed from Thomas Lowes dated [th]e 9th day of June 1739 being of [th]e yearly rent of 2s according to custome

2. We find & p[re]sent [tha]t John Slack ought to be admitted Tenant of a messuage & tenement called Crag in the Hay by deed from Robert Slack his father bearing date 30th day of June 1739 & [of] yearly rent of 10s according to Custome

3. We find that Daniel Stephenson ought to be admitted tenant of a cotage & parock[36] & p[re]mises Called Speight brig lying in the Hay by deed from Thomas Marshall dated the 4th day of Aprill in [th]e year of our Lord 1739 & of yearly customary rent of 1s 7d according to custome

4. We find and present That Barbara Fleming ought to be admitted Tenant of a messuage & tenement called Cowmire lying in Crosthwait of [th]e yearly customary rent [of] 13:4 [13s 4d] by descent from Richard Fleming her father dec[ease]d

5. We find and present that the late Jane Carter now Jane Show ought to be admit[ed] Tenant of one messuage & tenement w[i}th appurt[enance]s scituate at garths In the Hay of

Marquess[37] [of] yearly rent of 13s 1/2d during terme of her [nat]urall life in pursuance of last will & testament of John Carter her husband dec[eased]

6. We find & p[re]sent that [th]e said Jane Shaw ought to be admitted tenant of another messuage & tenem[en]t w[i]th [the] appurt[enance]s lying at garths aforesaid of yearly customary rent of 2s 9d during [th]e terme of her [nat]urall life pursuant to said last will of her said late dec[ceased] husband

Admissions of new Tenants at this Court
Rents Fines

1. And thereupon [th]e above named James German cometh into Court and taketh of the Lord the p[re]mises As to him before named according to custome of the Manour To have & to hold according to said custome yielding & paying as well [th]e yearly rent as [th]e fine in the margent and payable unto the Lord A piece of silver called a Godspeny & allso doing & p[er]formeing all other customes & services in what respect due and accustomed to be done
2: 0 6:

2. The before named John Slack cometh into Court and taketh of the Lord the p[re]m[ise]s as to yt to have Etc & payeth Etc And paying Etc and rending Etc
10: 0 1: 10

The manor of Kendal Barony is one where many records have survived. A total of 367 separate documents are listed on the Manorial Documents Register (MDR), scattered over five separate archives. *See* below for how to search the MDR.

In the sixteenth century both court leet and court baron were still reasonably thriving institutions, but after the end of the sixteenth century, a gradual and inexorable decline set in. The courts slowly became places of antiquated play acting, or dropped away altogether as their practical functions declined. This pattern was not repeated throughout the country in an even fashion. Some manors remained very important locally for the meting out of justice, particularly those petty offences to do with keeping hedges trimmed and fences mended, and other agricultural nuisances, for longer than might be supposed. The transfer of copyhold land from one owner to another also meant that the court baron had a functional purpose right up until the twentieth century.

Nevertheless, gradually the quarter sessions and the parish vestry took away the administrative work, and then the enclosure of the common lands, which also gathered pace in the seventeenth century, removed another prop. Enclosure of commons did away with the need to regulate cropping and the practices of common pasture, which was needed when land was used communally. Finally, the copyhold system was also in decline – no new copyhold could be created after 1660, and any change of the tenure to freehold or leasehold extinguished the copyhold status for that land once and for all.

In 1852 the Copyhold Act changed the law so that existing copyholders could demand enfranchisement, and many deeds of enfranchisement date from then. Copyhold was finally abolished completely by an Act of 1922, which came into force in 1926. The irony is that the manorial records most of us are going to use – that is, those taken from the seventeenth century through to the nineteenth – represent the survivors of a system that was actually in terminal decay, and had been in decay since the fifteenth century.

Notices in the local newspapers, now easily findable at Britishnewspaperarchive.co.uk and Findmypast.co.uk, give a flavour of the language and rituals surrounding the meetings of these ancient courts. Here is an extract from the *Ipswich Journal*, 18 April 1747, which shows that the court records of the manors of Reydon Hall, Shelley and Marks in Suffolk were in somewhat disarray.

> Notice is hereby given That General Courts Baron will be helden for the several Manors of Reydon-Hall, Shelley and Marks in the County of Suffolk at the following times and Places viz: For the said Manor of Reydon Hall on Tuesday the 28th Day of April instant at 10 o'clock in the Forenoon at Reydon Hall; and for the said Manor of Shelley and Marks the next Day at the same Hour at Shelley Hall.

> At which courts all the tenants of the said respective Manors are desired to produce the last Receipts for their Quit Rents and to pay the arrears thereof: And all Persons wanting to be admitted at either of the said courts and desired to produce their last Copies of Admission most of the Court Books and Rolls of the said Manors being lost or concealed. And any of the Copyhold Tenants of any of the said manors who are desirous (for the Preservation of the Titles) of having their last Admissions presented and entered into the Court-Books or Rolls hereafter to be kept for the said Manors may, upon producing their said last Admission at the said respective courts have the same accordingly done without paying any Fee or Reward therefore. And if any Person or Persons will give any Intelligence to the Steward of the said Manors where, or in whose Hands any of the Court Books or Rolls of any of the aforesaid manors are concealed, such person or Persons shall be handsomely rewarded.
>
> Peregrine Love, Steward.

Manors also produced many administrative records to enable the lord to run his manor and his estates in general as a business for the purpose of income. Some of the most useful to the genealogist and local historian are the estate surveys and the rental rolls. Beautiful maps may have been drawn up as part of surveying and describing the extent of the manor. Because rental rolls tend to list all tenants and their respective payments, a good collection of such rolls can be worth their weight in gold if they name all the tenants over a multi-year period. Sadly they will not list sub-tenants.

It is important to try to consult as many records as survive over a long period, and not just rely on a few years of rental rolls or court rolls for the period that your family was a tenant. By taking the slower path, even though your family may not be listed in all that you can examine, you will get to a deeper understanding of the place, regardless of whether or not you actually find the people you are searching for, and this will help all your research. (For more on finding records, *see* the section Starting Points for the Researcher on p.81.)

Common Lands and Rights

Originally both common lands and rights over common lands were part of the manorial system whereby the lord had his own demesne land for his own use, and the villagers used strip farming on various portions of the common fields to grow their own crops. In addition, tenants might also have had rights to collect wood from common woodland, or to let their cattle and sheep graze certain fields at certain times of the year. The lord of the manor had mineral rights on this land, but no right to graze his own animals. This is land subject to common rights.

Land grazed in common is land that is owned in common. This situation is found for example in the upland farms of the Pennines, where the grazing land on the hill tops is owned jointly by the farmers. Land grazed in common is not true common land.

Manorial waste, which I have mentioned several times, is open to public access, and was originally part of the lord's demesne, although not let out to tenants. Some of this land was not useful for growing anything, and was often heathland, verges, hedgerows or marsh. However, it was still useful for foraging, and manorial tenants were allowed access to this waste for grazing or to collect wood or turves. It may still survive: for example, verges alongside country roads may have originated as manorial waste, and may still sometimes be the subject of dispute as to upkeep between a county council and a local landowner.

Villages in the Sussex and Kent Weald often developed along common wasteland along the roadside. In the thick mud of the Weald, the cart tracks and roads would disappear into a morass in wet weather, including most of the winter, and strips of land alongside the road would be needed to widen the road so that carts could take to the side to bypass the muddiest parts. When the population expanded, these strips and bits of waste were squatted on by poor villagers, who built hovels and huts, which eventually turned into cottages; these would be followed by neighbours, and then a whole section of village was elongated down a 'street'. In the census, if you come across the word 'street' as the address, it could be an indication that the place had evolved just like this.

Under the various Enclosure Acts, villagers in some places were also granted allotments. This was because provision was normally made for people who would otherwise have been left without any land. This could be land set aside in allotments for the poor, or land used for the collecting of firewood, or peat, known as a fuel allotment. Some villages had stone quarries in common, and in that case then a stone allotment was made. These were used for the repair of the parish roads.[38] However, it is also certain that in many places the allotments that were supposed to be made, never in fact happened, and villagers could find themselves without any common grazing or land of any sort following an enclosure.

In 1600, some 27 per cent of land in England was common land. Common waste made up a further 4 per cent.[39] It was this 4 per cent of waste land that the landless poor did have access to, and could squat on. Even if private property was therefore the norm by 1600, if you do find any mention of 'common rights' in relation to an ancestor, you should look for surviving manorial records for the manor.

Was the Land Enclosed?

Enclosure was the process whereby either the common lands were emparked, surrounded by hedges or fences and brought under the control of the landlord, or fields were simply consolidated into larger and more convenient plots for more efficiency. The term 'enclosure' is therefore used to describe ways of consolidating land-holdings into larger units. This can be the enclosing of the open fields and commons and converting these areas of land to parcels of fields held by a smaller group of people, or the conversion of arable land to pasture and the occupation of the little strips of the commons by large landowners, excluding other users. However it happened, the process of enclosure tended to change the landscape in a major way, although the process was very scattered across England.

Large, open fields consisting of little parcels owned by many, were replaced with neat, ordered fields of a standard size, often bordered with a hedge, owned by the few. The reduction in the number of farms had an impact on the way the whole community looked. Also the enclosures of the eighteenth and nineteenth centuries often laid out a village in a whole new way, with small fields of wheat, barley and other crops giving way to larger fields of grazing animals surrounded by newly laid and neatly rectangular hedgerows. Some enclosures even caused the complete destruction of all the houses in a village, which were then rebuilt on a different site, usually by one landlord who wished to build a fashionable house surrounded by carefully designed parkland. One can only imagine the effect this had upon the poor villagers, although it is to be hoped that the rebuilt cottages were of a higher standard than those they replaced.

Enclosure awards and their related maps are legal documents recording the ownership and distribution of the lands enclosed, and although historic, are still used today in some legal disputes. They are therefore extremely important documents for the history of both landscape and society, as well as being useful to the family historian for the evidence they give as to individual landholdings and plots. Enclosure maps are held at The National Archives as well as in the county records offices. Some of them are very large and can be awkward to work with.

The process of enclosure of the common fields destroyed the common and open fields of the manor. These enclosures were gradual at first – some had even happened in the medieval period, followed by enclosures that took place when monastic lands were seized by the Crown after the dissolution of the monasteries in the 1530s, and were sold on to new landowners, as happened in the case of the land in Wensleydale owned by the monks at Jervaulx Abbey.

As the manorial system continued slowly to break down, the process of enclosure went hand in hand with its demise. Private enclosure agreements were drawn up between the landlord and the main farmers, and these would be an agreement to get rid of the old rights of common, by replacing scattered strips with an allotment of fields, thereby consolidating a farm's holdings and making it more efficient to work. If there was disagreement, then a private act of parliament would be necessary to force through the changes. In the cases where there was this disagreement, records were created and have usually survived. Enclosure became increasingly popular during the seventeenth and eighteenth centuries, reaching a zenith in the parliamentary Enclosure Acts of the Victorian period.

Most enclosures were brought about by groups of landowners

and farmers working together in order to improve farming methods. Much of this enclosure happened throughout our period, and most of the time there were no disputes. Unfortunately, the majority of this type of enclosure has left no record behind, although it might be possible to find an agreement, together with useful maps, in the landowner's estate papers. Any one enclosure may have taken up to ten years to complete, and so was a relatively slow process, with the landscaping changing over a period of time.

Despite the many privately agreed enclosures, there remains a good chance that if an enclosure award did take place in the parishes you are interested in, there will be mention of your family. Exactly how much that will help you progress your research will depend on the date of the award and whether the family were major tenants, and not sub-tenants, also whether they had common rights, if those rights were being extinguished.

If you do find a detailed description of the allotment awarded in lieu of common rights, and you are able to isolate this on the relevant enclosure map, you can then compare the location with a modern map. This should help you to follow up any copyhold land with manorial records, leasehold land with any estate records, and anything freehold with taxation and in probate records of the relevant court. Unfortunately the records do not normally point you to the spot where any particular family lived, just to plots of land. Nevertheless, by tracing land backwards and forwards up and down the generations, it is possible to link people together, and this can help prove relationships.

Historians continue to argue about the social consequences of enclosure, and you may have encountered the subject from the point of view of the poor villager being turfed out of his cottage by the wicked aristocratic landlord and forced to move to the nearest town. A powerful landlord could completely remove a village and all its labourers, if he held all the land. This type of scenario should always be considered when thinking about why an ancestor moved away from a settled rural existence, although it might not have happened exactly like that. While this did happen to some unfortunate folk, the other type of enclosure, where all the land-holders joined together, should be borne in mind as well.

Landlords who did act in a dastardly manner could get their

tenants evicted from manorial land by increasing entry fines, or by simply waiting until the end of the three lives – the lease held by most copyholders. Two deaths in quick succession could ruin a farming family, and that would be whether or not the landlord was set on getting the family off the land for his own purposes. Another trick was 'theft' of the manor court roll, in which case the copyholder may not have been able to prove he did in fact own the land.

Records of resistance to early enclosures during the Tudor period may be found in the Court of Requests, and the Star Chamber and Exchequer commissions and enquiries, all held at The National Archives. However, be prepared for hard work in using and interpreting documents from the sixteenth- and seventeenth-century courts. This kind of research is not for those lacking in resolve.

Of equal importance to the theme of place that runs throughout this book, and the topographical differences between those places, is the local administration of that place. In particular, knowledge of local administration and customs can help us to understand the relationship between the labourer, the tenant farmer and the ultimate land-owner. This relationship in turn helps us understand the context of the records.

Just as there are many regional topographical differences, so there were different administrative arrangements and customs local to each region, and even between villages in a region. Some of these customs, to do with the way the land was collectively cultivated and the types of produce grown or animals husbanded, are extremely ancient.

A Typical Farm of the Sixteenth Century

With my exhortations to consider the local, not the general, it is probably now foolhardy of me to consider whether there was any such thing as a typical English farm. What most farms of the sixteenth and seventeenth centuries had in common was their relatively small size compared with modern farms or even farms of the eighteenth and nineteenth centuries, and their use of a mixture of cattle, sheep, pigs and arable. They tended more towards subsistence, and less towards concentration on one or two crops or animals. To help illustrate this, I now introduce evidence from a probate inventory drawn up in Derbyshire in 1579.

Some of the most useful records for both family history and local history are records of probate, and not only for the relationships they help prove. Between 1529 and the late eighteenth century, many probate courts, which were part of the church court system, required an inventory of the deceased person's goods to be made shortly after death by two appraisers, usually neighbours. Probate inventories are a well-known source for rural history, but are less well known in family history. Of course, they are not confined to rural communities, but exist for town-dwellers as well, but because they list farm equipment and animals as well as furniture in the house, they are of particular use in allowing us a glimpse into the farmer's life. They are also in English rather than Latin, which is always useful.

Probate inventories were normally drawn up only a few days after death, and are therefore a good way of determining a date of death, although the final process of filing the final probate accounts was not normally done until about one year after a death. It was the job of the executor or administrator to file these accounts and to list all the payments from the estate. Many sums might appear in payments as the estate was wound up: rent, debts, funeral expenses and so on.

What follows is a transcript of the probate inventory for John Bichcroftes [Beachcroft], who lived and died in Hazelhurst, near Ashover in Derbyshire. The inventory was made on 24 April in the twenty-first year of Elizabeth's reign (that is, in 1579). The amounts are modernized, but the original spellings kept:

> This Inventorie mad the xxiiijth day of Aprill a. Re[igne] E[Lizabeth] xxith of all the goodes of John bichcroftes alias Whilright of hasleherst in the p[ar]ishe of ashover and praysed be James Swindel Edward bradshawe Thomas shawe and Richard norman

Imprimis	
towe bulluckes	£3 6s 8d
vi kyne	£8
v young bease	£3

viii weaning caulves	40s
for xiiii wetheres	56s
Towe shoeltes and ii piges	8s
for corn[n]e sown of the gro[u]nde	16s
for ii fether bedes iii matrices	16s 8d
for ii bolsteres iii coverlettes ii pillowes thre pears of blangettes & x peares of shietes	40s
iii panes on kettle and iii skeletter	20s
for on bras potte a posnet a chafindishe and one morter	10s
for vi candle stikes	3s
for xx puter dishes w[i]t[h] on hand basonn	10s
for xii sawsares vi pottichare w[i]t[h] on saltte	6s
iii cofares on fatte & ii drinke veseles	3s
for on table a foarme iii cheare ii stoules	2s
for a bacond Iron on speet apeare of golbartes a fyr shoull & on paear of tonnge	6d
iii kittel iii boutles w[i]t[h] all other implementes be longing to the house	12d
for ii sutes of apparel	£3
Summa totalis	£29 11s 10d[40]

I believe I have identified John's farm, still called Hazlehurst Farm, and lying at 245 metres above sea level below and to the east of the Matlock Road. The modern Ordnance Survey shows an area of small sloping fields, together with nearby woodland. The house was listed Grade II in 1995 as a seventeenth-century farmhouse, and a search simply using an internet search engine brought up more information, that it was part of an estate. Thus with one sparse probate inventory, a modern map, a search engine and some information about the area around Ashover, Derbyshire, it is possible to build up a picture of John's farming activities in 1579 in this part of Derbyshire.

That he was a small farmer (a smallholder in today's terms) is in no doubt. John's animals included two bullocks, six cows, five 'young beasts' – probably heifers – eight weaned calves, as well as pigs and sheep. His main interest was in cattle, with a total of twenty-one animals; he was not farming sheep as he had only fourteen wethers, which are castrated rams. Perhaps they were being kept for their wool. He also had two shoultes – possibly 'shoat', a young weaned pig – and two pigs. These were probably being kept for the table, rather than to be sold. Finally he had some corn, not a great deal, so this might be just for his own use, rather than for selling. The date being in April would mean that any stocks of corn kept over the winter for feeding animals would be used up, and if the weather was good, any farmer would hope to have his sheep and cows back out in the fields feeding on grass.

The total value of his 'goodes and chattles' (movable goods only; inventories do not cover houses or value land) was just over £29, and his house was very sparsely furnished to modern eyes. Two beds suggests perhaps there were only two bedrooms. Yet by contrast to many in Ashover, John was a rich man. In the kitchen and any outhouses, the pots and implements were also sparse. However, it is possible that only things made of metal were accounted for, anything of wood being more or less worthless. Therefore there may have been wooden spoons, and leather or wooden bottles for storing liquids.

Among the metal goods listed are three pans, one kettle, three skillets, one brass pot, a posnet (three-legged pot), a chafing dish, a mortar, six candlesticks, twenty pewter dishes and a hand bowl, twelve saucers, six potingers with one salt, two coffers, one vat and two drinking vessels, one table, a form, three chairs and two stools. Then we move on to the fireplace itself, with a back iron (metal fireback), a spit, a pair of golberts, a fire shovel and a pair of tongs. These fireside goods often feature prominently in probate inventories as they were relatively expensive and long lasting.

Stratas of Society

John of Hazelhurst Farm in Ashover tells us in his will that he was a yeoman. The terms 'yeoman' and 'husbandman' are often found in probate documents, wills and inventories, as well as sometimes in parish registers. So who was the yeoman, and what was his distinction from the husbandman? This was something that contemporaries knew very well, but which seems strangely elusive to us when we meet them in the records. Yeomen originally were the servants or retainers of knights, but by our period they had become the more well-off farmers. They had their own land, but this was more often copyhold or leasehold rather than freehold.

In an informal way the term 'yeoman' was also used to distinguish a person who was beneath the gentry class, but yet was more prosperous than the husbandman. In many areas the yeomen were also in farming-related occupations, such as malting and milling, or in the clothing trade as sheep farming was so closely allied to the wool trade. The yeoman might also sublet his land to others, and employed others as well. He often socialized with the gentry, and a yeoman's sons and daughters might marry into the gentry. A yeomanry family's landholdings could increase over the generations by useful marriages and consolidations and the joining together of farms. However, their sons could also slip down the social scale and become mere husbandmen. The husbandman then was on a lower level than the yeoman, and was a farmer of less land, was less well-off, and more of a smallholder, with no freehold land.

Tudor tax returns, known as the subsidy rolls, show that rural population in Tudor times consisted of five groups of people. Those at the lowest point on the scale were the destitute, and the very poor whose total wealth was less than £1. It is thought that these people made up to 25 per cent of a parish. The next group above had income in wages, and owned more than £1 in goods; they were mostly servants and labourers hired by the day. Next were those who owned more than £2, and who were poor farmers or husbandmen, also some tradespeople such as weavers. Above them came the richer type of husbandman, then the yeoman, and finally the gentry.[41] As feudalism died away, so during the sixteenth century came the consolidation of lands into increasingly larger holdings, and with this came the rise of the husbandman, the yeoman farmer and the gentleman.

So far we have been mainly talking about those who actually farmed a piece of land, rather than the landless labourer who can be so difficult to trace. People who were landless labourers are excluded from some kinds of records, but may appear in others, such as receiving money from the parish rates. They may also appear in the records of the court leet if they transgressed local customs or laws. Farm labourers also moved around the country, going from farm to farm, and might have been part of a large gang travelling south to north up the country at harvest time. There will be more about the work and migration of the labourer and the very poor in later chapters.

Victorian and Edwardian Attempts to Survey Landholdings

In 1873 an attempt was made to provide a complete listing of landholdings of over one acre, in what has become known as the modern Domesday. This resulted in the 1873 *Return of Owners of Land*, which was compiled from ratings records in an attempt to counter some of the radical questions being asked about British society by people such as Karl Marx – for example, that land was held by only a small circle of the élite.

In the *Return of Owners of Land*, holdings are listed for everyone with over one acre of land, and although it contained major inaccuracies, and had to be revised and reissued in 1883, it remains a valuable tool for finding out about landholdings, not just in England and Wales, but editions were also organized and printed for Ireland and Scotland as well.

The return is organized by county, and then by name of the owner, together with their parish of residence, and the acres, rods and poles of their holdings, together with its rental value. However, it does not say where those holdings are, thus making it very difficult to use as a local history source. When searching individuals with small holdings, one can make a guess that the people concerned are living near to their holdings, and then attempt to verify this by cross-checking with other records, such as the census – although of course people might have held land in other counties and sub-let their land for income.

When tracing individual small plots, the plot size can sometimes be a significant clue, because it doesn't tend to change over time – though of course the researcher will also need to have a name to link to the plot. The publication is available online at Ancestry.co.uk, and can be searched by both name and place. It is also available on CD as a book, and at thegenealogist.co.uk.

The outcome of this 1873 landholding survey was that it showed that just 11,000 people in England and Wales were landowners of more than one acre. This was significantly fewer than might have been expected by their ancestors of the Middle Ages and the start of our period, where so many copyholders, freeholders and tenants at least had access to their own land, even if the absolute ownership was with the Crown, or the lord of the manor.

It certainly seemed to be true that land ownership had, over the previous 300 years, become more and more concentrated into fewer and fewer hands. One of the lessons for researchers going backwards might be to expect that more of their ancestors held some land and farmed for themselves, even if only in a small way, than their research into nineteenth-century agricultural labourers might be leading them to presume.

It was not until the 1910 Survey of Land, also known as the Lloyd George Survey, that a nationwide attempt was made by national government to list owners and occupiers, and to delineate and value their exact holdings and plots of land, from the largest estate down to the smallest cottage and its garden. This hugely important survey produced maps and records that are extremely useful to local historians, although the tax that the whole endeavour was designed to raise, never came about.

Because the survey was undertaken in the period just prior to the 1911 census, it can be used together with the census to give a very complete picture of almost everywhere in England and Wales, although sadly with some large exceptions, such as London. The maps for the 1910 survey are held in the relevant county record offices; however, the most useful part, the field books, are only at The National Archives in series IR 58. It is well worth visiting The National Archives to use these records.

Starting Points for the Researcher

Some of the records discussed here are difficult to use, as well as being complex to find, so to start with the researcher should try to find out as much as possible from background reading and records that are easier to use. The most complete picture of rural landholding will only be built up if many sources are used together – and don't make the mistake of thinking that the ordinary labourer will not appear.

To make sense of the landscape and agriculture, the first and most obvious tool is a contemporary map at a scale that shows field boundaries. Choose one that will show contours, so that you have a sense of upland and lowland, and try to find a selection of older maps as well. Free online versions of many Victorian and later Ordnance Survey maps can be found at the National Library of Scotland website (https://maps.nls.uk/).

To search for a manor and its records, consult the relevant *Victoria County History* to find out if it is included, and if so, how the ownership of the manor descended. You can search The National Archives' *Discovery* catalogue online for a parish name plus the word 'manor', and use the Manorial Documents Register (MDR), also hosted by The National Archives. This allows you to search for any parish, and to find the name(s) of the manor associated with that parish; it will also tell you where the records are held (https://discovery.nationalarchives.gov.uk/manor-search).

The online version does not yet cover the whole country, although it comes close, and the MDR can also be consulted at The National Archives in person. However, many of the entries in the MDR were made many years ago, and it is always wise to search the local county record office catalogue and other online catalogues, such as Access to Archives, also hosted by The National Archives through their *Discovery* union catalogue. Work on the MDR is ongoing, and new discoveries of manorial material are being made all the time, so do not give up hope that one day something may turn up that will be relevant to your own ancestors. Because these records were private records, they may also still be in private hands.

Probate inventories are a very useful source of information for people's house interiors, furnishings, farming equipment, cattle and even pots and pans, as we saw in the example above. Although they do not survive for all wills, there are so many of them that do, that it makes sense always to search for them in the sixteenth to eighteenth centuries. Nowhere else, except perhaps in Chancery records, do you get such an intimate glance into people's everyday lives. Many of the inventories from these centuries were drawn up in respect of property in rural areas, and they were not just for the richer farmer and gentry, but survive for very humble folk. Probate records were created and held by the church courts prior to 1858. There is no overall national index to these records, so you will need to search to find where the diocesan record office is (for example, for Derbyshire it is in Lichfield).

However, many indexes to probate records have been printed and published, and increasingly these are found online at the major data websites such as Findmypast.co.uk, which allows access to about ninety separate indexes. But these are usually only indexes, and if you wish to see a will or an inventory, then you will have to access them at the record office. If you cannot find an inventory for your ancestor, it can be worth looking at the inventories of his or her contemporaries from the same village or nearby, or even use the probate documents from a group of villagers to discover more about links, kinships and ways of living.

If you are hunting for individual farms, or even plots of land, then don't ignore the more modern sources. Even if you have no farming ancestors in 1910/11, it is still very worthwhile looking at the 1910 survey, as it is the most complete survey ever undertaken of land ownership and tenancy in the UK. Every landowner is available, and also the occupier, and a complete delineation with description of the property in the majority of cases, although there are some gaps. In addition, the exact acreage is given.

If you can identify individual farms (for example by name, as in the Hazlehurst Farm example) then you will be able to see all the fields associated with that farm in 1910. This then allows you to move backwards in time again, perhaps by combining census information and using an enclosure award or the tithe records from 100 or more years prior to 1910. Before this, manorial records (if they survive), probate records and records of the parish chest may also help.

Title deeds, which usually deal with the conveyancing of property, are often quite well name-indexed, at least for the main parties, and it is well worth searching for surviving deeds very widely. As private documents, many of them have been deposited in the county record offices by solicitors – they are therefore found where the solicitor had his offices, rather than where the land actually lies. Again, *Discovery* catalogue is invaluable in this regard, as well as the surname: try searching using the parish name only to find other documents for the same plot(s) of land under different ownership.

By widening the focus to the whole village, you will gain a far more detailed and intimate knowledge of the village and any farmlands or even quite small plots associated with an ancestor. Because the 1910 survey gives both landowner and occupier for the whole area in a set of field books, it may also be possible to work out kinship links between some people – for example if you are researching a relatively rare surname. However, it would not be possible to use the 1910 survey as a starting point if you don't already have a good idea of the location of the farms or plots you are interested in.

There is a comprehensive guide to parliamentary enclosure awards by W.E. Tate: *A Domesday of English Parliamentary Enclosure Acts and Awards.* Copies of the awards and papers are in The National Archives in the series MAF 1 and MAF 25.

Older printed county histories and topographical histories will also help you to see a county through the eyes of contemporaries. Descriptions of features from the eighteenth-century antiquarian authors such as Hutchins for Dorset, and Hasted for Kent, can be invaluable. However, an antiquarian's writing and family trees always require a skeptical eye, as they can contain inaccuracies. Be careful not to take them all at face value. The first detailed maps also come from the eighteenth century – for example John Rocque's map of Middlesex in 1754 – and these are also valuable to pinpoint farms and properties existing prior to the Ordnance Survey of the nineteenth century, although they are unlikely to be drawn to scale accurately.

The tithe map and its apportionments are a good starting place to find the cottages and garden plots of most, as well as the larger parcels and the bigger farms. We look at the tithe in Chapter 4.

For the Victorian period, Geraldine Beech and Rose Mitchell's *Maps for Family and Local History, The Records of the Tithe,* and *Valuation Office and National Farm Surveys 1836–1943* (PRO Publications and Dundurn Group, 2nd revised edition, 2004) will act as a guide.

Manorial records are not very well covered by the genealogy literature, however the most readable and accessible account is a very old one and can be downloaded from the internet for free: N.J. Hone, *The Manor and Manorial Records* (London, 1906). More advanced and experienced early modern researchers will appreciate P.D.A. Harvey, *Manorial Records* (British Records Association, revised edition 1999).

4

The Church and the Tithe

The Parish Church

The parish church lay at both the social and religious centre of village life, whether the village and the parish were one and the same, or whether the parish included more than one village or hamlet, scattered or nucleated. It is certainly true that not all parish churches are geographically in the centre of a village; in some places they are isolated among fields. But wherever the physical buildings were located, the church was more than just a place of worship: it was a place where parishioners would gather every week. This was probably the largest gathering some of them saw on a regular basis, aside from visiting the local market day in the nearest larger settlement, or perhaps an annual fair.

For a largely unlettered community, the church was not only where people had religious worship, but also where they heard about the news of the area and of the world, such of it that arrived. The clergyman in the earlier period may have been the only person, aside from any local gentry and possibly a farmer or so, who had any education and who was able to read and write. He was therefore in a position of huge authority.

Having said that, we should recognize that for some parishioners, the parish church could be a long walk from home, particularly in the north of England where parishes were much larger than in the south. As populations expanded, chapelries were set up; however, as late as 1838 the situation in Wensleydale was such that the Church Building Society was reporting that:

> ... nearly the whole of Wensleydale is in the parish of Aysgarth, endowment £137 – twelve townships, with nearly six thousand

> inhabitants, and five chapels; but still many of the parishioners are so widely separated, as to be unable to partake of the services or duties of the church.[42]

The medieval church was a legal and religious entity with similarities to a country or a state. It had laws, law givers and lawyers, and it kept prisons. This great state was broken by the Reformation; however, it retained some of those stately functions for a very long time, and it is hard to over-estimate the importance of the church and the parish to our rural ancestors, and not just in a purely religious way. Church administration created records specific to each parish; these contain the names of parishioners, and thus should always be considered a useful hunting ground for genealogists.

Church administration was naturally not confined to the rural parish and village – it obviously operated in towns and cities as well. However, because of the unique importance to village history of some of these records, particularly the records of tithe and glebe, a dominant part of this chapter is devoted to them.

Someone had to pay for the day-to-day running of the parish church and its fabric, and for the upkeep of its rector, vicar or curate. These payments were quite apart from other sums collected from the parish via the rates. There was no salary from the church authorities for the clergyman. He had to rely on the tithe (originally a tenth of a parishioner's produce from the land) and any money he could get from what are known as glebe lands, as well as donations collected in church. 'Glebe' simply means a piece of cultivated land, but in relation to the church it means a discrete piece of land cultivated for the benefit of the clergyman.

These records of tithe and glebe are hugely useful to the local and family historian for what they can tell us about the owners and occupiers of land, and can be used in conjunction with the other records already discussed in the previous two chapters. They are also more often to be found in connection with rural parishes than those in towns, and thus have a special significance for the history of the countryside, rather than the town, where payment of the tithe was very widely ignored. With the glebe, the Sunday collection and the tithe, the church collected rent money from a few, donations from many, and placed a tax in kind on everyone to pay for the clergyman. These amounts collected from the parishioners were known as the clergy benefice or living.

Each parish church had a patron. Historically the patron was the landowner owning the land on which the church was erected. The patron had the right to appoint the clergyman, subject to the bishop's approval. This patronage was therefore a property right, and it was possible to sell it. Every parish had a patron. In the past, the patron could have had a huge amount of influence over a community's affairs through a choice of clergyman sympathetic to their values and politics. And the clergy were often under the thumb of a patron, as the novels of Jane Austen testify. *See*, for example, the odious Mr Collins under the sway of Lady Catherine de Burgh in *Pride and Prejudice*.

When searching for places in Lewis's *Topographical Dictionary* you may have come across a reference to the value of the 'living' for a parish, using a mysterious source called the *King's Book*. This refers to a survey undertaken by Henry VIII in 1535 as part of the process of trying to account for church possessions during the Reformation, in order to tax the clergy. It is also known as the *Valor Eccliesiasticus*, or *Liber Regis*. The full survey was printed by several publishers in the eighteenth century, and it is now possible to read John Bacon's 1786 updated version online at a website maintained by the Hathi Trust.[43]

The entry for Bredhurst in the *King's Book* is as follows:

> Bradhurst C[uracy] (St Peter) A chapel to Holingborne. Rec[tor] Hollingbourn Patr[on] John Cauntley 1783. 37l. 17s. 6d. certified Value. Exempt from the Archdeacon of Canterbury.

This provides us with the useful information that Bredhurst (previously spelled Bradhurst) was a chapel to Hollingborne, the patron (landowner) was John Cauntley in 1783, and the annual value of the living was £37 17s 6d. In addition it tells us that this parish is outside the jurisdiction of the Archdeaconry of Canterbury, and that the rector is at Hollingbourne.

The Datchworth entry is as follows, in a slightly different style:

> [yearly value in King's Book] £14 13s 4 Datchworth R[ectory] (All Saints) Prox. Episc 4s.4d. Earl of Essex, 1709. Clare Hall, Cambridge [yearly tenths] £1 9s 4d

And Aysgarth, in North Yorkshire, which is a parish that includes our Abbotside, appears under the heading 'Livings Discharged' – that is, with no tax to pay, with a clear yearly value of £42 14s, and in the *King's Books* at £19 6s 8d:

> Askarthe, alias Aisgarth [Vicarage] (St. Andrew) Val. In denar. Numerat. Abb. De Jorrevall £19 6s 8d. Abb. Jorrevall, Propr(ietor) Trinity College, Cambridge.

There then follows a useful list of chapels in Aysgarth: Askrigg, St Oswald, Hardraw, Hawes, Lundes and Stallingbusk, together with their values and livings. This would be useful to help a researcher identify chapels and records that may not be in the parish church. Jorrevall is an older name for Jervaulx Abbey.

What Henry VIII's survey of 1535 revealed was the very uneven nature of the amounts available to a clergyman. Most rectors and some of the vicars had an adequate recompense, but many of the rest did not. Rectors, vicars and curates could be very dependent on their parishioners, and on the fees set for baptisms, marriages and burials as well as donations. Livings were found to be uneven across the country, with the clergy in the south generally having less land and less income.[44] Of course the survey was quickly out of date, yet continued to be used as the legal basis for many arguments about the livings of the clergy.

Glebe Terriers

The glebe or parish terrier is a detailed listing of lands and church properties set aside for the benefit of the clergyman. 'Terrier' is simply another term for a written survey. Thus, glebe land is similar to a manorial lord's demesne land. Where glebe terriers exist they can provide very useful lists of local names because this farmland was often rented out to local farmers. Just as with demesne land, glebe lands could include strips in the common fields, and therefore can provide a great deal of information if manorial records are lacking.

In the days before land registration or maps drawn to the correct scale, and recognized plot numbers, land was described by reference to the occupying neighbours. This means that records such as glebe terriers not only contain the names of tenants but can also contain a note of the occupiers of the land next door to the glebe. For example, strips of glebe may be described as 'such and such lying on the south side of Joe Fishe and to the north of Jane Owen and to the east of William Gregory.' Such descriptions usefully bring in the names of many local field occupiers.

Terriers were not drawn up very regularly, usually only under particular circumstances, so they can at best only provide a snapshot; even so, it is a highly useful one. The survival of these lists is itself very haphazard; many parishes have none, and it would be fortunate to find more than one or two for a single parish. Not all livings were well endowed with glebe lands, or even had any at all, thus where it was lacking, clergymen had to rely on tithes for the major source of their income. Some terriers also include a description of how income from tithes and fees is calculated and collected.

In 1571, under Canon 87, a general survey was made of church land in every parish, and bishops were directed to oversee the compilation of terriers of glebe land and to keep these in the diocese; in 1604 this was made a more formal requirement.[45] There was no overall direction as to exactly how the terrier should be laid out, so this was left to the individual clergymen. The bishop was supposed to gather in the terriers when he made his periodic visitations around the parishes in the diocese. A copy of the survey could also be kept in the parish chest, and occasionally copies appear within parish registers.

More usefully for the researcher, some dioceses appointed special surveyors of 'Church Glebes and Possessions within the Diocese'. Lincoln diocese did this in the years 1605–7, and all the surveys made under the Lincoln surveyor are set out in the same way. This allows comparison between parishes, which is of use to the local historian. In Hertfordshire, information from the Hertford record office catalogue says that:

> A large number of glebe terriers of 1638 were fully transcribed in the Hertfordshire Genealogist and Antiquary ed. William Brigg, (3 vols, 1895–1898). Further original glebe terriers were purchased from Messrs. Sotheby's in 1937 and are catalogued as 21328–21333. These are for Ashwell 1638, Caldecote 1638 and Hinxworth 1638, 1686 and 1724.[46]

This gives interesting evidence of the archival history of this type of parish record, as well as alerting us to the fact that there was a large-scale survey undertaken in 1638, and then further surveys of 1686 and 1724. As with parish registers, glebe terriers from many parishes unfortunately found their way out on to the antiquarian market-place, and are still turning up, to be collected by the county record offices where possible. It is therefore well worth checking not only what might be with the parish records and the diocesan archives, but in other large collections such as the British Library.

The most useful glebe terriers usually start with a description of the church and the churchyard, including the parsonage or rectory house. This includes everything in the church, all its fabric, furniture, plate, books and the bells, and information about the churchyard with a note if there are any obligations to repair walls. The parsonage house is described in detail, including what the building is constructed from, and information about outbuildings. In the 1638 Hertfordshire examples, the church itself is omitted, but there are descriptions of each parsonage house and its gardens and outbuildings, and this is followed by a description of the exact location of the glebe land. These describe all the boundaries, and whose land is abutting.

In a typical example from the village of Kimpton, Hertfordshire, in 1638, the wording for each plot shows how it is possible to use a glebe terrier to reconstruct the occupation and ownership of large parts of a parish. If the researcher is fortunate, there will be a large, scattered glebe and many small landholders abutting, and the terrier can be used for useful genealogical clues; for example:

> Three Acres in Churchfeild buttinge on the South side of the Kinges highway and the West side buttinge upon the land of John Hill, and the North Side upon the land of Robert

> Gouldsmith, and the East side upon the land of the widdowe Chambers.[47]

The 1724 Hertfordshire terriers, also printed by William Brigg, are fuller and contain information about the tithe revenue, give details of any tithe-free land, as well as arrangements for tithe collection. They give the missing information about the fabric of the church, the books and bells, and also include a list of fees, which were charged for things such as marriage, burials and so on. That for King's Langley also includes lists of charitable donations for the poor. The lists of fees are particularly interesting, and give good evidence as to the difference in cost of being buried inside the church and outside, as well as the different rates for marriages:

> Item fees due to the Vicar are as followeth tenn Shillings a Marriage with Licence five Shillings with Banns 6d for Churching 6d Registering every Child Baptised 1s for publishing Banns of Marriage and 2d a head for offerings for every one of the age of 16 years. A Noble for breaking the ground in any part of the Church, except the Chancell and a Noble also for burying any Corps in the Church and Ten shillings in the Chancell, two shillings for breaking the Ground in the churchyard.[48]

Therefore, in King's Langley the fee for a marriage with a licence was double the price of a marriage with banns, at 10s, and with banns 5s, with another 1s for each publication of banns. If bride and groom came from different parishes, then publication of banns would add on 2s or so, depending on the second parish's charges for banns, making a marriage with banns 7s in all (a considerable sum in 1724, when farm wages might be only 7s a week).

A noble was a medieval coin equal to 80 pennies, or one-third of a pound. For anyone wondering about whether their ancestors had to save up to be married, the answer is here: if they were a poor labourer, then yes, they did. Occasionally a vicar would have a 'cut-price' day, often on Christmas Day, and it is possible to find several couples being married on the same day because of a reduced fee. It was the thorny question of fees for marriages that partly caused some of the so-called clandestine marriages of the early eighteenth century, whereby a clergyman might undercut other nearby churches, or turn a blind eye to those from outside parishes in order to attract couples to his church for the fee income.

The Hertfordshire 1638 and 1724 glebe terrier examples all end with the signatures of the vicar, churchwardens and sidesmen (if any). Although the terrier for Datchworth is not included in the printed terriers quoted from, nevertheless there is a terrier from 1607 in Hertford Record Office, which is transcribed by Jane Walker in her book *Datchworth Tithe Accounts*. Her work shows that the glebe land in Datchworth was spread between 10 acres of fields immediately around the Rectory house, a small piece of ground around the church itself, and then also in many scattered strips in the common fields to the north of the church, the total amounting to over 24 acres.[49]

The Tithe

A tithe is literally a tenth, and the word is the root of the Anglo Saxon 'tithing', which was one man in ten; in the manorial court leet, one householder in every ten – the tithing man – was responsible for reporting misdemeanours to the court, and the word has come to mean a tenth of anything. The tithe was an ancient yearly payment in kind to the clergyman, made at Easter, of a tenth of each parishioner's produce. It was a very practical way of dealing with the problem of providing food and income for the incumbent priest in a time when there was a lack of physical money in circulation, and when the church itself did not offer a salary or any kind of wage to clergymen. Tithe payments in some areas made up a substantial part of a clergyman's income.

Because the parish needed to delineate its boundary in order to collect tithe payments from a set area, it can be argued that the area of tithe and the parish boundary are one and the same. It is possible that parish boundaries thus originally arose out of the need to set out clearly which lands were for the use of which church.

If a rector was in the parish, then he collected this tithe or was paid it, and his house was also known as a 'rectory'. In the

Middle Ages many benefices were owned by the monasteries, and the monasteries themselves were entitled to the tithe, but also had to provide the spiritual care that the relationship demanded. This spiritual care they contracted out to vicars, who then lived in vicarages. After the monasteries were dissolved by Henry VIII, the monastic benefices passed to the larger landowners and they became 'lay rectors', entitled to receive tithes. This passing of the tithe to a large landholder must have seemed deeply unfair to the poor parishioner, as it meant some of his hard work in husbandry and agriculture had to be given up for the benefit of the richest people in the country.

Tithes were payable on animals, agricultural crops and so on, and are often classified as either 'great' or 'small'. The great tithe was made up of corn, hay and wood, and was directly related to land rather than individuals, while the small tithe was any other produce from the land including animals, hens, eggs, market garden produce and so on, with the small tithe payable by all people. The great tithe was usually, although not always, payable to the rector, and the small tithe payable to the vicar.

Payment of tithes to absentee rectors, or where the land was poor and the farmers' livings precarious, caused a great deal of bad blood between the clergy and the farmers, with many legal disputes. The parish historian W.E. Tate gives many examples of lawsuits brought in a very non-edifying way by vicars for a tithe on such things as fallen apples, wild cherries, and even the stubble in a wheat field.[50] Newly appointed incumbents sometimes started off a relationship with their parishioners by drawing up lists of tithe payments, and seeking to resurrect payments that had previously been ignored.

If a clergyman did pursue his rights in this way, new items could be added to the tithe list, and one can imagine the dismay of the poor cottager being told that they now had to give up every tenth hen or laboriously tended cabbage. Adding to the general confusion and dissatisfaction of the tithe payer, by the nineteenth century tithes increasingly did not end up with the clergy, but because of land transfers had become payable to the lay rectors – in other words the large landowners.

Naturally the payment of produce was difficult to organize: it required the church to keep a suitable barn or fields, and to be prepared to handle animals and grain alike. Thus from quite early on, the tithe of produce in any one area may have been replaced by a money payment. This tended to have happened in those places where enclosure of the common fields had previously taken place – indeed, an objective of the Enclosure Acts was to get rid of the tithe. Sometimes the tithe was replaced by an allotment of land, and sometimes by a payment. In addition, religious dissenters argued forcefully against payment of the tithe at all, although some Puritans counter-argued that it helped the clergy attend to their spiritual flock without having to worry about money. By the end of the eighteenth century, the system had become a confused and iniquitous mess – yet despite all the piecemeal and local enclosures and payments, many English country parishes were still paying some tithe in kind.

However, it had become apparent that something had to be done, and a general commutation of the tithe to a money payment was necessary across the whole country. Luckily for the landlords this could be coupled with a move to end the open field system in the name of agricultural improvement. This would mean that produce could no longer be collected, but instead a money payment would be made, just like a rent. This was called the 'tithe rent charge'.

After several failed attempts, finally the commutation of the tithe to an annual money payment was made law in England and Wales with the great Tithe Act of 1836. In addition, the new tithe rent charges were no longer to be subject to local variation, as had long been the custom, but were fixed over the whole country each year, according to the moving national average price of corn calculated over the seven previous years. If corn prices rose, the tithe rent charge rose; if they fell, the rent charge fell.

Tithe Maps and Apportionments

It is the records created by the 1836 Act that are of most value to family and local historians alike, and one of the reasons they are of the utmost importance is the record of occupation of the humblest bit of land, thus ensuring that not only are the farms included, but small cottages and gardens as well. The lists of landholders and occupiers in the apportionment act as a kind of land census. They also record the use of local field names, which is fascinating for landscape historians, and also very useful for the genealogist if a field name from the tithe apportionment can be matched with a field name in a probate document, a manorial court document, or a conveyancing deed.

The tithe records fall into three kinds: files, maps and apportionments. The only downside for the researcher is that because of those previous enclosures, the 1836 Act maps and apportionments cover only about three-quarters of parishes in England and Wales, rather than all.

After the Bill received royal assent on 13 August 1836, three tithe commissioners were appointed. The work was very challenging, involving the whole of England and Wales and every parish and township. Their first job was to find out to what extent any commutation of tithe for money had already taken place, and this meant sending out written enquiries to all parishes and townships listed in the census returns. The results are now at The National Archives in the series IR 18, called Tithe Files.

Unfortunately, the returned answers to enquiries were weeded by earlier archivists, and the remaining contents are hit and miss as far as family historians are concerned. When a quick agreement was reached, there is little material, but where there was disagreement and a compulsory award had to be made, then there could be plenty of interesting documents about the exact nature of the tithe, and the relationship of the clergyman with his parishioners, as well as detail from meetings and draft awards.

Meanwhile each tithe owner had to advertise publicly a general meeting of landowners in order to come to a joint agreement for the commutation. These notices were placed in the local papers, for the purpose of bringing together the local landowners and drawing up an agreement for the commutation of those tithes to monetary payments. Just such a notice appeared in the *Kentish Gazette* of Tuesday 14 August 1838, and shows that the curate of Bredhurst, Kent, was the only person collecting the Bredhurst tithe.

> I, the undersigned, being the Sole Tithe Owner within the Parish of BREDHURST in the county of Kent, whose Interest is the whole value of the Tithes of the said Parish, do, by

this Notice in writing under my hand, call a PAROCHIAL MEETING of LAND OWNERS within the said Parish, for the purpose of making an agreement for the General Commutation of Tithes within the limits of the said Parish, pursuant to the provisions of an Act passed in the 6th and 7th years of the reign of his later Majesty, entituled "An Act of the Commutation of Tithes in England and Wales."

And I do hereby give Notice, that such Meeting will be held at the BELL PUBLIC HOUSE, in the said Parish, on WEDNESDAY, the 29th of August, at the hour of Eleven in the forenoon. – Given under my hand this 4th day of August, 1838.
THOS. ANDREWS, Perpetual Curate of Bredhurst

The process of agreement and apportionment for Bredhurst took two years, even though there were only seventeen landowners and the parish is tiny, being only 599 acres, 7 acres of which were waste. If there was no agreement between the tithe-owners and landowners, then under the Act an award could be made by the tithe commissioners.

After the initial enquiries had been made, the tithe commissioners had to survey and draw up a map of the exact area that was titheable. Surveyors were therefore contracted and despatched all over England and Wales to produce the relevant maps. The detail in the maps can be wonderful, showing the exact position of plots, and with each plot given a number so that it may be related to the list of owners/occupiers on the apportionment. They may show all field boundaries and may perhaps even plot trees. However, these maps can be cumbersome to use, sometimes being very large and tightly rolled. Originally, lists of landholders and occupiers were attached to the map, and sown in: this part is known as the apportionment.

The maps fall into two classes: first and second. First-class maps are highly accurate, drawn to scale, and sealed and signed by the tithe commissioners, and can still be used as accurate legal documents; however, second-class maps are much more variable, and unfortunately make up over 80 per cent of the total. Originally the commissioners had made attempts to provide maps of a high standard throughout, but in practice this proved impossible.

Naturally there was often no suitable map already in existence, and the expense of new maps had to be met by the landowner.

Although the surveyors of the maps were given detailed instructions by the tithe commissioners, they didn't all pay attention to them, and the results are mixed, as might be expected from such a huge task. Trying to insist on uniformity would just have delayed the whole process too much. Second-class maps should therefore not be taken as an accurate scale representation of buildings and plots, as the main purpose was to show boundaries. For this reason they often omit roads, and other features as well. However, although they may lack the detail needed by the lawyer or the landscape historian, when used with care by the genealogist, they can still be very useful, and when used with the apportionment (which includes the size of the plot), can provide astonishing insight into an ancestor's way of life.

The Bredhurst map is dated 1839 and surveyed and drawn up by A. Doull of Chatham. On the map is noted: 'July 27th 1840. This map was deposited in the Parish and produced at an Appeal meeting held this day'; it is signed by the assistant tithe commissioner.[51] This tells us there was a dispute over at least one aspect of the map or apportionment; however, they did come to an agreement as the catalogue description for the Bredhurst Tithe File[52] says that 'An agreement and apportionment were made for this tithe district' – which means there is less likely to be any correspondence existing. Where the words 'award and apportionment' are noted in the catalogue, this notes a disagreement that the tithe commissioners had to rule on, and thus correspondence may exist.

After the enquiries and the surveying and the agreement between landholders or the award made by the Commissioners, came the final step in the process, which in a handful of localities took up to another fifty years or so, and this was the finalized tithe apportionment. This was the actual amount of payment each tenant was henceforth liable to pay annually to the tithe owner. In Bredhurst's case the tithes were all payable to the perpetual curate, Thomas Andrews. The apportionments are important records as they detail the amounts of land occupied, by whom, and the money payments.

The apportionment for Bredhurst, containing a list of the landowners and occupiers, a description of the fields and plots and what was being cultivated, together with the plot sizes, was finalized and dated 7 September 1840, less than two months after the appeal meeting on 27 July 1840. Thus the process was completed.

For the genealogy researcher, the main records of interest are likely to be the maps and apportionments, as the lists of landholders and occupiers in the apportionment act as a kind of land census, which may show an ancestor's name and his cottage or farm (although not all occupiers may be listed). However, those who are dedicated or researching the whole history of a village may also want to follow up any cases brought by individual clergymen to court, and to search within IR 18 for any surviving correspondence and for any parish terriers, which, as we saw above, can sometimes list tithes payable. Tithe maps may also exist from earlier periods, pre-1836. There can be great variation between places as to what was collected.

Did everyone pay the tithe? No, there had always been widespread evasion in the larger cities, and depending on the area of the country, early private enclosures had also brought an end to tithe payments. Tithe maps were only rarely drawn up for urban areas, because the tithe was a payment in kind, and in any event widely ignored in London and other urban places. The rectors of the Midlands and the North had often supported enclosure of open fields in order to abolish the tithe. Most enclosure acts extinguished all tithes in a parish, with the land being parcelled up between the larger landowners and the incumbent. Where this happened there was a change in the relationship between the clergy and their parishioners, and they became landowners and not tax collectors.[53]

Tithe maps and apportionments can now be easily found online. The county of Cheshire was one of the pioneers in putting together a search engine for names and places, allowing any plot to be seen on a tithe map and also on the 1875 Ordnance Survey and other maps. This is a very valuable tool for those with Cheshire ancestors, as it is available for free. Following this, searching for tithe maps and apportionments outside Cheshire has become much easier due to the digitization of the maps held by The National Archives by thegenealogist.co.uk, a paid-for subscription website (thegenealogist.co.uk/tithe).

The apportionments are more consistent than the maps because they were written on to pre-printed forms. The example apportionment entry below is from Great Budworth in Cheshire, a village that proudly declaims itself to be the most picturesque in Cheshire. The whole of the apportionment was downloaded and saved as a spreadsheet from the Cheshire Tithe Maps Online; however, while the online Mapping function has been much expanded, the apportionments now have to be specially requested (https://maps.cheshireeast.gov.uk/tithemaps/).

There were 382 plots in the parish and township of Great Budworth paying the tithe. The map itself is dated 1845. In the Great Budworth example there are around a dozen major landowners. It is possible to build a complete picture of the land use and occupation in the village in 1845, and the usefulness of this is that it can be directly compared to both the 1841 and 1851 census entries. The plots have their field names – some of them no doubt very ancient, or descriptive of a past purpose, for example 'Brittains or Hanging Hill'. It is possible to reconstruct all the cottages and houses, and there are many descriptive field names, such as 'Gorsty Hey', described as a clover meadow occupied by Edward Grange and owned by Rowland Eyles Egerton Warburton, one of the major landowners in the area. The table below gives the detail for this entry including the area – 4 acres, 2 roods and 24 perches.

Ref: EDT 173/2	Plot Number 120	Field Name Gorsty Hey	clover meadow	4	2	24	Rowland Eyles Egerton Warburton	Edward Grange	Great Budworth

It is also interesting to spot those areas of land being used for things other than agriculture; for example, at the time of this apportionment there were five public houses in Great Budworth: the Cock, the George and Dragon, the Saracen's Head, the Ring O'Bells and the White Hart. The smallest plots are all of 1 perch for single cottages, and the largest are those of the park and lands owned and occupied by the main landowner James Heath Leigh, occupying Belmont Hall (now Grade 1 listed), built in 1755 and lying in over 7 acres of grounds. It is still owned by the Leigh family, although it is now a school. A tithe map may be the first time the researcher has come across information about the local aristocratic or large landowner, and this could be a valuable tool in helping to discover more about the history of the place and the landholdings.

East Sussex has also put tithe maps and apportionments online, and more information about the maps is available there, although the map functionality is not quite as good as with Cheshire (https://apps.eastsussex.gov.uk/leisureandtourism/localandfamilyhistory/tithemaps/).

Free transcriptions for the County of Kent are available on the web pages of the Kent Archaeological Society. The forms for Kent are set out in a similar manner to Cheshire, although with some minor differences. The following table is an extract from the entry for Bredhurst:[54]

Owner	*Occupier*	*No.*	*Description*	*Cultivation*	*Area (acres, rods, perches)*
Alexander	James	70	Cottage & Garden	Garden	0.0.25
Barnes	Harvey &	71	Cottage & Garden	Garden	0.0.29
	Ambrose				**0.1.14**
	Naylor				
George	George	57	Winch Mill	Arable	14.1.20
Frederick	Nethercoat	58	---	Firs	0.3. 5
Douce Esq	Cooke	59	---	Arable	0.2. 0
		60	---	Pasture	0.0.22
		61	Winch Field	Arable	4.1.15
		62	Wood	Wood	1.1.26
					21.2. 8

As can be seen from the Great Budworth and Bredhurst examples, the apportionments are standardized and consist of printed forms containing columns for the landowner and occupiers' names (because until the passing of the Tithe Act 1891 the payment of tithe rent charge was the owner's liability), as well as the other details. After a preamble, a detailed apportionment of the aggregate tithe rent charge then follows. The plot numbers relate to numbers on the map. In Bredhurst the number of tithe-paying owners is only seventeen, one of whom is the Crown. The occupiers are moderate farmers or small cottagers, as we might expect from this small, out-of-the-way parish.

It would be a great mistake to think that these were the only people living in Bredhurst at the time; the 1841 census has 138 souls in Bredhurst. Thus, if we put the tithe apportionment together with the 1841 census information, we find that the cottage of Ambrose Naylor, an agricultural labourer aged fifty-two, actually held six people, all members of the Naylor family.

Kent had a long history of tithe disputes and was a county that was still paying the tithe in kind, with crops at the end of the eighteenth century. It was also one of the places where clergymen were physically attacked during the notorious disturbances known as the Swing Riots of the 1830s. Nevertheless, the whole county was surveyed and apportioned completely within ten years, with the last awards being made in 1848, the majority of them by agreement. In total the Kent tithe surveys contain a record of the ownership, occupation and use of 974,706 acres of land, amounting to 98.1 per cent of the surface area of Kent *c*.1840. [55]

There are sometimes codes to the right-hand side of the apportionment, which relate to activity after the document was originally drawn up. 'AA' means 'altered apportionment', and you may find more information about an alteration to a boundary or ownership in IR 29. 'CR' means a compulsory redemption of the rent charge. This would have been a lump-sum payment to 'buy out' the rent charge, and no tithe would be payable after the redemption. You may also see other notations:

CRA	corn rent annuity
KA	voluntary redemption
M	merger

When the landowner was also the tithe owner, an individual was liable to pay tithes to himself, which is obviously a piece of nonsense. This was normally resolved by a process known as merging the tithes (or tithe rent charge) in the land. The land thus had no monetary rent charge associated with it, and this continued when or if it was sold to a new owner. There were many such mergers, and this brought about a situation where some land was free of all rent charge prior to the 1936 abolition of the whole system.

OA	order for apportionment of tithe redemption annuity
R	redemption (of tithe rent charge by lump sum)
RA	redemption of tithe rent charge by annuity

Matching the Tithe Map With Older Records

And what about Hazlehurst Farm in the parish of Ashover, which we met in the probate inventory of John Beachcroft in Chapter 2? Because of its name, this farm was easy to find in the tithe records using both the search engine at thegenealogist.co.uk, and the local knowledge that I had already built up from my earlier search for it. The Ashover map is dated 1849, and Hazlehurst Farm is clearly named on the map.

In 1849 the occupier was James Wragg, a tenant farmer, and the owner was Mary Ann Gladwin. It had just over 71 acres of land, a mixture of arable, pasture and meadow over nineteen fields, with field names very suggestive of mixed farming having been carried on over these fields for many, many hundreds of years, just as the inventory of John Beachcroft suggests that he, too, had a small mixed farm. Thus there is a field called Calf Doles, and another Calf Yard, there is Stubble Close and Cow Leys, Little Meadow, Barn Close, Yew Tree Close, Well Close and Wood Close. It is a neat collection of small fields encircling the house, with a total annual rent charge of £4 10s, and 5d payable to the Rector of Ashover.[56]

It seems entirely possible that these are more or less the exact same fields that Beachcroft was farming back in the sixteenth century, probably with the addition of a little more land. When looked at with the aerial photographic view of Google Maps or Bing maps online, the hedged field boundaries from the 1849 map are still apparent today, with only the growth of woodland into one field a major difference. This seems like history one can almost reach out and touch, and it should enthuse any family historian to think that they could identify and walk in the same fields as their ancestor.

For the genealogist, the main question is going to be, how accurate are the names as to ownership and occupier of the lands? What don't these lists tell us? An 'owner of land' meant any person in possession or receipt of the rents and profits of land, so it is almost certain that some mortgagees and tenants for life were assumed to be owners at tithe commutation. It would be wise to check the parish rate books, and also the census to build the most accurate picture. The 1851 census also gives the acreage for each farm, if you can trace forwards.

It is hit and miss as to whether you will find anything at all for the parish you are researching. Unfortunately there were many districts in which no apportionment was made, although the tithes were commuted under the provisions of the 1836 Act. This is because either the amount involved was negligible, or there was a special award, and/or the redemption or merger of the tithe rent charges. Obviously, if landowners could get away with not having to bear the expense of a map and a formal apportionment, then they would.

The 1836 Act was not completely the end of the tithe story for those who had to pay the rent charge. The annual payment of the tithe was cause for food, drink and socializing in many villages. In his eponymous diary the Reverend Kilvert describes a tithe audit and dinner held in the parish of Bredwardine, Herefordshire, on Tuesday 5 February 1879:

> Today was the Tithe audit and tithe dinner to the farmers, both held at the Vicarage. About 50 tithe payers came, most of them very small holders, some paying as little as 9d. As soon as they had paid their tithe to Mr Heywood in the front hall they retired into the back hall and regaled themselves with bread, cheese and beer, some of them eating and drinking the value of the tithe they had paid. The tithe-paying began about 3pm and the stream went on til six. At seven I sat down to dinner with the farmers.[57]

W.E. Tate tells us that by 1886, 11,787 tithe apportionments had been made and only twenty-four parishes were left with tithes as payment in kind.[58] There was a further Act in 1891 that changed the rent charge from being the tenant farmer's annual responsibility to being the landlord's or the owner's responsibility. Of course, the owner simply put up rents in order to cover their increased costs. By the 1930s there was agitation for complete reform. Two further Acts in 1918 and 1925 had failed to fix equitable rates; while the 1925 Act allowed for the gradual exemption of all tithes payable to the church by way of a sinking fund, the lay tithe with all its iniquities remained. All tithe was finally abolished in 1936.

Occasionally you may come across surviving tithe accounts in amongst the parish chest records and normally held at the relevant county record office. Tithe accounts exist in some quantity for Datchworth due to a particularly diligent and methodical clergyman, who kept a running account of the tithes he received from 1711 to 1747; these are now edited and transcribed by Jane Walker, as previously noted.[59]

Changes in the Authority and Administration of the Parish

The start of our period just after the Reformation coincides with the start of a period of gradual increase in the civil responsibilities undertaken by the parish. In many ways these reforms took away some of the power of the old manorial courts – *see* Chapter 3 – and gave them to the parish. In 1555, the repair of highways fell to the parish, and local able-bodied men were supposed to work six days a year on their upkeep. It introduced a new set of parish officials called the surveyors of the highways, elected by the ratepayers. Henceforward the ratepayers were to become increasingly important.

From 1536, legislation had required parishes to provide for their 'impotent' poor, whether orphaned, sick, disabled, too old to work, or for some other reason unable to work. In 1572, the ratepayers had to choose new 'overseers of the poor', to be added to the parish officers. The Poor Law Act of 1601 gave real authority to those overseers, in cooperation with the churchwardens, to raise and spend money on poor relief, again to come from the rates. We look at some aspects of the Poor Law in relation to the village in Chapter 5.

Two more types of parish record were created from these administrative duties, although by no means restricted to the village, being equally as important in the town or city. Nevertheless they may play a role in the breaking down of a family history research block, as well as showing the character of a place. They are the churchwardens' accounts and the vestry minutes.

The Churchwardens' Accounts

Churchwardens' accounts are among the earliest of surviving parish records and pre-date the Reformation, but unhappily, like many of the records being discussed in this chapter, their survival varies very much from place to place. The churchwardens were appointed to be the guardians of the fabric of the parish church. They may also have been known as stewards, or church reeve, and they have very ancient origins, at least as far as back as 1167. Wardens were elected or chosen from the local people annually, and presented their accounts at Easter each year. In some places there was a system of rotation amongst all male householders, in other places one or two yeomen or tradesmen families dominate in these, as well as other parish offices.

As always, it helps to know about the idiosyncracies of individual places. In some places the churchwarden's accounts give a great amount of detail in the day-to-day running of the parish, and mention many local people. In others, they are less useful and are sparse with names. Churchwardens were responsible for the nave of the church, the churchyards and other parish property. However, upkeep of the chancel of the church was the responsibility of rectors and the 'impropriators', often leading laymen in the area.

Essentially the accounts are lists of payments for items for the church, together with receipts for payments made. They regularly include rent received from properties, church running costs, such as provision of communion bread and wine, cost of the visitation by the bishop, cleaning and repairs, payments to mole catchers and dog whippers, and maintenance of bells. There will be payments to local carpenters, builders, people repairing bells, and building projects, sums received from locals for burial, and rents received from glebe and other lands. If you are lucky, many parishioners' and local tradesmen's names will appear.

It is always worth going through the churchwardens' accounts and the parish registers together when researching families, as the one may shed light on the other. In some places the churchwardens' accounts contain payments to paupers. The bigger the parish and more prestigious the church and its buildings and land, then the greater the possibility of extensive accounts that are rich in names.

An example of the richness of these records comes from the West Sussex village of Billingshurst. Billingshurst is a large parish and has a good run of surviving records, which have been well catalogued. The accounts survive from 1520 to 1639 and have been transcribed, and as well as showing the changing history of church liturgy, customs and beliefs, and the furnishings and arranging of the church, they also provide little insights into the daily life of the parish. For example, they include rent from tenants including parish cows being let out and parishioners standing surety, and many regular payments for work to the bells. In one instance there is the cost of a journey all the way to Reading in Berkshire on the business of bell repair, letting of the seats in the church including a request from a woman who attended the altar for a permanent seat by the church door for her lifetime; other expenses include for a plumber to come from Chichester to repair a gutter, also many payments for wax and candles, and regular payments to workmen, including for their drink. Donations include money given to 'maimed soldiers'.[60]

The 1729 churchwarden's accounts for the parish of Coughton in Warwickshire featured in the Warwickshire Archives Document of the Month, and is illustrated at https://www.ourwarwickshire.org.uk/content/article/churchwardens-account-book-coughton-1729. It includes payments to remove dogs from the church, and for the killing of pests such as sparrows, rooks, foxes and even hedgehogs, known as urchins, as well as interesting charitable payments: 'gave to 30 Men taken by the Turks 6d' – presumably there was a collection being made – and also 'gave to 2 Scotch Men that had been robbed 6d.'

The example from Coughton lacks the full details of names of all the recipients of the payments, however the churchwarden's accounts from Wirksworth in Derbyshire are replete in parishioners' names from the 1660s to the mid-eighteenth century. Payments made for hedgehogs, fox heads and ravens frequently occur, naming all the people involved, including some women, as well as many other interesting payments such as the payments to the regular washerwoman for the surplices, Mary Huttlescutt, in the 1680s. A transcription by John Palmer exists at a private website for the records of Wirksworth, created from his detailed study of the parish (http://www.wirksworth.org.uk).[61]

There is an online project in conjunction with Warwickshire University to list all surviving churchwardens' accounts, as well as transcriptions and printed editions. Called *The Churchwardens' Accounts of England and Wales*, when complete it will be a wonderful resource to finding these fascinating documents, as they are not usually featured among the genealogical useful documents most often found online. The project can be found at https://warwick.ac.uk/fac/cross_fac/myparish/projects/cwa/.

The Vestry

As more administration came into the hands of the parish, the parish needed more organization, and matters in general came to be run by a meeting of parishioners known as the vestry. There was no statute creating the vestry, it was a meeting that simply evolved from about the late sixteenth century. The first known use of the term comes from a manor court roll in 1507, and meant a form of assembly or getting together of parishioners.

The rise of the vestry in many ways mirrors the decline of the manorial courts. In some places it took on some of the functions of a manorial court, with voluntary officials such as constables, surveyors of the highways (called stone wardens in some places) as well as the all-important churchwardens. Once there was a regular parochial meeting occurring, then it became a community of the parish, recognized by Justices of the Peace, and with its own voice.

The history of the rural vestry diverges from the urban vestry due to population expansion in urban areas. This expansion of urban parishes put increasing pressure on the voluntary officials of the vestry, and increasingly officials were selected by the JPs rather than being elected by parishioners. Vestries tended to fall into two types: either they were very large gatherings of all-male ratepayers, all of whom were elected to run the parish (open vestry); or a kind of family oligarchy rose up, whereby one or two families monopolized the positions (closed vestry) – which of course led to abuses. The parish minster was often the chairman. However, there was also a third kind, a vestry that was neither entirely open nor entirely closed, but was something in between the two.

After 1689 the vestry had the right to make byelaws on matters of parish concern, and whether the parishioners turned up to the meeting or not, these laws were binding on them. The vestry also had the right to impose local taxation, so it was very much the supreme constitutional body within the parish. Only male ratepayers were entitled to attend and vote at vestry meetings.

The local Justice of the Peace (magistrate) was key to the functioning of the parish, and before the mid-eighteenth century he undertook much of his work at his own house or the local inn. Often a local larger landowner and a member of the gentry, the JP was very probably the landlord of the parish officers, with all the possible abuse of power and inhibiting effect that would have entailed. He had the right to inspect the vestry minutes, and had oversight of many things such as licensing, and all the questions arising from Poor Law disputes. We shall look at a specific Poor Law case in the next chapter. The vestry had responsibility for the poor until 1834, when the Poor Law guardians were created.

A closed vestry was the more common type in rural areas, overseen by a few inter-related families, and where the whole vestry might consist of the parson, the local squire, the inn-keeper and one or two local freeholders. These closed rural vestries had no formal procedures, did not suffer from outside interference, and because the majority of parishioners were unrated labourers, they were definitely not representative of the people as a whole. It is understandable that in the larger parishes there is greater likelihood that formal records of vestry meetings were taken, while in the smaller parishes, things may have been decidedly more informal and without proper recording. Many rural parishes would fall into this latter category.

The *Victoria County History of Essex* has a detailed account of the vestry of the parish of High Laver: the minute books survive from 1657, although detailed minutes vary, depending on the interest of the clergyman writing them up. Only a handful of parishioners ever attended, sometimes only two and sometimes as many as seven.[62]

Could dissenters and non-conformists hold parish office? Mostly, we don't tend to consider looking for records of non-conformist chapels and their registers until our own searches in the Church of England parishes have proved negative, and then it is normally in connection with baptisms or burials. When a family has been found to be non-conformist, it would be easy to suppose that they then had nothing further to do with the Church of England in their own parish. Yet it is possible that at least in the seventeenth and eighteenth centuries, parish officials may also have been dissenters. This has been found in Datchworth in 1719, where a group of parish officials gave notice that they would be meeting for religious worship at a house on Datchworth Green.[63]

I have also found the interesting example of the eighteenth-century painter Johann Zoffany, a German émigré and originally a Roman Catholic, serving on the parish vestry in Chiswick, Middlesex, where he lived with his family. It seems that in some cases the need for parish officers overcame any religious sentiments.

The subject of non-conformity is a large one, too big to go into in any depth here, so the researcher is recommended to read about the subject in one of the many guides available for genealogists.

In order to pay for all these new officers and tasks, the payment of parish rates became compulsory in 1601, with the introduction of the poor rate to support the poor of the parish (*see* the next chapter for further detail). In the mid-seventeenth century, a further rate was imposed for the upkeep of the highways in the parish. The ratepayers were both the wealthy (if any) in the parish, and anyone else who owned property worth £10 per year. Rate books are found in parish chest collections and are very useful for building a snapshot of the community from given points in time. Rates were normally collected twice a year, and we look at them again in Chapter 7.

Complaints about paying the rate were heard at the Quarter

Sessions. This newspaper article from the *West Kent Guardian* on 2 April 1836 tells something of the desperate struggles that could surround the setting of a rate:

> The parishioners of Boxley in 1834 determined to rate several small cottages to the poor-rate, that had not previously been rated. The rates, however, have not been paid in a great many instances, and the magistrates of the Bearsted sitting issued distress warrants against the defaulters. On Thursday last, two persons from Maidstone attempted to execute one of these warrants at a cottage near Bredhurst and to distrain upon a pig, as the cottage was locked up. About 20 of the neighbouring wood-cutters assembled, however, armed with their axes and woodbills, and declared that they would cleave the heads of the distrainers if they laid their hand upon the pig. The amount of the rate was about 10s., with about 13s. expenses; and the cottagers, who, it seems, are hardly able to keep themselves, declared that they would die rather than allow their little property to be taken. The warrants have since been returned to the magistrates, with the reasons why they could not be executed.

Both vestry minutes and churchwardens' accounts can range from annoyingly sparse to astonishingly useful for genealogy. They can confirm someone's residence in the parish, or they can give useful detail that is missing from parish registers, such as local workmen being paid, payments to widows and the poor, expenses for carriage of the poor out of the parish, and even important entries such as the following from West Dean in West Sussex, which could open up a whole new area of research into a family:

> ... to consider levying a voluntary rate to defray the expenses of parishioners wishing to emigrate to South Australia: details of such families; estimates of expenses of outfitting them; emigration certificates to be requested from the Government Emigration Office (9 Park Street, Westminster), and if approved by the Board of Emigration, overseers to order outfits etc., 1846.[64]

Starting Points for the Researcher

The records discussed in this chapter are of most genealogical use when used in combination with other records, such as the census, parish registers or manorial records. Using a selection of different maps for the same area will help you to work out how the landscape has changed over time. You may find yourself needing a map that clearly shows parish boundaries to help orientate yourself and see the shape of the parish. A quick guide could be *The Phillimore Atlas and Index of Parish Registers* (available to buy, or on Ancestry.co.uk) or the parish boundary maps available at the Familysearch.org. Using a modern online aerial map such as those provided by Google or Bing can also be helpful, but should always be used with other maps that show boundaries and topographical features.

One set of tithe maps with apportionments is held by The National Archives (series IR 30 and IR 29), together with the tithe files (series IR 18). Other copies are held locally, normally at the county record office. However, tithe maps and apportionments for many places are now available as scanned images on the internet, and a search engine using the parish name and the term 'tithe' should find whether the parishes you are interested in are available online as images or transcription for free.

The subscription website thegenealogist.co.uk has the most complete coverage and indexing together with original images. Normally you will need to use both the maps and the apportionment together, and in fact they are technically one document – they have just been separated for more efficient storage. If you are looking for a specific person or family name, then start with the apportionment and progress to the map to see where the plots are. If you know the plot or farm name, then you can start with the map.

Churchwardens' accounts and vestry minutes are normally records that were kept in the parish chest and are now at the county record office. Glebe terriers may also be there, or can be found as part of the diocesan administration. All these records are less likely to be online than parish registers or tithe maps and apportionments; however, they could have been previously published by one of the many county-based record societies, as is the case with Buckinghamshire, Berkshire and Wiltshire Glebe Terriers, all published by their respective county record societies. A simple way to check quickly what exists in printed book format is to use the British Library main catalogue online and search for 'glebe terriers'.

When searching for original records, use The National Archives *Discovery* catalogue to search The National Register of Archives with the search terms of the parish you are interested in, plus the word 'glebe' or 'tithe': 'Bredhurst AND glebe'. This will return results from repositories around England and Wales, as well as anything held at The National Archives.

A very comprehensive discussion of all kinds of parish chest records is given in W.E. Tate, *The Parish Chest* (3rd edition, re-published Phillimore, 1983); although admittedly a little old-fashioned in approach, it gives many interesting examples from the records. Tate provides much interesting history and background to all types of parish record; however, he is less good at describing how genealogists or local historians can use the material. A more genealogy-based approach is found in Stuart Raymond's *Tracing Your Ancestors' Parish Records* (Pen & Sword, 2015).

5

SUPPORTING THE POOR

In this chapter we meet another family, this time in the Hertfordshire village of Datchworth. Before that, we start with some background about how parishes supported the poor in the days before any kind of welfare state. It is a story of local assistance by and for local people, and of how 'belonging' to a certain place came to have a legal meaning and could result in the forced physical removal to your place of belonging.

Did the very poor in early modern English society actually starve to death? It is an interesting question raised and debated by historians and demographers. Naturally, if you had a small plot of land and could keep a cow and some chickens, life on the margins of subsistence might be terribly hard, but you and your family were unlikely to starve to death. The manorial system of common rights for grazing, foraging in the hedgerows and collecting sticks for firewood also helped. The right to glean the fields after harvest could also provide a little help for the poorest.

One of the ancient ways of making sure that the population within an area could not outgrow the food available was the widespread use of social norms to restrict marriage age, and thereby total population. These social norms placed huge pressure on poor young women, many of whom never married. This proportion of those who did not marry rose from 5 per cent in the mid-sixteenth century, to perhaps 20 per cent in the first part of the seventeenth century, and continued at over 10 per cent.

Of those who did marry, genealogists should not expect that pre-Industrial ancestors usually married at a young age. Marrying couples were normally in their mid- to late twenties, the average age for women in the mid-seventeenth century being almost twenty-seven years. It was important for a man to be able to support his wife and children, so he needed a wage or land that would enable him to support them, something that did not come easily to the young. We should expect that the majority of the poor married late and practised pre-marital abstinence.[65]

But what if you did not have any land, and could not keep animals? What if the commons were enclosed? What if the only way to make a living was by muscle, working on someone else's land, and you were subject to being laid off, taken ill or simply get old and unable to work? The first port of call was probably always to seek help from family, and failing that, loans and gifts from friends and neighbours. However, a reliance on those who might also be equally poor is obviously insufficient in times when everyone is affected by harvest failures or job losses.

England was unusual in Europe in developing a national system of poor relief from the time of Elizabeth I, which was based around the parish. Each parish was to be responsible for their own poor. This system had evolved gradually over many years and with much alteration of law, and depended on an older, medieval way of dividing up the poor into those who were 'deserving', and those who were poor because of some moral defect. England's able-bodied village labourers also usually had alternative methods of earning a living, by migrating to the towns where there was a chance of employment. Yet a growing economy during the sixteenth century meant that inequalities were growing too, and when the whole economy took a turn for the worse, or certain parts of it did, then there was widespread misery.

There is plenty of evidence that the authorities did usually manage to get money into the poorest hands, and that actual starvation of individuals was something rare, to be remarked upon and blamed upon individual's actions rather than inefficiency of the system. And people did not regularly starve in large numbers in England, evidenced by studies that have shown that poor harvests were not regularly followed by a rise in death rates.[66] However, that is not to say that life on the margins was not incredibly hard, and there were certainly periods of hunger and extreme want. It was not only the lack of plentiful nourishing food that the rural poor suffered from when times were hard, but year in, year out, the cottages and hovels that they lived in were notoriously broken down, leaky, cramped and insanitary. In many areas it was quite common for two families to exist together in a two-room cottage.

Each harvest was vitally important, and naturally there would be some differences in harvest around the country, depending on the local weather conditions. There were continual and continuing harvest crises, for example in the 1590s, in 1622–3, and again in 1630–1. One of the ways that the authorities tried to alleviate times of harvest crisis was by issuing 'dearth' orders, whereby measures were taken to make sure local grain markets had enough provision, and prices were controlled. The price of corn was crucial because this dictated the price of bread, which the poor relied on as a major part of their diet. When the corn price rose, then people suffered.

These actions to impose prices and move grain around became normal in times of food scarcity in the countryside; they were imposed by local magistrates, and where they were not put in place, crowds would quickly gather to demand and to physically stop grain moving out of the district and to force its sale to the poor.

Food 'riots' remained one way that the poor of England attempted to secure fairness in the market-place. An example of this comes from Sussex. During the summer of 1756 there was heavy rain, and the harvest was poor. During the following winter of 1756 and into 1757, the price of corn rose and there was widespread hunger as prices rose beyond wages. In more than 130 parishes over the whole breadth of the county there were disturbances. In Lewes, the county town of Sussex, a mob of people from the surrounding villages marched into town and broke open a warehouse full of corn, whereupon the local merchant who owned the warehouse offered to sell them the wheat at 5s 6d a bushell, a price they could afford and which satisfied them. They collectively bought 7 or 8 bushells and went on their way. Farmers in Sussex were also sent threatening letters, some of which were published in the press:

> You covetous and hard-hearted Farmers, that keep your Stacks and Mows of Corn to starve the Poor, if you will not take them in and sell them that we may have some to eat, we will pull them down for you by Night or by Day, signed Jack Poor, Will Needy and Will Starve.[67]

The Old Poor Law

As well as having to deal with the sick, the aged and orphans among their own parishioners, the movement of bands of unemployed vagrants from parish to parish was a real problem. Before the Reformation, the monasteries had traditionally taken on the role of providing alms and support to travellers on the road, and legally the manor was supposed to provide help for their tenants, although in practice it left the duty to the church. A number of medieval laws had required that beggars should be returned to their home parishes, and many harsh punishments for vagrancy existed. A raft of legislation took place following the Reformation, but a couple of Acts in particular formed the basis of what became known as the Poor Law, and are important to genealogists because of the records that the laws produced.

Parish overseers of the poor were appointed by Justices of the Peace from 1597 to 1598. This was followed in 1601 by what came to be called the Great Poor Law Act. This ordered that the parish churchwardens and two to four substantial householders be nominated as overseers of the poor for that parish, to be funded by a local tax (the poor rate). It included various other orders, such that beggars and vagrants were to be sought out and put into a house of correction. This treatment was also to be meted out to women who had illegitimate children, and any parent who left a child chargeable to the parish.

At the heart of the Act of 1601 was the idea that vagrants would not have a right to claim any relief from a parish they had arrived in, and the idea of the *deserving* poor was paramount. A woman pregnant out of wedlock was not deserving of support by her fellow parishioners. However, the ordinary labourer in his home parish who had worked hard and was now disabled, *was* deserving.

The administration of the Poor Law can be thought of as having three tiers. At the day-to-day local level were the parish overseers and their decisions, paying and creating records of payments to the poor in their parish. These records are held locally. In the middle were the Justices of the Peace or magistrates at the quarter-sessions courts, and many, many kinds of questions and problems were referred to them by the overseers, creating another set of records, again held locally; while at the top was national government with an over-arching oversight. With the growth of local newspapers from the eighteenth century, many cases that were referred to the quarter-sessions and petty-sessions courts were also reported in those newspapers, which can now provide a happy hunting ground for historians and genealogists.

The 1601 Act was followed in 1662 by the Act of Settlement and Removal. The original Act of 1601 had prevented those who had newly settled gaining instant handouts, and instead they had to wait one month before being able to receive relief from their new parish. Of course this did not stop people from moving, and parishes from still being overburdened by an influx of incomers. The new Act meant that not only vagrants but anyone arriving in a new parish who was likely to become chargeable to the parish (in other words, was an ordinary labouring person) could be removed by the Justices within forty days of their arrival, unless they met certain strict criteria.

He or she could be, and were often, removed back to the home parish, which was defined as the place where the migrant was last legally settled. Any parish receiving someone under a removal order whom they did not consider to belong to their parish could appeal to the local Justices at quarter sessions, and if it was not resolved the case could then go to the Assize Courts. Thus more records were created, all of which are of much use to the genealogist. The Act of Settlement recognized the fact that the earlier legislation had been almost impossible to administer in the north of England, due to the sometimes very extended size of the parishes. Thus from 1662 every township or village could appoint its own overseers, as well as collect its own poor rate.

Records of Settlement

For the family historian the records created by the system of settlement are a real boon. Settlement certificates, settlement examinations and removal orders were formally recorded, and any disputes were, of course, taken to the courts.

Settlement in a new place was only gained via a number of different qualifications. This gave rise to records called 'settlement examinations', whereby the overseers of the poor and the Justices formally interviewed incomers to the parish, township or village, and recorded the reasons they believed themselves to have settlement there, or to discover where they did have settlement.

However, people did need to move about, and the Act of 1662 also provided that people could take jobs in other parishes if they held a certificate of settlement. This would show that their parish of settlement would be willing to take them back if they lost their job or otherwise became a liability on the parish. These certificates had to be obtained from the churchwardens and overseers of their legal parish of settlement, and signed before a Justice of the Peace. However, this did not mean that everyone who moved did obtain one, and in practice their survival is very patchy. Country districts seem to have been generally far stricter as regards requiring settlement certificates from incomers than towns, probably because there was less work available and less housing stock.

While the certificate simply states that a person has a legal settlement in a parish, an examination is far more interesting from a family history point of view, often with lengthy detail about the person, their spouse and their children, including where they had lived in the past. Some parish officers were very officious in seeking out the incomers and examining them, and others were not. Many examinations were of people who were perfectly entitled to be in the parish, and thus the discovery of an examination does not mean that someone did not remain in the parish; in many cases it seems that the overseers were satisfied that the person concerned would not become chargeable. Alternatively they might be ordered to obtain a certificate from their actual parish of settlement.

In addition, the 1662 Act, together with an amending Act of 1691, more closely defined what settlement meant. Those who had settlement had one of these qualifications: they were:

- unmarried and had worked in the parish for 365 days or more (this qualification brought about short contracts for servants and farm labourers);
- a woman married to a parishioner, in that wives took their husband's place of settlement;

- a child born legitimately, under seven years of age, whose father lived in the parish;
- a child who was illegitimate and who had been born in the parish;
- someone apprenticed to a master in the parish;
- a resident of forty days, after having given the parish authorities written notice of his intention to receive relief (after 1691);
- were born in the parish where parents had legal settlement (but only until another method of settlement took over, for example, they were apprenticed);
- paid the rates or rented a house worth £10 per annum (the vast majority of houses were much less than this);
- served in a parish office;
- had previously received poor relief in that parish.

These Acts of 1662 and 1691 reduced the mobility of the population, although historians are divided on how much – we look at this some more in Chapter 8. It can be complicated working out what the situation was at any point in time due to the several sets of legislation from the period 1662 onwards, after which there were many tweaks and changes.

It was the duty of the churchwardens and overseers to make regular enquiries of people coming into a parish as to their settlement. If there were concerns about those being examined that they could become liable to poor relief, then the overseers could bring the person before the Justices to be questioned, often at petty sessions. If the Justices were not satisfied, a removal order was issued. These orders directed that the people concerned return to the parish where they did have a legal settlement. Naturally, removal orders were the subject of many legal disputes, as parishes sought to dispose of the unwanted to another parish. Disputes often went to the local courts of petty sessions and quarter sessions. Some were removed who were not even claiming any relief from the parish, but it was not until 1795 that an amending Act meant that removal could only take place if relief was actually claimed from the parish.

The following is an example of a settlement examination taken from the records of Earl's Colne in Essex:

> the examination of Jas Edwards taken upon oath touching his last legal place of settlement the 6.1.1748 who saith he was born at Earls Colne or White Colne and that about twelve years ago he let himself for one year to one Jas Ward of the Heath parish in the town of Colchester in the said county and served (torn) let himself to the said Jas Ward for one other year at the yearly wages of 20s and served the greatest part of the said last year and received about half a guinea of his said wages and that he heard say by the neighbouring people that his said master Ward resided there by a certificate from London and further says then he went and lived with his mother in White Colne where she resided in (torn) he says he has heard she paid no parish rates in White Colne and that he was bound apprentice to Thos Livermore of Hedingham Castle who as this examinant hath been informed resided there by a certificate from Ketton and served his said master about four years and hath never done anything since whereby to gain settlement sworn the day and year above before me (torn) the mark of (torn).[68]

More amending acts followed those of 1691, which further restricted the movement of people.

The Poorhouse and Outdoor Relief

Knatchbull's Act of 1723 gave parishes the right to provide poor relief in specially built workhouses, and to require the poor to work in exchange for their upkeep. It also enshrined in the law the idea that the workhouse was to provide a deterrent – in other words, workhouses were only to be for those who could definitely not provide for themselves, and were not the kind of place that any right-minded person would want to present themselves at. However, Knatchbull's Act made the provision of workhouses entirely voluntary, and there was no compulsion on any parish to provide one. Not every parish, particularly those in the countryside, could afford to provide a workhouse, but nevertheless by the 1770s nearly 100,000 people were housed in workhouses, about 15 per cent of those people being in London.

Life in the workhouse varied very much between parishes;

inmates could have been set menial tasks in prison-like surroundings, accommodated in single-sex wards in the bigger workhouses, while others were said to be much more comfortable, providing some form of education and clean clothing as well as simple medical care, and with visitors allowed to come and go. Naturally, many people died in the workhouse, particularly if they were there for medical care, as workhouses very often provided the only kind of free medical aid it was possible to get, and thus very sick people naturally ended up there. Many more died because the houses were insanitary, and care was non-existent. Nevertheless, the workhouse as an institution was supposed to provide food, and not deliberately cause the death of inmates by neglect.

Because workhouses were expensive to set up and run, they tended to be a feature of towns in the eighteenth century and were mainly absent from the countryside. What the village could and did provide was a poorhouse, and provision for poorhouses in the village parish had been a feature of the Poor Laws prior to Knatchbull's Act. The poorhouse was one or more cottages or tenements rented by the parish specifically for housing the poor, paid for from the rates and under the supervision of the overseers. The attitude prevailing at the time was that any person who had to live in the poorhouse was irresponsible and unable to support themselves. Because it was expensive to fund these houses, many parishes also continued the long-standing practice known as 'outdoor relief'.

Outdoor relief was simply a monetary payment made to top up a person's income or wages, administered individually and accounted for in the overseer's accounts. Lists of outdoor relief feature many widows' names, with regular pension-like payments paid for by the rates. These can be an excellent way of tracking women after their husbands have died, or even discovering a man's death, a record of which might be missing from the burial register, by reason of his wife suddenly appearing as a widow, or because she receives payments made from the overseer's accounts for his burial.

As well as pensions, many other types of payment were made, such as payment for doctors or medicine, including expenses for removal, obtaining legal opinions on settlement cases, burial payments, and payments for items such as spinning wheels, granted to poor women so they could spin wool and thereby earn money. These can be found in what are known as the parish chest records, now at the county record offices.

Overseers' accounts are well worth searching through, as many names are mentioned within them, particularly where small, regular payments are made. It is possible to trace people, to distinguish between two men of the same name, and whether they were in work at a specific time, by the payments made to them under 'out-relief'. These accounts also provide a testament to the activities of the parish, sometimes the only way that we can get to know about the day-to-day activities that involved our ancestors.

Until the New Poor Law of 1834, the laws of 1601, 1662, 1691, 1723 and 1791 made up the backbone of what we now call the Old Poor Law, and which ruled the lives of the poorest and thus many of our ancestors. The parish was meant to provide in cases of the *deserving* poor, and the laws of settlement were a crude way of ensuring that a parish would not be over-run with poverty-stricken incomers who would then demand food and lodging. In practice, the interpretation of the Poor Law, which was loosely worded, as well as the exact way it was administered in rural locations, differed greatly throughout England. In that sense it is similar to the manorial system, which also differed in custom from area to area and from manor to manor. One parish should not always necessarily be taken as representative of the whole.

Importance of Justices of the Peace and Quarter Sessions

The sessions courts originated in the fourteenth century and were overseen by the Justices of the Peace. The Justices have a history dating back to the thirteenth century, with increasing powers over the years to deal with the less serious criminal cases on behalf of the King. Furthermore, as the manorial court leet system died away, they took on many functions of civil administration, such as oversight of the relationship between masters and apprentices, administering taxes and oaths, the upkeep of highways, and oversight of the poor law system.

The Justices always met four times a year, at Easter, Trinity, Michaelmas and Epiphany (January), and this is how the records are organized. In respect of village and rural matters, these meetings were held in the county town (though some boroughs and towns held their own separate sessions). As well as the quarterly business of the court, sessions records may contain a large number of documents enrolled or deposited either with the court or with the Clerk of the Peace under a very long list of statutes, all of which provide information for the local and family historian. Their records consist of minute books, which summarize the court business; sessions rolls, which include the evidence put to the Justices; and order books, which show the outcome of each case.

The Justices were eminent men of considerable power in the county, appointed by the Lord Chancellor, and since the eighteenth century on the advice of the Lord Lieutenant of the county. Men were qualified by their property holdings rather than their knowledge of law. The Clerks of the Peace and their deputies, if they had them, were the people who actually administered and organized the system. Clerks of the Peace even had charge of the records, such that in Gloucester one diligent clerk actually purchased the lease of a building out of his own pocket to keep the court records in. It seems he was reimbursed.[69]

Quarter-session records are among those that are lesser used by the family historian, usually because they lack good name indexes. Nevertheless, the courts covered a huge range of business, and should be better known as a vast trove of local material. However, these records can be difficult to search and to handle, in some cases being bound in large rolls. They are held at county level in the relevant record office, and in some places survive in an unbroken run back to the sixteenth century, although it is more often the case that they have gaps or start later. Their importance for the Poor Law in deciding on many cases of settlement and removal and other matters is immense, and as we shall see below, the Justices expected that if things were going wrong at the local level, they would be appealed to.

The Eaves Family of Datchworth and a Notorious Case

Deserving and ordinary parishioners were thus able to apply to the overseers of the poor in their parish for relief in the form of monetary payments known as 'relief', for food, firewood and, in the parlance of the times, 'the necessaries of life'. In some parishes, out-relief also consisted of putting the supplicant to parish work, in clearing overgrown hedgerows, mending roads and other suitable labouring jobs that were for the common good. Overseers were elected every year by the vestry, or appointed by a local JP, and were usually men of good standing in the community. In practice, the job of overseer was often undertaken by the tradesmen, the shopkeepers and the smaller farmers, and in small communities there were often limited numbers of these, so the same few people would find themselves elected year after year. Not surprisingly, sometimes things could, and did, go very wrong.

To find out more, we now need to imagine ourselves in the Hertfordshire village of Datchworth in the year 1768. King George III is on the throne, William Pitt the elder is coming to the end of his term as prime minister, and in August Captain Cook sets sail on board HMS *Endeavour* on his way from Plymouth to the Pacific Ocean. And what of Datchworth? It is a straggling, mid-sized parish 28 miles north of London, with a small community around the church, a village green with other houses at a mile's distance, and several further flung hamlets and farmsteads; a middling kind of place of mixed farming and woodland, with one prominent absentee landowner: Catherine, Vicountess Townsend.

There is a resident rector, the Reverend Edward Smith, who arrived in 1748 and will stay until his death in 1785, several larger farmers, some tradespeople such as carpenters and butchers, a vestry of some eight or nine, and only one churchwarden and one overseer of the poor, John and Samuel Bassett, brothers and carpenters. There are maybe some 350 to 400 people living in around seventy or eighty houses (based on the 1801 census); some labouring families share a cottage with another family. There is not too much happening day to day except for the chores of farm, field and daily life, which include fetching water from the many ponds. Most people do some work in the fields, including the youngest children. There is no school.

Into this scene steps a poor labouring family called Eaves, man and wife married for fourteen years with four children, aged fourteen down to three years old. James Eaves had married Susanna Pegrum in Datchworth on 21 October 1754 following banns; their marriage is recorded in one of the new printed marriage books brought in after Hardwicke's Marriage Act. They were noted as both being 'of the parish'. Susanna must already have been pregnant, for on 16 March 1755, their first son James was baptised in the church. Another boy, William, was baptised on 4 December 1757, and then daughter Sarah (noted as Ives in the register) on 9 May 1762, and finally, their youngest, Susanna, on 6 October 1765.

James was probably the same James Eaves who was baptised at St Paul's Walden, Hertfordshire, in 1725, the son of James Eaves, a husbandman. This elder James died in 1730 at the age of forty. Interestingly, he was also baptised at St Paul's Walden at the age of forty, his age being added to the baptism information in the St Paul's Walden register; so the family were presumably dissenters of some kind, or extremely lax in their church attendance. How the younger James came to Datchworth is not known; he probably arrived looking for farm work and having found work, was able to stay, and so gain a settlement in Datchworth.

Wife Susanna Pegrum was also an immigrant, presumably also having been a farm servant of some kind prior to her marriage. There are Pegrams and other variations of the name living in nearby Broxborne, Braughing and Westmill in the first half of the eighteenth century, so it seems possible that she belonged to this family. Both James and Susanna appear to have gained settlement in Datchworth prior to their marriage, and this is mostly likely due to being hired for work by local people. As we will come to see, James did have a sister living in Datchworth as well.

Into this picture also steps one Philip Thicknesse, a well-known figure in Georgian England; a friend of society artist Thomas Gainsborough, and an eccentric campaigner and inveterate meddler in various causes, he made so many enemies that he was harshly lampooned in contemporary cartoons and known as 'Dr Viper'. Thicknesse had taken copyhold of a cottage or several cottages on

Datchworth Green, thus giving him an interest in village affairs and making him an unusual (for Datchworth) gentry ratepayer. If he had not, then the Eaves family story would almost certainly have been lost to history, because in 1769 he caused a case to be brought against the Datchworth parish overseers in the court of King's Bench following publication and widespread publicity of his polemical pamphlet *An account of the four persons found starved to death in D[atchworth] in Hertfordshire 1769*, which is now in the British Library.

In the third week of January 1769, the bodies of four people were found in the tiny decrepit hovel that was Datchworth poorhouse, having apparently starved to death. Those bodies were of father and mother James and Susanna Eaves, and daughters Sarah, aged seven, and Susannah, aged three. The third child was William, and he was still alive. Let's walk back to the events in the eighteen months or so leading up to this grim discovery, and what happened after that. This account has been constructed from witness statements among the court records of King's Bench.[70]

Up to Michaelmas, 25 September 1767, James Eaves was renting a house from carpenter Samuel Bassett, but the rent had not been paid and so Bassett told him that he would be evicted; but the rent was still not forthcoming, and on 25 March 1768 Eaves and his family left or were evicted from the house of Samuel Bassett and removed themselves to William Nash's house. They either left some broken-down bits of furniture in the road – an old table or stool, a piece of a spinning wheel and an old bedstock – or they were evicted and their furniture placed in the road. Whatever the sequence, it was agreed that the furniture remained by the side of the road for some weeks or months.

At Easter, Samuel Bassett was elected overseer, and his brother John, churchwarden. At around this time Eaves came to Samuel Bassett complaining of a swelled leg and saying he was unable to work. He was offered help from the local apothecary, and relief was provided to him. His leg was not better until June. On 12 June 1768 the whole family left Datchworth to go and work in the hay harvest in the districts round about, with the eldest son earning 3s a week. After the hay was in, they returned to Datchworth, with the exception of the eldest son, James, who was now in constant work, and lodged with William Nash again. Then they all went harvesting the corn and gleaning; James Eaves as a harvestman would have earned 16s or 18s a week with board and lodging. When all the corn harvest was in in the autumn, James Eaves took work with Datchworth farmer Mr Stevenson.

On 25 September 1768 or just after, they were turned out of Nash's house. Then it was said that James Eaves slept chiefly in one of the outhouses belonging to his employer, farmer Stevenson, and his wife and children at a neighbouring cottage; but soon after harvest they were turned out of the cottage and were obliged to seek some other lodging – but again they were turned out. Then they came under the barn wall of farmer Stevenson and complained they had nowhere else to go, and Stevenson said that he pitied their condition, and permitted Susanna and her children to lie in his stable for some time. However, Datchworth labourers George Warby and William Nash together, put a different light on this sequence:

> ... after the hay harvest was over the said Eaves and his family returned to ... William Nash's house, and then the said James Eaves went to corn harvest work to Joseph Stevenson of Datchworth, and Eaves wife and children went a-gleaning ... the said James Eaves his wife and family were so abominable nasty that this deponent William Nash and his family could not bear them in his house.

The Eaves family then went to live with the Ellis family. In the autumn James Eaves was at work ploughing for Stevenson and also taking threshing work elsewhere. Then Ellis in turn chucked them out, and they all turned up at Stevenson's, where Susanna Eaves was told to apply for relief. The reason for all these evictions were, in the words of Warby and Nash:

> James Eaves and his family being so filthy and nasty that they made use of the bed chamber where they lay as a necessary house (toilet), and the said Benjamin Ellis would not let them stay any longer in his house and ... saw the said Eaves family in Mr John Bassett's granary which ... is warmer and more comfortable than most of the cottages in Datchworth.

Churchwarden John Bassett agreed that in November, Susanna Eaves and the children put themselves in his granary, which was full of clean straw, and there they stayed until applying for the poorhouse. Witness George Parcelles said that Susanna and her children were in a poor and starving condition around this time, and about two or three weeks before Christmas Susanna Eaves applied to Samuel Bassett the overseer for relief, telling him that she and her children were in a starving condition – but Bassett refused to give her any relief, and told her she should be sent to the House of Correction. Samuel Bassett disputed this, and says that the family went into one of the poorhouses at Burnham Green, while James Eaves and his son continued in full-time work.

Witnesses differ on the exact dates: one account says that at the start of December a place for the Eaves family was found at the poorhouse located in Burnham Green at the far end of the parish. The poorhouse was already being lived in by another family, called Hanchett, and this family made a strong complaint that with all ten of them in the house it was unbearable – they could not even lie down at night. The second family were given use of an unoccupied house owned by Philip Thicknesse. Thomas Hanchett and his daughter Sarah said that the Eaves family were emaciated at this time.

All this time, from about 15 November until the end of December 1768, James Eaves was not with his family every night, as he had taken work with farmer Robert Young of Holwell, a few miles distant. He returned to Datchworth only on Saturday night and for Sunday. Witnesses say he appeared to be well during this period.

Around 14 December Samuel Bassett is said to have refused to give the family relief, but he denied this, while witness Elizabeth Ancell said that during December she visited the family in the poor house several times. On 3 January 1769 farmer Young of Holwell was told that James Eaves had 'the itch' very badly, and was not coming to work. On Friday 6 January – old Christmas Day – James Eaves junior, who had been living a few miles away with his employer in Tewin, walked over to visit his parents but found them very ill; he returned on Sunday 8 January.

At some point Widow Harrod made application on behalf of the Eaves family to Samuel Bassett for relief for them as they were ill, and Samuel Bassett claimed he then visited them, and gave them 2s 6d. He also asked Martha Chalkley to go to Widow Harrod and Sarah Smith, two poor women living on the green nearby, to go and take care of them and get them tea 'it being usual in the said parish as in other places ... to employ the healthy poor to take care of the sick'.

James junior states he went to the house of Samuel Bassett to ask for relief, but Mrs Bassett was abusive, saying: 'Send them relief, send them a halter to hang them, let them die and be damned'; he then met Samuel Bassett himself, who refused relief.

The 12 January is about the last time the neighbours who made statements say they saw the family alive. Prior to that at least three women were 'frequently' bringing various things to the Eaves – tea, wine and balm tea are mentioned – but having seen Samuel Bassett enter the house, they did not make a further visit. Elizabeth Ancell said that on her last visit James Eaves was delirious, and they were all so emaciated she was afraid to visit again. Ann Bond and her mother, and also Martha Chalkley, were asked by Samuel Bassett to arrange things for the family. However, Catherine Lowin stated that she often saw the boy William at her door begging for bread and in a semi-naked state. When asked why he could not go to work, he said no one would have him as he had no clothes, and the parish would not clothe him.

It is hard to be sure about exact dates, as the witnesses were not questioned, they only gave written statements; however, it seems that the Eaves died on about 20 January, and that the coroner's inquest was heard a day or two subsequent to this. They were buried on 27 January 1769.

Thicknesse (*see* above – property owner) was outraged at what had happened, and as well as publishing his pamphlet in February, he lost no time in writing letters to many local newspapers to further publicize the case:

> The following melancholy Tale is strickly true; I write not from Report, but from the Evidence of my own Eyes, and what adds to the Concern I feel is, that the dismal Scene happened in our own Parish, and almost within a Gun-shot of my House. My Servant informed me this Morning, that a Man, his Wife,

> and three Children, had perished for Want in one of the Poor-Houses, and that the Floor of the wretched Hovel was covered with their naked and emaciated Carcases. Scarce able to believe him, I went to the Place, where, in a Hovel of one Room only, the gable End of which lay quite broke open, and exposed to the Severity of the Weather, and a Window Frame at the other unglazed and uncovered, I saw four of the emaciated Bodies lying upon a little Straw quite naked; for they had neither Cloaths nor Covering when alive! The third Child (a Boy about eleven Years old) is yet living, but unable to stand, or give any Account how long his Father and Mother, Brother and Sister, had been dead, tho' otherwise sensible.
>
> Upon enquiring among the Neighbours, I am informed they were taken ill on Saturday three Weeks, that they had no Relief that they knew of, till Thursday was sev'nnight, when one of the People, called Overseers of the Poor, came and left them Half a Crown; the poor Family, however, seemed too far gone, or too tired with their wretched Condition, to wish for Food or Life; for they only desired a Faggot and a Candle to be bought; which Faggot, Candle and Part of the Change of the Half-Crown, was, or was pretended to be found in the House, and likewise a Piece of Bread. It is said to be found there by the same Overseer who relieved them with it.
>
> I will only add to this Relation, that several other poor People in the Parish, are in an almost starving and dying Condition. I have forbid the Burial of these unhappy, I should have said happy People, till an Inquest has been taken; and I could wish some humane Man, learned in the Law, will inform me by a Letter directed to P. T. at Mr Davis's Bookseller, in Piccadilly, what other Steps are to be taken in this Case, to prevent for the future such Acts of Negligence and Inhumanity; where my Name many be known to those who either from Curiosity or Humanity desire to know it.[71]

In his pamphlet Thicknesse says that it was written by himself as 'one of the jurymen on the inquisition taken on the bodies, printed for the benefit of the surviving child.' He tells us that they had 'perished from want of food, rayment, attendance and a habitable dwelling.' According to Thicknesse's own account, after he had visited the scene he then foiled an attempted cover-up.

When word got back to the parish officers that the family had perished, the officers are said to have removed the bodies on a cart and were transporting them to be secretly buried before an inquest could be held. It was at this point that Thicknesse happened across the grisly transport and stopped the men. He wrote to the Rector of Datchworth, the Rev. Edward Smith of Clare College, Cambridge, to remind him of the consequences of the 'dark transaction'. The bodies were then taken to the church, and the next day were examined by a local surgeon brought from nearby Hatfield, who, according to Thicknesse, commented that he 'had never seen bodies so emaciated'.

Whatever the real facts, Thicknesse was in absolutely no doubt as to whom he thought were responsible: the parish officers for having let the situation occur, and then for attempting to cover it up. His pamphlet says:

> ... in no kingdom are the Poor more hardly dealt with than in this; especially in extensive but obscure parishes where scarcely any gentleman reside. In these it is usual for three or four upstart necessitous freeholders to combine to form a vestry and engross the whole power of every kind in their hands.

This was something of an exaggeration and hyperbole on his part, as the situation in other countries was different to that in England. Nevertheless, the overseer and churchwarden of Datchworth at this time *were* two brothers, John and Samuel Bassett, both of them carpenters. Would it be better to have upstart freeholders? Or the gentry?

Following the inquest, the Datchworth parish register records the burials of the family on 27 January 1769 as 'James Eaves, Susanna Eaves Senr, Sarah Eaves and Susanna Eaves Junr'. Meanwhile, Thicknesse's pamphlet and letters to the papers, together with an appeal for donations for the poor of the parish, had seen the case widely reported in the press, and a huge amount of food was collected from various donors and sent to Datchworth. The *Kentish Gazette* of 22 February 1769 reported:

> Sunday last one hundred and forty-four pounds of beef and mutton, one hundred weight of bread, and three pounds four shillings in money were distributed to the poor of Datchworth in Hertfordshire, being part of the relief being humanely sent by unknown persons in consideration of their unparalleled hardships and distress.

Thicknesse would not let it lie; having asked for legal advice in his open letter to the press, he then caused a case to be brought against the parish overseers at King's Bench, which was the superior criminal court in England. Meanwhile, this widespread publicity caused some consternation for the main Datchworth landowner, Lady Townsend. She immediately wrote to one of the local JPs and asked for an investigation and explanation, and it was his subsequent testimony to King's Bench that probably saved the Bassetts' skins.

Thicknesse busied himself interviewing various witnesses for a prosecution, and arranged for them to swear their versions of what had happened at his house in front of a local commissioner of oaths on 24 April. Eight witness statements were sent up to King's Bench, and on 27 April, the brothers Bassett were ordered to 'show cause' why a rule should not be made against them. The order was despatched post haste to Datchworth and pinned up on their front doors the next day, a Friday. The witnesses for a prosecution were as follows:

Joseph Stevenson, farmer of Datchworth, an employer of James Eaves
George Parcelles, servant to Joseph Stevenson
Catherine Lowin (wife of Joseph Lowin, labourer), neighbour on Burnham Green near the poor house
Ann Bond, of Datchworth (wife of William Bond, labourer)
Elizabeth Ancell of Hatfield (wife of Thomas Ancell, labourer), daughter of Ann Bond
Thomas Hanchett and his daughter Sarah, who lived in the poor house
James Eaves, of Tewin, son of the Eaves

Naturally this shocked and frightened the brothers Bassett, who claimed that the family had died of a fever known as 'gaol distemper', and proclaimed their innocence. On Sunday 29 April they went to local JP Thomas Browne for advice. He told them to contact Mr Hall, an attorney in Hertford, and the next day Mr Hall got his London agent to send the copies of the witness statements on which the order had been made. These did not arrive until Wednesday 3 May.

On Thursday 4 May the brothers both arrived in London and swore an oath at an attorney's chambers that they needed more time to reply. This was granted. They had only a short time to gather their supporting witnesses and put their own case, which also had to be sworn in front of another local commissioner of oaths, this time at Welwyn on 16 May, before their witness statements could be sent to London for the King's Bench decision.

Those witness statements from the court case at King's Bench survive at The National Archives in series KB 1/17/6, and they shed a very interesting light on the situation, with much fascinating background that could be applied to the situation of many other rural labourers. They also allow us a unique and fascinating insight into village life, with people who would otherwise only be known as a few entries in surviving parish registers. Witnesses for the defence were:

Arthur Warren Esq., of Marden in Tewin, late of Datchworth
John Smith of Datchworthbury, farmer
William Pennyfather of Digswell, farmer
Robert Young of Holwell, gentleman
Sarah Smith, pauper spinster of Datchworth
George Pyner Bisse Esq., of Codicotbury, JP
Edward Smith, Rector of Datchworth
Thomas Browne Esq., of Camfield Place, JP
George Warby, butcher of Datchworth
William Nash, labourer of Datchworth
Samuel and John Bassett, carpenters of Datchworth (the accused)

The first three make statements about the Bassetts generally being of good character and good parish officers. Robert Young testified that he employed James Eaves from 15 November to 31 December 1768, when he appeared to be in good health. He never heard him complain of poverty.

George Warby and William Nash together gave evidence of the wanderings around the parish of the Eaves family, and said that the Eaves never paid rent. They had bad habits and were very filthy and nasty. There was also a dispute between the Bassetts and Stevenson regarding tithes, and this prosecution was carried out by spite and envy. If the Rector would let Stevenson have his tithes again, there would be an end to the dispute.

Sarah Smith testified that she lived with Widow Harrod, and heard from Martha Chalkley that she (Martha) had been sent by Samuel Bassett to get the Eaves some tea and wood and what was necessary, and had bought a bundle of firewood, a candle and a quarter of sugar, but no tea as they had tea. The change was left with them, which amounted to four 6 penny pieces (that is, 2s). Widow Harrod claimed to be ill, and was not able to give her story. The death of the family was as a result of 'the itch' and gaol distemper, and they were not starved, as 1s and bread and dripping were found in the house after their death; furthermore the boy who was now living (William) was immediately afterwards taken care of by the overseer of the poor.

George Pyner Bisse Esq., of Codicotbury, JP, and Rector Edward Smith, said that farmer Joseph Stevenson was a bad overseer when he had the task, and the Bassetts were good characters. Bisse said that he was the nearest residing magistrate to the parish, and no application to him for relief was made on behalf of the Eaves family. Furthermore, he casts dispersions on the character of Thomas Hanchett, as he was committed to Bridewell by him (a local prison).

The Rector said that he had refused permission for the bodies to be buried until they had been seen by the coroner for Hertford, and that the warrant for burial said that 'it was found they died a natural death'.

John Bassett, churchwarden, maintained that he continually gave the family victuals and money; however, the wife did not keep herself and the family clean, and neglected them. He thought the deaths were caused by mercury ointment for the itch or some other infectious disorder.

Samuel Bassett said in his defence that he himself had arranged with the local poor women to take care of the family, 'it being usual in the said parish as in other places ... to employ the Healthy poor to take care of the sick.' He didn't hear of any complaints, and assumed that they were well. He was very much astonished to hear of their deaths, and immediately went to the poorhouse; finding this to be true, he ordered the widows Harrod and Smith to take care of the two surviving children, which they did; however, one of them died that evening.

He also said that from information he had since received, he believed that the deaths were caused by improper applying of mercurial ointment for the cure of the itch, or that they died of an infectious disorder, which it was generally supposed that they had. Moreover, James Eaves' own sister who lived nearby was too scared to visit him for fear of catching the infection.

Thomas Browne Esq. of Camfield Place, JP, says he employed Samuel Bassett as a carpenter in repairing a house of his in the occupation of Joseph Stevenson. He gives the most powerful testimony for the defence, saying that himself, together with George Boyner Bisse and the Revd Mr Rooke, are the only Justices who act for the Hundred of Broadwater, which includes twenty-three parishes. He is constantly at petty sessions and never heard of any complaint against Datchworth. He lives within 6 miles of Datchworth.

Lady Townsend heard of the case in the newspapers and asked him to enquire into the matter, which he did. He casts dispersions on Stevenson's testimony because he was long 'at variance and enmity with the Bassetts'. He says that Mr Thicknesse is the sole prosecutor of the Bassetts, and calls on Thicknesse to bring a prosecution to the assize, and that if so he would personally put up money for the defence. He also says that Elizabeth Ancell, her mother Ann Bond and Catherine Lowin had made their affidavits at Thicknesse's house, and that they were paid to do so with the promise of an order of 1 guinea for clothes made with a draper in Hertford. He does then slightly overdo it with this statement, that he:

> ... constantly attended the petty sessions and other business for this said Hundred as well as for the County, and that he this Deponent always believed and does believe that the poor were better taken care of in that parish than in any parish in the said Hundred and this Deponents reason for such belief is that this Deponent never was applied to at his own house which is within six miles of the said parish or at the petty sessions with any complaint of the poor of the said parish against any of the parish officers of the said parish and this deponent further saith that upon the unfortunate Affair (which has given rise to the Charge against the Bassetts) being in the publish newspapers He this Deponent was Applied to by Lady Townshend who has an Estate in this parish to enquire very particularly into the circumstances of it which he accordingly did by ordering the two Bassetts, two substantial farmers of the name of Smith (who were on the Coronor's Inquest taken on the Body of Eaves his Wife & Two Children) tenants to Lady Townshend, Mr Atkinson The Coroner and Joseph Stephenson (which last was this deponents tenant as aforementioned) to attend this deponent at this deponents house which they all did and that after the strictest examination it did not appear to this deponent that there had been any neglect either in the said Churchwarden or Overseer respecting the said Eaves and his family and that this deponent is very well assured the said Stephenson would omit no circumstance that would affect either of the defendants as the said Stephenson hath long been at variance and enmity with them both.

The case was obviously further complicated by accusations from witnesses for the defence that farmer Stevenson 'had it in' for the Rector as well as the parish officers due to a long-running complaint about the tithe. The defence also sought to discredit Thicknesse's witnesses by saying that Thicknesse had paid very handsomely for them to swear their statements. With a defence as strong as this, no capacity for the court to question the witnesses, and all the local big-wigs on their side, it was not so surprising that the case against the Bassetts failed, and they were completely exonerated.

> On Tuesday last, Cause was shewn in the Court of King's Bench, for John Bassett, Churchwarden, and Samuel Bassett, Overseers of the Poor of Datchworth, Hertfordshire, why an Information should not go against them, they being charged with Neglect of Duty, in suffering a poor Family there to be starved for Want of Necessaries: When upon a full Hearing of the Matter, the Court was unanimously of Opinion, that there was not the least Ground for an Information, and order the Rule to be discharged.[72]

Why didn't their neighbours come to the aid of the Eaves family in those final weeks, and what did they really believe? Gaol fever (typhus) was known to be very infectious and deadly, so that would undoubtedly have kept people away. If they had been infected with typhus then their symptoms would have included fever, lassitude and diahorrea, and this could be expected to have weakened them considerably, particularly if they had little food and no access to clean, fresh water. It may even have been the cause of death. Typhus spreads by fleas in unsanitary situations, and was known often to be fatal. However, this does not explain why they had no clothes in the middle of January (if this is indeed true).

James's own sister was said to be nearby. What was she doing? Was the whole parish on the brink of starvation, as claimed by Thicknesse and hinted at by the newspaper reports of donations of food to the poor? The burial registers suggest not, as more births are recorded than burials in 1769, and for most other years in the 1760s. Could the parishioners speak out against the Bassetts? Were there some deep-seated 'getting even' with them for past injustices? Did Thicknesse really bribe the witnesses?

It did not seem to be disputed that James Eaves was in regular work right up until the end of December, so why was he so emaciated by 20 January? Why could they not get regular lodgings, and was it true that they kept 'filthy' habits? Perhaps the fate of the Eaves family depended on a little of everything: not much nearby family, fear of contagion and general neglect, as well as a generally unliked family who had become more than a bit of a nuisance to everyone. There was no question of them not having legal settlement in Datchworth, because if they had not, they could have been forcibly removed to their parish of settlement, thus passing the case along to another parish. Certainly, the tiny poorhouse seems to have been in a shocking condition, and this was the responsibility of the parish officers, and ultimately the ratepayers.

Dr Edward Smith, the rector at the time, had been at Datchworth since 1748, and was to die there in 1785. He was also granted dispensation to be vicar of St Paul's Walden for the period 1761–1775. Unfortunately it seems to be true that the overseers at Datchworth had something of a history of not making proper provision for the housing of the poor. On 17 March 1653, the Hertford County Records sessions rolls show that William Pennyfather and William Meade, churchwardens and overseers of the poor of Datchworth, were called to the court to answer for 'disobeying an order directing them to provide a house in their parish for the habitation of James Kittsey.[73] As for the other records of the Datchworth parish chest, these are sadly missing for the right time period, maybe even deliberately destroyed or never kept securely in the first place.

The case of the Eaves family, as with any real-life story, is complex, and shows that even when in full-time work, wages were not always enough to cope with feeding a family and illness. Although living conditions were in general far more squalid than would be tolerated by most of us today, there were limits to what others could be expected to put up with. There have always been people, for whatever reason, who could not get on with their neighbours and who were constantly evicted.

Through indirect evidence, some of the most interesting facts for family and local historians emerge: that the Justices obviously expected appeals to be made direct by the poor to them; that bad characters committed to a local Bridewell prison were known of, and this would make any evidence they gave suspect. Also the casual way that everyone seemed to accept the terrible state of the cottages in Datchworth, so that a granary full of straw would be a preferred place to stay in an English November. That it would be acceptable to have two families in a one-room poorhouse. The way that agricultural labourers moved around a neighbourhood, working at different farms at different times of year. The fact that the bread-winner could live in at a farm, while his wife and younger children were left to find whatever they could. That the mistress in Tewin would not let her thirteen-year-old employee have a day off to visit his sick parents. That out-relief had to be applied (begged) for, and could be given or withdrawn on a whim. The attitude that a boy of eleven should be out at work to provide for his family. Finally, that evictions and movement from lodgings often happen on one of the quarter days: 25 March, 25 June, 25 September, 25 December.

These fascinating and contradictory witness testimonies show that eighteenth-century justice was very far from perfect, and that the parish officers and the JPs all stuck together, and their words must have carried very strongly with the King's Bench. In the end it came down to who could be best believed as to whether or not relief was given, and what the cause of death was. Witnesses for the prosecution were quite easily rubbished, but neither can we be entirely sure that envy, spite and maliciousness did not also come into play against the Bassetts.

It must be remembered that this story cannot be found in the parish chest records for Datchworth, but only came to light due to publication of the Thicknesse pamphlet, his publicity campaign in the newspapers, and most importantly the legal action taken at King's Bench. This makes it extraordinary in many ways.

The New Poor Law

In 1834 the Poor Law system was reformed, and became known as the New Poor Law. This changed the law from one that was mainly organized parochially, to one that had a national focus. One of the most important results of the New Poor Law from a researcher's point of view was a new arrangement of parishes into local districts called Poor Law unions. The Poor Law unions then became the basis for the organization of civil registration districts (from its start in July 1837), and the enumerator's districts in the census (from 1841). Under the New Poor Law the old system of out-relief that had been so important to many, including those such as the Eaves above and the Izzards of Rotherfield discussed below, lost its central role. It was no longer to be paid to the able-bodied, although in reality some provision was still paid in many places, particularly in the North, until a further prohibitory order of 1844.

The main effect of the New Poor Law was that workhouse provision was centrally organized and expanded, and the poor had to apply to enter the workhouse where they were set to work for their board and lodging. If some of the prejudices against the Eaves family were because they were not 'deserving' of relief, and should have been more prudent with whatever money they had, then these very old-standing attitudes did not get swept away by the new system.

The old settlement rules were also adjusted and simplified, and a year's employment and the service of a parish office were no longer possible ways to gain settlement. In practice, the local records of settlement become increasingly sparse as the nineteenth century progressed, and the researcher is lucky to find any surviving settlement material from the period after 1834, although records of the workhouse start to become more and more useful.

The Story of Jesse Izzard

The story of Jesse Izzard of Rotherfield in Sussex is all too typical of a nineteenth-century agricultural labourer existing on the very margins of making ends meet, and spans the two systems of Poor Law. It also shows how much can be reconstructed for a person's life using Poor Law records in combination with many other sources. It uses overseers' accounts, relief payments and workhouse records at East Sussex Record Office, combined with details from the tithe maps, the census, civil registration and parish registers.

Jesse was born and baptised in the Sussex parish of Rotherfield in 1805 and died in the Union workhouse in Uckfield, in April 1887. He worked all his life as an agricultural labourer, and had eight known children, all of them baptised at Rotherfield.[74]

In 1813, when Jesse was a child of eight years old and almost certainly already working in the fields all day, the Reverend Arthur Young, a clergyman from Sussex, reported to the Board of Agriculture his findings as to the state of the County of Sussex. Writing about the poor, he says that:

> ... the present state of this class of people is in many parts of England inferior to what every humane person would wish ...

> Too many of their houses are the residence of filth and vermin; their dress insufficient. [75]

However, this is contradicted earlier on by his statement on stone and flint cottages:

> In the Weald of Sussex they are in general warm and comfortable, and many of them built of stone; and on the Downs with flints. Certainly, the lower class of people are here in much more eligible circumstances, than in many other parts of England which might be named.[76]

Jesse married in 1827, and by 1829 had one child; at this point in time things were stable for Jesse and his little family. Then came a period of agricultural depression across the country, when wages for the labouring man in particular were very depressed; new machinery was being brought in, and unemployment threatened. These factors sparked many disturbances across the country, which became known as 'the swing riots'. On 15 November 1830, men from Rotherfield were caught up in these riots, and Jesse was probably with them. Sussex newspapers reported that labourers from Rotherfield broke into the house of the vicar and demanded half his tithes.[77]

Subsequently, during the next few years, Jesse is mentioned in the overseer's accounts for Rotherfield as being periodically one of a list of men who were paid either out-relief, or for parish work such as 'grubbing', which was clearance of wasteland, verges and so on. He was also put to work on the roads.[78] More children were born, and Jesse and his growing family were constantly on the edge of being able to cope. During this period they had moved house several times, probably in search of cheaper rents, or possibly, like the Eaves, they had been evicted.

In 1834 Jesse was out of work again, and appealed to the parish for payments from a local charity: this was granted at 2s, and then sometime later at a further 3s.[79] In April 1835, Jesse was sent to prison for two months for stealing a small implement worth 2s (perhaps to sell).[80] Naturally his wife and family were in a very bad position. She then applied to the parish for money, and just before all out-relief was stopped, was granted 6s, which would hardly have been enough to feed her and the children, and to pay rent.[81] Out-relief in Rotherfield was suspended in May 1835 as the New Poor Law came into effect. No more payments of out-relief appear to have been granted in Rotherfield. In November 1835 the Izzards' little boy died, aged just four years old.

After these tragedies there were some very tough periods for Jesse and his family. In 1848 potato blight came to Rotherfield and was very severe. This is the time of the Irish famine, but it is little known that it also affected people in England as well. More children were born, but there were also more deaths of children to endure, when in 1857 two of Jesse's children died within days of each other of some infectious disease.

However, by 1861 the two eldest sons were out at work and thus contributing to the family, so at last the family entered a period of relative ease; this lasted until Jesse's old age and the eventual death of his wife in 1881. They continued to move within the parish fairly regularly, but by 1871 the eldest son lived next door to them, and one of the sons had bettered himself by joining the police force and had moved away to London. Jesse was still working on the land at the age of seventy-five, and he must have been fit and strong. However, there came a time when he could no longer look after himself, particularly after his wife died.

Jesse was admitted to Uckfield Union workhouse in 1884, where he continued to live until 1887, when he died as an inmate.[82] He most likely became infirm and unable to look after himself, and his family did not, or could not, take him in. Regrettably his younger son William, who was the police officer in London, was summoned to the petty sessions court in Lewes for failing to support his father, was found guilty, and the Poor Law Union was able to force the docking of 2s from his wages to help pay for Jesse's upkeep.[83] This was a kind of means testing. Frederick, Jesse's elder son, was in Rotherfield all the time, but presumably his wages were so low he could not contribute to his father's upkeep or take him in. No doubt this story and variations on it were played out in thousands of other similar cases up and down the country.

The need for the very poor to steal in order to support themselves is ever present throughout history, and the juxtaposition or use of Poor Law records, together with criminal records, is something that could be of interest to many researchers. Many of these tales of theft are for really small and low value items.

As well as the story of the Izzards comes this little case from the Kent village of Bredhurst in 1848:

> Sarah Ferminger, a middle-aged woman, who stated that she was from Bredhurst and that her husband was at work charcoal burning at Cobham, was brought up charged with stealing a child's frock from the shop door of Mr Clift, pawnbroker, Chatham. The prisoner committed the robbery about an hour before Howes, the constable, brought her before the bench. She was seen to take the article by two witnesses; she, however, denied it and said that she had picked up the frock in the street. The Bench committed her for trial at the assizes. The prisoner said that she had four small children at home by themselves, and inquired what was to become of them. The bench directed the constable to proceed immediately to Bredhurst and communicate with the overseer or some other person, the circumstances of the woman and her children.[84]

Starting Points for the Researcher

Most Poor Law documents are within the records of parish administration known as the 'parish chest' and thus at the relevant county record office; they are usually now also available to search through by online catalogue. All the material should be organized in the catalogue by parish. To discover payments of out-relief you may need to use both churchwardens' and overseers' accounts. There may also be documents recording charity monies paid regularly to the poor, as many parishes did have a local charity that paid out small sums to the very poor, so these are worth searching for. Vestry minutes may also be helpful, and again are found with the parish chest records.

Not many parishes have large amounts of settlement examinations, but where they exist they are so helpful in establishing where people have moved from, and in shedding light upon their lives, that they must always be sought out. Any removal orders will usually also be found with these documents, but could be with the receiving parish or the removing parish, so it is worth checking both if known. Look for the local petty sessions and quarter sessions records in case a removal order was disputed; this often happened, and may give a clue as to whether a removal was permanent.

Unfortunately, many sessions' records remain unindexed, therefore unless you have an exact date for a removal order, speculative searches could be very long-winded. A partial name index to quarter sessions was available on the old Access to Archives website, which is now part of The National Archives *Discovery* union catalogue. If you find material in this, remember these records are not held by The National Archives, they just provide an online catalogue. An example of what could be found comes from Surrey quarter sessions:

> Easter Sessions, 1766, catalogued as QS/6/1766/Eas
> Item 11: Removal Order William and Elizabeth Reese and children from Carshalton to Swansea, Glamorgan, South Wales.

This roll, and any other associated documents to do with the case, is held at Surrey History Centre, in Woking.

Other places to search for petty and quarter sessions records are the printed editions published by the county record societies, or sometimes by the record office or county council, as in the case of the volumes of session rolls extracts published by Hertfordshire and used in the case of Datchworth above. Online books can be searched for at The Hathi Trust (https://www.hathitrust.org) and also at Internet Archive (https://archive.org).

Newspapers can help locate and unlock the all-important dating of sessions cases if they are online and indexed. Using a simple surname plus place parish name, search on the British Library's collection of local newspapers available on British Newspaper Archive online: this can be an extremely rewarding way to discover interesting cases. Try searching online newspapers with terms such as 'sessions' plus the parish name, or simply the county name plus 'sessions'. Take a note of the sessions date, and then go to the relevant sessions court roll to discover more information.

Newspapers are also extremely helpful not only in highlighting individual cases, but also in providing evidence of the attitudes of the authorities and the administrative process of the law. They may be worth browsing issue by issue.

Not many cases will end up in the records of the King's Bench as the Eaves case did. In the event that you do trace a case into the higher courts of the County Assize or King's Bench, all of which are held at The National Archives, then their dedicated research guides on the Assize, the King's Bench, and generally on records for tracing criminals, will be helpful. All the research guides are online (https://www.nationalarchives.gov.uk/help-with-your-research/).

To read more about records of the Poor Law, as well as other parish records, W.E. Tate's *The Parish Chest* (Phillimore, reprint 1983) remains a major authority. Stuart A. Raymond's *Tracing Your Ancestors' Parish Records* (Pen & Sword, 2015) also has a very useful section on Poor Law records. David T. Hawking's *Pauper Ancestors, A Guide to the Records Created by the Poor Laws in England and Wales* (2011) gives many examples of transcribed records, but not so much background. There are many other books on Poor Law available both from a social or legal history point of view, as well as those aimed at family historians.

6

Work and School in the Countryside

Countryside Work and Crafts

The countryside and villages were not just a place for farms and agricultural labourers: there were trade and industry too. Both farm and village have always needed the trades and occupations that help support the growing of food and the making and repair of buildings and equipment: blacksmithing, wheelwrighting, carpentry and butchery, for example. In addition, some villages had a semi-industrial workforce from the medieval period: for example, the iron workers of the Sussex Weald, the tin miners of Cornwall and Devon and the salt producers of Cheshire. Quarrying and brick making were scattered throughout the countryside wherever the stone or clay was of the right kind. Coal and lead mining were not urban occupations, but existed hand in glove with agriculture, often in remote and thinly populated places. Therefore, there is no set of rural occupations that fits all possible villages, and depending on the area, available work might vary greatly.

As well as working in the fields, those villagers who were agricultural labourers took on a variety of crafts and subsidiary occupations, depending on gender, to help eke out a living, as wages were usually very low and agricultural work seasonal. These secondary occupations and crafts might include weaving, spinning, lace making, hat making, straw plaiting, knitting and basket making. Many jobs were seasonal and fitted in with a variety of other occupations – thus the charcoal burner might also work as an agricultural labourer, while the wheelwright might run a local beer shop and do some carpentry as well. Once again, account needs to be taken of the local situation: people may have been occupied in many different activities within the countryside before the mass movement into the towns and cities, and the growth of the factories during the nineteenth century, which tended to kill off the village craft.

In the nineteenth century it is thought that craftsmen and tradesmen were typically one-fifth of all those in employment.[85] Arable areas such as the south Midlands, Bedfordshire and North Hertfordshire often included crafts centred on by-products of the field, such as straw plaiting and weaving, and straw hat making. The male knitters of Wensleydale in North Yorkshire were using the by-product of the local sheep, which were the predominant stock animals of the upland farms.

In many places, villages in the early part of our period supported the wool and cloth industry, which became so important for national fortunes in the medieval and early modern periods. East Anglia was one centre of the cloth industry and of weaving; however, the weavers of towns and cities such as Norwich, Colchester and Sudbury depended on all the nearby villages in their localities spinning yarn for them. In the West Country a similar interdependence of town and country also supported the cloth trade. The cloth-making areas of Wiltshire had plenty of dairy farmers who managed to make broadcloth in their spare time. Clean running water was needed to run the fulling mills, and with them also came dyers and weaving. By the mid-eighteenth century as weaving competition intensified from Yorkshire mills, cloth making went into decline in the west and the southern half of England.

Knitting on a frame was also an occupation in both town and village from the early seventeenth century onwards. The mechanical frame to knit stockings was invented as far back as 1589, and from the eighteenth century could make cotton or lace items of any kind. The use of knitting frames started in Nottinghamshire and spread to Leicestershire and Derbyshire, so that by the eighteenth century these counties contained 85 per cent of all the frames. These frames were used domestically, and whole families were occupied in frame knitting at home before a more industrialized approach developed. In just one example, Kimcote, a parish and village in Leicestershire, had a population in 1851 of 603, many of whom were occupied in framework knitting.

The inhabitants of those villages that were near to the sea or to rivers, to fens and osier beds, would have been involved in many crafts that went hand in hand with fishing or waterside activities, such as fish preparation, eel catching, basket weaving and reed cutting.

Woodland areas had their own specific jobs, many of them undertaken on a part-time basis: bodging or wood turning, making trugs or basic furniture such as kitchen stools or chairs, as well as looking after the woodland and timber, felling trees and sawing in wood mills. Horses would be used to drag felled logs from wooded areas to the roads. Charcoal burning was another job for the woodsman, and often supported a local iron industry such as in the Forest of Dean and the Sussex Weald and at places such as Bredhurst on the North Downs of Kent.

When the village lay within the estate of a grand house, the upkeep of the house and grounds gave work to many villagers as domestic servants, gardeners, coachmen and grooms. The rectory or parsonage and the gentry houses (if any) also employed their own servants, and any household that could afford it would have employed at the very least a local woman to come in during the day to cook and clean, or a live-in maid-of-all-work. The larger farmers were the main source of employment in many villages, with the farmer higher up the social scale than the tradesman. Tradesmen, carpenters, wheelwrights, blacksmiths, butchers and shopkeepers came next in the hierarchy, and following them were the more skilled labourers, such as horse-team drivers, then the general agricultural labourers.

Some people stood quite apart from the local community – for example, gamekeepers were often isolated and usually from outside the area. They were usually loathed by the local community and could command higher wages in recompense for the danger of their work as they were often set upon by local gangs. Their references had to be impeccable, and their backgrounds were closely inspected.[86]

Occupations recorded from the 1851 census, together with *Kelly's Directory* of 1850, for one Hertfordshire village included builder/bricklayer, wheelwright/carpenter, beerseller, saddler/harness maker; miller, grocer/draper/shopkeeper, butcher, boot or shoemaker/cordwainer, blacksmith, baker and tailor. Many of these small-scale enterprises were family businesses, and they came under increasing pressure as the nineteenth century went on, with competition from new factories and mass production.[87]

In addition to horses and wagons owned and used by individual farmers, villages might also have had independent carters for hire, and blacksmiths for shoeing the horses and making many general items of ironwork. The carter could be seen as the forerunner of a local taxi or 'man-and-a-van' service, providing lifts for both people and goods around the district. The blacksmith was an important component of any rural society, taking the position of local 'mechanic' with the blacksmith's forge in many areas evolving in the twentieth century into a garage and petrol station. Blacksmiths were often positioned centrally near to a pub or inn, so as to be near to the horses of passing travellers who might need a shoe replacing.

On the farms there were two types of labour, depending on the character of the district. On some farms the farm servants (both men and women) lived in, and were hired by the year on an annual wage (to get around the settlement laws), while on other types of farm the farmer relied more on casual labour hired by the month. This second type was more typical of the southern counties, and is what we saw in Datchworth in Chapter 5. In the more heavily populated southern and eastern part of the country live-in farm servants only accounted for about 10 per cent of the farming labour force in the mid-Victorian period, but they were up to 40 per cent of the labour force in the northern districts.[88]

As with all research into the past, context is everything. The history and geography of an area would have helped to shape the occupational structure, depending not only on land ownership but also on whether the area was wooded, or arable, or mixed pasture. For example, the area around Cranbrook in Kent had generally kept its medieval or even older woodlands, and had been settled later than surrounding areas. Farms and hamlets were not established until the twelfth or thirteenth centuries, and all of them are thought to have been enclosed from the start, therefore there was no common land or manorial waste. There was pasture not arable, and the woods gave work for carpenters, charcoal burners and iron smelting. When this was coupled with the Kent practice of gavelkind or inheritance among many, whereby not just the eldest son inherited land, it resulted in smaller farms with a larger population to support, and thus extra labour provided a suitable environment for the development of local woodland industry.[89]

The distinctive windmill or watermill for grinding corn into flour was a feature of most landscapes throughout our period, perhaps in almost every parish. The corn miller was often a person of relative wealth and importance, as the milling of corn was a crucial part of the economy, with the staple diet being bread for most people. Grain that was not sold by the farmers to larger brewers or other businesses usually had to be sold to the nearest miller because transporting it too far would be inefficient. Thus a miller with a local monopoly could dictate a price.

Some mill owners further consolidated their position by being both farmers and millers. Many watermills were used for the cloth trade, being fulling mills or silk mills, and mills could be converted from corn to fulling and back again, depending on economic circumstances. The fulling process involved wetting the cloth and beating it to shrink and thicken it, thus producing a thicker, more waterproof fabric.

The history of the small Somerset village of Over Stowey provides an illuminating example of the interconnectedness and sheer complexity of geography and historical occupation. A watermill is recorded there in the Domesday Book of 1086, and at one time there were at least five separate fulling mills, some of which spent time as grist mills or were converted to and from other purposes. Clothing and fulling were joined by dyeing and tanning using local oak. A silk mill was constructed in 1812 to 1816, which was said to employ hundreds of women and girls; however, it only lasted a few decades. A pottery existed in the thirteenth century and again in the sixteenth. Bricks were also made locally. Meanwhile local woods provided work for charcoal burners, and broom making was also locally significant.[90]

Those parishes where there was manorial waste and where the vestry system was open rather than closed, tended to have many cottagers along the roadsides, in the woods and on scrap bits of land; these were occupied by day labourers, mole catchers, pedlars, casual workers of all kinds, perhaps wildfowlers, hurdle makers, as well as poachers and others scratching a living as best they could out of sight of the main parts of the parish. In the Headington area of Oxford, just such an area was researched by the editor of *Village Life and Labour* (History Workshop Series) in an essay called 'Quarry roughs, life and labour in Headington Quarry, 1860–1920'. This quarry area was near a wide area of wasteland that was used for camping by gypsies. Both the quarry dwellers and the gypsies lived a life literally on the edge of the parish and officers of the law.[91]

Both widowed and married women also operated cottage laundries from home, taking in washing from others. In Hampstead, Middlesex, before it became fashionably gentrified in the early nineteenth century, there were rows of cottages doing just this, many of them using their nearness to the big city of London as a source of unlimited customers.

Notwithstanding these other occupations and all the craftwork that was also taking place, farming employed around half the labour force in a typical rural location, with about a fifth being taken up by trades and crafts, around one-tenth being domestic servants, and the rest being farmers, the gentry and professionals, and others specific to the location.[92]

Social Status and the Farmer

Within the occupation of 'farmer' there was, not surprisingly, a wide disparity of status, size of farm and relative wealth. Farmers might be wealthy freeholders or prosperous tenants, or they might be poverty stricken on poor land, with only the immediate family employed. The 1851 census was the first that recorded how big a farm the farmer was working. You may have seen in the occupation column comments such as 'Farmer of 100 acres, employing five labourers'; and the notes given to the enumerators are worth looking at more closely for what they tell us about who those labourers might be; for example, the notes say:

> ... the number of labourers returned should include waggoners, shepherds and all kinds of workmen employed on the farm,

> whether they sleep in the house or not; and when boys or women are employed, their number should be separately given.

However, there was no definition of 'farmer', or a limit on size, so that smallholdings of one or two acres are shown as 'farmed', when in fact they might have been market gardens, or some kind of secondary occupation for someone who mainly carried on another activity or trade.[93] It is always going to be worth combining other records such as tithe and the rate books with the census to get a better idea of the exact size and worth of a farm or smallholding.

As we saw in Chapter 3, in older documents you will come across the terms 'yeoman' and 'husbandman' in relation to someone who was obviously farming. Social rank in the countryside based upon a study of probate records always went titled ('gent' and above): 'farmer', 'yeoman', 'husbandman', 'labourer'. The terms 'yeoman' and 'husbandman' originally had definite meanings, with the label of 'farmer' hardly being used prior to 1730; but gradually original meanings were lost, so that by the eighteenth century they can only be said for certain to be alternative terms for 'farmer'.[94]

In the eighteenth and nineteeenth centuries you may still find the term 'yeoman' being used to distinguish someone who was at a higher level of status than a tenant farmer or husbandman. However, the general term 'farmer' increasingly replaced both these terms. The tenant farmer who rented a small number of acres on an annual agreement was often little more than a smallholder and was liable in bad times to move down to the status of labourer. On the other hand a labourer could, with luck, move up to the status of farmer; therefore, great caution needs to be taken when trying to distinguish people with common names in the same area using occupational terms alone. Again, you will need to use a variety of different records to put an ancestor's working life into the right context, and to recognize that he could move up, but was equally or perhaps more likely to move downwards, both economically and socially.

The Farm and Its Work

Jobs on the farm were driven by the seasons: ploughing, cultivation, drilling, weeding, harvesting, stacking and threshing for crops, coupled with the husbandry of animals. The farm itself might employ not just the farmer and his family, but also a shepherd, a man for the cattle, women for milking and for butter and cheese making, someone in charge of the horses and wagons and the plough team, and many general casual labourers for the long list of fluctuating jobs in the fields.

The start of the agricultural year was in the autumn, after harvest. This was the time when tenants changed property and the farmer started to plan for the growing year ahead. In some areas of the country, hiring fairs were held in the local county towns to make it easier for the farmer to find new hands. Such fairs were either around Michaelmas (29 September, or in some places 10 October, after the Gregorian calendar change in 1752 moved Michaelmas forwards) or Martinmas (10 November). Farmers and labourers would mingle in large crowds, with the labourers wearing tokens that reflected their experience. In some places female domestic servants carried mops, hence the fairs are sometimes referred to as 'mop' fairs.

For the single person, who is often the most difficult ancestor to track, the importance of the hiring fair and the pull of the local market town cannot be overstressed. It is also important to consider the seasonality of agricultural work, and the fact that both men and women were engaged in it, factors that might help you to understand how an ancestor met a spouse, or the migration from one district to another. In the 1851 census some 143,000 women were recorded as agricultural labourers, and in general it is thought that the census returns significantly underestimate the numbers of women engaged in farm work.

Whether one had steady work or not depended entirely on location – those who worked for one farmer or on one estate for almost the whole time, and those who moved around year by year, or worked seasonally only. The latter had a much more precarious existence.

Winter was a quiet time on the farm, with short days and less to do in the fields; jobs for winter included some animal husbandry, hedge laying, ditch digging and clearing, liming and marling of fields to improve fertility, and the picking of winter crops such as brassicas and some roots, in the areas where they were grown, such as Bedfordshire. There was also winter ploughing and threshing to finish. Ploughing was heavy and skilled work, particularly on clay soils, often involving teams of horses that needed to be handled correctly. It is not just a question of following along behind the horses: a plough has to be 'driven' at the correct angle and in a straight line by the ploughman, as well as being pulled through the earth by the horses. The ploughman was often accompanied by a ploughboy who was learning the skill, but a youngster was not strong enough to be left on his own with the plough on a heavy soil.

In late winter and early spring lambing would begin for the shepherds, while in arable areas spring was when the work really started and the labour force on the farm increased, with sowing of crops, stone gathering, and weeding of all crops, either by horse or by hand hoeing, which was often women's work. In early summer was the hay harvest, and work then built up in a crescendo to the most important time of the year, which was Lammas (usually celebrated between 1 August and 1 September): the main harvest period. Harvest times would depend on location, the height above sea level and latitude, with the more northerly districts being the last to harvest.

Harvest work took place in all daylight hours, often involving a whole village or a professional harvest gang in cutting, raking, stacking and carrying. As the exact period of harvest varied from district to district depending on weather, soil and sowing times, it was possible for large gangs to work the fields for a lengthy period of time, starting in the southern districts and moving slowly north as tasks became ready. Maude Robinson in her memoir of a Sussex farm remembers gangs in Sussex in the mid-Victorian period:

> However ample the supply of labour for the rest of the year, it was impossible for the ordinary staff to manage the harvest, and crowds of Irish labourers came to England at this season, sleeping in the outbuildings as the hop-pickers do.[95]

Evidence of other long-distance walks to find harvest or summer mowing work appear in Armstrong's *Farmworkers* (1988) and Samuel's *Village Life and Labour* (1975): kilted Scottish workers walked to Norfolk and back; grain was harvested in Herefordshire by Welsh mountain folk; gangs from the western counties of England worked their way down to the southern ones; and men from Derbyshire walked to London and back, working all the way.

The witness statements from King's Bench in the case of the Bassett brothers and the Eaves family also gives important evidence as to the travels made by workers more locally around the North Hertfordshire area for harvest work, with men and boys or whole families absent from their home villages as they travelled from farm to farm.

Wages and Conditions

Wages for farm workers were very low. For example, wages in Datchworth in the Eaves case in 1768 were testified as being 3s per week for boys, and 16–18s per week for a harvestman (the time of year when the labourer could earn the most). These amounts hardly changed for a hundred years, as Edwin Grey in *Cottage Life in a Hertfordshire Village* reported that teenage boys could earn between 3s 6d to 5s per week, and adult agricultural labourers 11–13s weekly in summer and 9s or less in the winter. Head ploughmen, cowmen or shepherds earned more at 15s per week.[96]

In some districts wages included board and lodging for the unmarried, or farm cottages let out by the farmer at a low rent. For those living in, who were almost always unmarried and the majority of them under twenty, with most of the rest being in their twenties, there were no evenings out or days off either, except for Sunday, when farm servants might be expected either to attend church with their employer, or to sit and listen to their employer reading the bible.

Maude Robinson, in her slightly rose-tinted memoir of a Sussex farm in the 1860s, remembered:

> ... it is strange to realize what excellent and contented servants had incredibly low wages. One quite capable of simple farmhouse cooking, management of the dairy and butter-making, had only twelve pounds a year, paid quarterly, lest she should squander it.

> When my father took the farm there were only six cottages, and these he reduced to five, as he would never be responsible for a dwelling with less than three bedrooms, but in after years, the milk trade needing more labour, seven more cottages were built. The older ones were rent at 1s 1d week – I think the newer ones were 1s 6d, and every man had as much garden as he could cultivate and was encouraged to plant fruit trees. With this, although wages were what would not be considered scandalously low, from 10s to 18s a week according to skill, the labourers were very comfortably off and I remember no real poverty. They could have gorse for fuel, and I remember one man saying with great satisfaction when winter set in, 'Yes, I've six boys, but I've got a sack o' taters put by for each of them'.[97]

In many places the right to the tiny spilled grains of corn in the fields after harvest, known as the 'right to glean', was an age-old custom and a great help to the poor labourer. This work was traditionally for women and children. Robinson again:

> In the old days we children spent much time in the harvest field picking up the scattered corn and giving our bunches in turn to the women and children who toiled all day. I have known an industrious woman with well-trained children pick up in one harvest season eleven bushels of wheat![98]

In 1786 a case brought to the Court of Common Pleas heard evidence surrounding this right. It was brought in connection with a male Norfolk labourer who was accused of trespass in the fields outside his own parish. The case was of interest to farmer and gleaner everywhere because although the right to glean was an ancient custom, it was not actually on any statute. Was there such a right, or was it simply an indulgent custom? The Justices agreed that there was a right for the poor to glean after the harvest was cut and taken away in their own parishes, but not outside their own parish.[99]

Although the work was hard and physical in the fields and woods, with the English working day being twelve hours long, from 6am until 6pm, and longer at harvest time, yet foreign visitors of the time noted that the English labourers took more breaks, talked to each other a great deal, and worked a shorter, less strenuous day than their foreign counterparts. Of course it was extremely difficult for the farmer to oversee all the labourers in all his fields, and while there were opportunities for breaks and chatting, no doubt the work was often back-breaking, monotonous, cold and wet and generally physically very tough.[100]

A distinct period in the history of the village started with the mechanization of labour in the fields, and the subsequent reduction in demand for men and women working in the fields. At around the same time, there was a gradual change from the system of hiring labour for a year, to one of casual work and hiring on demand. This was something that took more than 150 years to fully play out. The introduction of the threshing machine around 1800 was an important part of this early mechanization, and farm labourers quickly realized that their jobs and life on the land were considerably threatened by this machinery. They began to organize themselves over this, and in the 1830s threshing work played a large part in riots and social unrest, which became known as the 'swing riots', as the threshing machine could thresh the same amount of wheat more quickly than a man and at half the cost.

Inevitably men and women lost their jobs. The poor relief system came under increasing strain due to a combination of all these factors, particularly in the south and the main arable districts, and is one of the reasons why agricultural wages, the price of corn, unemployment and the question of relief for the poor were all considerably intermeshed.

Furthermore, a process of farms becoming more consolidated was occurring. As early as 1831 the number of farms was reduced by three-quarters, and each individual farm was much bigger.[101] In arable areas a large rural workforce was only necessary at harvest time, thus as harvest work disappeared many villagers were obliged to find some other kind of trade or craft to fall back on during the slower months. But the increase in mechanization and industrialization also meant that all kinds of crafted goods could be made cheaply in the factories, as a result of which all the cottage crafts went into decline. More efficient harvest methods also meant that there was less spilled grain to glean for.

All these factors coming together over the nineteenth century were a serious blow for the poorer village folk, and led to mass migrations of rural populations away from the countryside into the towns in search of work.

Brewing, Malting and Public Houses

One other common occupation in the village needs to be mentioned, and that is of the inn or public house, and the associated activities of brewing and malting. The village pub is a very old-established entity, and the drinking of ale or beer, both home-brewed or in the local public house, is equally ancient. In the days before a safe water supply – Datchworth, for example, was supplied only by pond or well water until the 1930s – beer was safer to drink than water because the brewing process involves boiling.

Originally the ale of England was made only with malted grain, water and yeast, without hops, and this is what made it 'ale'. However, hops gradually made their way into the brewing process during the fourteenth and fifteenth centuries, brought over by the Flemish. When hops were added to ale, the resulting liquid became known as 'beer'. From being something that was a common hedgerow and garden plant, hops began to be planted in English fields where the land was suitable, particularly in the south and the West Midlands. By 1665 hops were being grown in fourteen counties, and a central hop market was established in Southwark on the south bank of the Thames. In Kent it is still possible to see many old oast houses, which were used for the drying of hops.

Apart from water and yeast, the other ingredient of beer is barley (other cereals can also be used), which can be grown in many places. In order to be suitable for brewing the barley grain first has to be malted. The malting process involves soaking the grain in water until the seeds are just germinating, and then quickly drying or roasting them to halt the germination. Traditionally this took place in large drying rooms in buildings known as maltings, where the grain was spread out on the floor and raked over. Once the grain, or malt, is prepared, it is then milled to crush it.

The beer-making process therefore starts with malting and the specialist skills of the maltster. On a brewing day the milled malt is put into a large vessel known as a mash tun, and boiling water is added to fully soak and steep the malt. This results in a liquid known as 'wort'. The wort is then drawn off and boiled in another large vessel known as a copper, where hops are added. From there it was traditionally transferred into an open vessel where yeast was added (or a wild yeast hopefully made its way in), and the process of fermentation could begin. The whole process takes about seven days.

Thus there were home-grown supplies of common country ingredients in the right place, and an ancient process of malting and brewing that was well understood by many country folk.

Brewing equipment is often a feature of sixteenth- and seventeenth-century inventories, and most farms throughout our period would have brewed their own beer, and farms in the apple country of the western counties would have made their own cider. Before the rise of the large breweries in the eighteenth century, brewing was mainly domestic, and was the role of women – hence the term 'ale wife'. Only as the process became industrialized did it lose its domestic identity and become almost exclusively the preserve of specialist male brewers.

What we tend to think of as a traditional inn was more often a feature of the towns, normally situated on an established transport route, providing a space for change of horses, rooms for travellers, and hot food. Most villages did not aspire to such grand or large establishments – but what they almost all had was a village ale house. This was equally as ancient as the inns, dating at least from the medieval period. Traditionally an ale house did not hold a licence to serve spirits, but that was fine, as throughout most of our period most people drank beer. All those who could afford it, including small children, drank 'small beer' at meal-times, much as we might drink water or tea, or have a soft drink. Small beer is a weak variety of beer made from the left-over contents of the mash tun, after the first brew has been taken.

The village ale house was joined at the start of the nineteenth century by the establishment of many beer shops (the brewing of beer for sale came under the Beer House Act of 1830, and licences were relatively cheap and easy to obtain). Then it was possible to brew just enough to set up shop in a cottage front room, or maybe to brew only for a special occasion annually; for the rest of the time villagers made their living in the fields, or as tradesmen.

The Village School

Throughout most of our period, village children would be lucky if they could get any instruction at a local school. The children of agricultural labourers were needed to work in the fields from the age of ten for boys, and younger children were used for some jobs such as crow scaring, stone picking, potato harvesting, and of course gleaning. For the girls, helping at home looking after the younger children was also expected from a very young age, perhaps as young as five and certainly from eight or nine. For most children, schooling was something that had to be fitted in around work.

Towns and cities had grammar schools, and there were many 'dame' schools, which might range from a handful of village children being taught the three 'r's plus study of the bible by a retired soldier, to larger establishments where a couple of spinsters taught girls to sew and undertake domestic duties, as well as to read and write. The dame schools were normally paid for by the parents and were completely unregulated.

Charity schools that gave a free education to the poor in the seven to eleven age group, or partly free basic education, also existed in some places, often organized in the eighteenth century by the Society for the Propagation of Christian Knowledge. It was from these schools that our concept of primary education derives.

From 1780 Sunday schools started to appear, and in the early nineteenth century more structured education in village schools started to be established; sometimes a schoolhouse was also built. Conditions varied very widely. For some reason the inhabitants of Bedfordshire in the 1840s had the lowest male literacy rates in the country. Lancashire schools were not as disciplined, nor did they have as many pupils as Yorkshire ones, and Northumbrian schools were judged to be dirty and ill-disciplined.[102]

The authors of the parliamentary report known as the 'Commission of Employment of Children, Young Persons and Women in Agriculture' (House of Commons, 1867) found that boys were generally employed full time in agriculture from the age of ten. They would not become ploughboys until they were a bit stronger, from the age of twelve upwards, and in areas of heavy clay soil, fourteen years. Of those in school, it was not at all uncommon for boys to leave school early in the spring and not return until late autumn. In fact this was encouraged, for then the boys would have their own money to pay towards their education in school when they could attend. Nevertheless, the commissioners found that parents' desire for the provision of education in the countryside was strong.

There was no compulsory education for any child until 1880. The 1870 Education Act brought in a national system of schooling outside the various religious groups, with teaching that was required to be non-denominational, and the establishment of school boards. Schools that were already established continued, but over the years came under increasing control from these school boards. However, it was not until 1880 that education between the ages of five and ten became compulsory for all children and within inspected schools, and not until 1891 that this schooling became completely free. There was therefore a period when children were supposed to be in school, but their parents were meant to provide for some of the cost – no doubt a burden to an already stretched budget. Not surprisingly there was a lot of truancy, and children still worked many hours outside school.

Finding surviving attendance records of village and local school pupils as far back as the eighteenth century might be unlikely, but is much more common from the mid-nineteenth century onwards. If any survive they are likely to be in the local archives or in the county record office, and on a few of the data websites such as Findmypast.co.uk and Ancestry.co.uk. Try searching by parish and the words 'attendance register'. However, the lack of early attendance records for genealogists to pore over is made up by some early nineteenth-century parliamentary reports, which give good details of the existing schools and the numbers attending. These reports are available online.

The information from the *Abstract of Education Returns 1833*, published online by the Hathi Trust[103], gives us a wonderful flavour of the state of things at the three locations of Bredhurst in Kent, Datchworth in Hertfordshire and Aysgarth in Wensleydale in North Yorkshire. Note that 'males and females' does not mean that all the school attenders were children, as sometimes adults were attending in order to gain a better education. The emphasis on 'day school' is an indication that in many districts there were also night schools for those who could not attend during the day.

The entry for Bredhurst tells us that in 1833 the parish population was 147, there was one Sunday school, where fourteen received free instruction. In Datchworth, by contrast, the population was 593 and there was a single day and Sunday school, which was founded in 1820. It was attended by nineteen males and forty-three females daily, and by twenty-four males and fifty-nine females on a Sunday. It was supported by subscription, and payments from the pupils totalling £35 per year. What is not stated is that this school was established by the National Society for Promoting Religious Education, together with a local subscription for the building among the large landowners of the parish, and was one of the earliest in Hertfordshire, and even in the whole country. What is clear from the report is that the children and adult pupils were paying for their own education, a situation that was not uncommon.

The situation in Wensleydale was quite different, with many small schools scattered around the dale in the many townships of the large parish of Aysgarth. The village of High Abbotside, with a population of 589, had two daily schools established in 1833, for thirty-five males and twenty females who were paid for by their parents. Even the tiny hamlet of Thornton-Rust, population 158, had two daily schools, a Calvinistic and a charity school. Newbiggin, population 122, also had a daily school:

> ... containing 2 children [it] is endowed with a field, the rental of which is £6 6s per annum; it is observed that the School would be better attended, but that the inhabitants of the township are dissatisfied with the master, and that some of the trustees are dead, others refuse to act.[104]

The reason we still have a long summer break from school is because the farmers and parents successfully argued that the children must be free in the summer weeks to help with the work of getting in the harvest. Nevertheless, the increasing amount of free or nearly free education in the countryside during the nineteenth century meant that it became increasingly rare for villagers to be completely illiterate, or if they were themselves, then at least there was someone in the family who could read and write well enough for simple tasks such as filling in a census form. Maude Robinson again:

> I have heard my father say that at the time of the 1861 census every single cottager asked him to fill up the papers, but by 1881 only one cottage had no inmate capable of doing it.[105]

Starting Points for the Researcher

When researching the occupations of people in the past, it is necessary to take into consideration that occupational titles as used in parish registers or other kinds of document, particularly prior to the statistical undertakings of the Victorian census, were used as a way to identify people, and were not necessarily descriptions of a person's actual job. Women's occupations must have been heavily under-reported, as they were only referred to in relation to their male relatives or by marital status as someone's wife, widow or as a spinster. The absence of women's occupations in the genealogical records thus leads to some interesting anomalies – for instance, apparently no one was spinning the wool into yarn to be used by the thousands of male weavers.[106]

There being no national list of people and their occupations, except for the census, which starts the detailed recording of people in 1841, there is no one record source that is predominant prior to 1841. Yet occupation is a distinguishing factor between people, particularly in an area where a surname is common. Thus almost any kind of document that mentions people might include an occupation, and occupations should always be recorded by the genealogist, together with the date and on which document it is found. Parish registers, poor law records, churchwardens' and overseers' accounts, probate records, tithe and enclosure and some types of court record: all of these could be useful. Flavours or hints of the many types of local work can also be found in exactly the same local or parish records when they are read in their entirety, rather than just in the search for specific people. Occupations often occur as asides and incidental to the main points of the record keeping, and it is noticeable that burial registers often give male occupations.

Once the genealogist is working with the census from 1841 onwards, male occupations become far more obvious, although the census does not tell us about those who had multiple occupations. The census was only taken every ten years, and during that time an occupation might change, a farmer could slip down into being an agricultural labourer, and the agricultural labourer might appear as a farmer.

Trade directories, which appeared more often than every ten years, can be used to try to supplement the census. Long a feature of town life, trade directories underwent a period of expansion to cover rural areas during the mid-nineteenth century. Pigot's Directory started covering individual counties from the 1830s onwards, and Kelly's Directory achieved a nationwide coverage during the nineteenth century; these are therefore very useful in tracking down people to one place at a point in time. However, trade directories must be used with some caution. They do not cover women's craftwork carried out in the home, and tend to feature the kind of tradespeople that people buying the directory would be wanting to look out for – the principal inns, the wheelwrights, the nearest blacksmith, the miller, the post office, and information about the local gentry and church. Labourers are not listed.

The census will be the most important evidence for occupations for the nineteenth and into the twentieth centuries – and don't forget that civil registration certificates (birth, marriage and death) also record occupations. Court cases reported in the newspapers will normally include occupation, and of course probate records may do so as well. For any occupation that needed a licence issued by a magistrate, such as inn-keeping or peddling and hawking, and even midwifery, there may be lists of licence holders in quarter-sessions records.

Any lack of definite detail about the ordinary agricultural labourer in local records is in some cases made up by the nineteenth-century parliamentary reports and papers published by the House of Commons or House of Lords under various names and dates as commissioners' reports: for example, the 1843 reports of Poor Law commissioners on the employment of women and children in agriculture, or the 1867 Royal Commission on the employment of children, young persons and women in agriculture, both of which are readily available online. British History Online has a full list of commissions, and also the officials from 1815 to 1870, from which one can pick a commission report from the 'index to commissions' to investigate further.[107]

Using such reports, the researcher can turn to generalities about parishes and counties in order to make sense of the types of work their ancestor may have undertaken in those localities. Some names are given where people have been interviewed; however, don't expect to find your ancestors appearing, as it is the background detail of the daily working life of the agricultural labourer that gives the local historian and genealogist plenty of food for thought, even if their actual ancestor is not named as such. In this way it is possible to understand vividly the situation of their surroundings, and what was happening to the folk around them. In his book *My Ancestor was an Agricultural Labourer* (Society of Geanalogists, 2007), Ian Waller also gives a useful list of parliamentary papers to search for.

Other things to seek out are diaries of local people (published and unpublished), as well as village histories, which when read in conjunction with social histories of the times can prove very enlightening. Even memoirs and diaries written by rural people in other areas of the same county will give the enquiring genealogist plenty to think about. Some excellent general reading about rural ways and people can be had in books such as Flora Thompson's *Lark Rise to Candleford* or Laurie Lee's *Cider With Rosie*. And it is possible to hear the voices of labourers in *Ask the Fellows Who Cut the Hay* by George Ewart Evans, who interviewed older rural workers from the East Suffolk village of Blaxhall in the 1950s. Other contemporary diaries such as Kilvert's or Thomas Turner from Sussex, or the far more famous and political Cobbett's *Rural Rides*, can all be put to good use in providing background context for everyday rural life.

Surviving school records may be found at the relevant county record office, while some are online at Findmypast.co.uk and Ancestry.co.uk.

7

The Whole Community: Lists of Villagers and the Victorian Census

Anyone interested in the history of a village will be interested to know how many people lived there in the past. The ideal situation for historians, demographers and genealogists would be for a whole community to have been accurately counted, named and described on an annual basis. Obviously that is a historian's fantasy, but failing that, it would be good to have complete lists of people at certain points in time. The nineteenth- and twentieth-century censuses go part-way to this research nirvana, but for all other periods we are forced to rely for most of our community-wide information on incomplete sources and estimations.

This chapter looks at some early lists of taxpayers, and contrasts that with information from the census, and how the work of demographers and statisticians can aid the family historian. To do this we will be considering records that were created and held at a national level, rather than locally.

Both parish registers and manorial records, when they survive, have been used by demographers working in early periods to try to reconstruct a whole community. In some areas they have been able to estimate successfully and closely numbers of people over long periods of time, and using the figures gained have attempted to extrapolate them to regional and national numbers. However, the problem with both sources has always been the incomplete recording of people: not everyone living on a manor or in a parish is always recorded in all places, and this is compounded by patchy survival of the records themselves. Counting women is particularly difficult as they tend to be invisible in any source that only includes male householders.

Apart from parish registers and manorial records there are other sources that have been used as recognized lists or 'counts' of people from medieval times onwards, starting with the Domesday Book of 1086 and moving into military lists and tax records. Occasionally complete lists of parishioners can be found among other parish chest material. Again, these sources do not include, or rarely include, women, and therefore estimates of the female population have had to be made. This problem of counting all males and females over the whole of England was only fully solved by the first census of 1801.

We have already seen how the local administration of the manor and then the parish very slowly becomes more and more taken over by the civil administration of the county, and finally by central government through their wish to count people in the census and civil registration reforms during the early nineteenth century. And the growth of central government went hand in hand with tax-raising powers – even though most of our village ancestors hardly knew what a central government tax was.

From 1538 up to 1801 sources for the population of places are often ecclesiastical. The Bishop's Census of 1563 counted communicants, but only parts of it survive. The ecclesiastical census (the Compton Census) of 1676 provides by parish the number of Anglicans, Protestant dissenters and Roman Catholic dissenters. Visitation records – by the bishop on his journey around his jurisdiction – also often have estimates of population. Military muster rolls are useful sources for the sixteenth and seventeenth centuries, as they tend to include all able-bodied men. Manorial extents can sometimes list the heads of families and could therefore also be used to estimate the total population. The Protestant returns of 1641–42 provide a count of all males over the age of eighteen who swore allegiance to the Protestant religion, organized by parish.

The Hearth Tax

For most people in British history there was no such thing as an income tax. National attempts at regular income tax were started in 1798 to pay for the Napoleonic wars, but came to an end in 1816. Income tax was reintroduced by Robert Peel in 1842, but only the wealthy paid. Until the nineteenth century there was no regular direct tax by government at all. Tax was raised to pay for exceptional things and special events, such as wars. These special taxes gave rise to a set of records called the 'lay subsidy rolls'. The Tudor lay subsidy was a tax on wealth discovered by individual assessment, as laid down by scales and thresholds by statute. Much of the useful early lay subsidy collection was prior to our period, and is of less general use to genealogy as it only concerned the relatively wealthy. However, these taxes were a precedent for a much more useful (and easy to use) tax to the genealogist: the hearth tax.

The hearth tax was a tax on fireplaces in the house, also referred to as chimney money, and a recognition that houses throughout the nation had changed from the style of a medieval open hall to what is recognizably a modern house with a chimney stack, two floors and separate rooms, perhaps each with its own hearth. The tax was first introduced in 1662 by Charles II as one of a number of ways of getting him out of a big financial hole. From the very start it was beset with problems. It was collected only fifty-four times, the last time being in 1689. The idea was that the wealthier the person, the more rooms they had in their house and the more fireplaces, the more they would pay; however, it did disproportionately affect the poorer householder.

The tax was set at 2s per hearth per year, 1s to be collected twice a year on Lady Day in March and Michaelmas in September from any householder who paid local rates, and where the house was worth more than 20s rent per year. Those who had small cottages or hovels worth less than this and who were not ratepayers, or who had belongings worth less than £10, did not have to pay; also industrial hearths were exempt. However, people did have to apply for exemption certificates, signed every year by the minister and one of the churchwardens or overseers, and many lists of hearth tax payers (after 1663) also include those who were exempt, which makes them a very valuable source for the whole male population in a location. Heads of household did, of course, include some women, mainly widows. This makes it as complete as possible as a list of heads of households in any one place. The only other listing of men that would be comparable are the local militia lists.

The first set of assessors were the local constables who reported to the sheriff of each county; however, very soon the collection system changed to collectors appointed by the Treasury, known colloquially as 'chimney men'. This changed again in 1666 when it was farmed out to large financiers, who made their money by organizing the collection and taking a cut. None of these systems was entirely successful from the Treasury's point of view, and it had to resume collection itself in 1684.

The hearth tax was very much hated by the people who had to pay it; it may have been widely avoided in some localities, and the collection of the tax was complicated by a certain amount of lack of clarity as to who was chargeable. It was particularly hated that strangers would have to come into a person's house to appraise the hearths, while the chimney men who were strangers to the district were likely to be less forgiving to the poorest. Those who refused to pay were liable to be charged and might appear in quarter-sessions records; certainly there are plenty of instances recorded of collectors suffering verbal abuse and threats as they went from house to house, and in some cases physical attacks were made and even murder.[108]

Records of the taxes collected are now held in The National Archives in their E 179 series, which currently forms part of a separate database searchable by place. The 'E' of E 179 stands for 'Exchequer'. A few county record offices also have material, so it is worth double checking if there are local records that are not held by The National Archives. The original records in The National Archives are organized first by county, then by hundred, and finally by parish and village. The most complete surviving set are for the tax of 25 March (also known as Lady Day) 1664. People are not listed alphabetically, but mostly as a 'walk' around the location, and for some town or city locations it may be possible to reconstruct a street; however, for most smaller places this is very problematical.

Fortunately for the researcher many of the returns are available in transcribed and printed form, and increasingly on the internet. To see whether the returns have been printed for your county of interest, visit the website of the Centre of Hearth Tax Research, who are gradually making lists available online, albeit slowly due to the huge amount of work involved in transcribing these early documents.

You should always make certain if there are any printed

or transcribed returns for your area before heading off to The National Archives, because unless your reading of 'secretary hand' is good, you will find the lists of names difficult to interpret. The very first set of returns I looked at were in the then public record office in Chancery Lane. They were for Surrey, and were delivered to me in the original bag of the tax collector. As a very green researcher at the time, this was rather overwhelming and I retired all but defeated by the old handwriting, although extremely excited by the original bag. I then discovered that the very returns I had been struggling through had previously been transcribed and were available in book form on the library shelves. This was a good lesson, and one that I have never forgotten.

Displayed below is an extract from *Kent Hearth Tax – Lady Day 1664* (transcribed by Duncan Harrington) to show a typical parish entry.[109] In this case, Hawkinge (modern day Hucking) and Bredhurst are listed together, and it is not entirely clear which column relates to which, or if they are mixed together.

Hawkinge and Bredhurst

Chargeable		**Chargeable**	
Robert Staple	3	John Allen	4
Thomas Figg	3	George Allen	2
John Doe	2	Robert Woollett	1
Richard Kempsall	2	Robert Austen	2
Edward Carter	1	Thomas Wedd	2
Henry Staple	2	John Lemmon	1
Thomas Longe	6	George Nash	3
John Saywell	2	William Paine	6
Thomas Bird	1	Widdow Hodgeskin	2
Richard Weston	2	Jonanthon Sawyer	2
Widdow Hudsford	2	Thomas Cox	1
Robert Knight	3	Robert Packham	2
Thomas Champion	2	Thomas Bunton	2
Emanuell Cooper	3	Richard Trey	6
John Chambers	2		
Not Chargeable		**Not Chargeable**	
John Wood	2	Lawrence Fryday	1
Humphrey Dunkin	1	James Knowles	2
Widdow Goulden	1	Richard Wise	2
Nicholas Miles	1	Robert Andrewes	1
William Frowd	1	Stephen Willard	1
William Jorden	1	Stephen Cheesman	1
		Henry Staple Borsholder	1

In Hawkinge and Bredhurst in 1664 (shown above) you can see that Thomas Bird has one hearth and is chargeable for the tax. Only three houses have six hearths, and there are plenty of cottages with only a single hearth. One of the immediate problems of the way the original is displayed and listed is shown: which list is Thomas in? Is he living in Hawkinge or in Bredhurst? Or are both places combined? There is indeed a Thomas Berd in the Bredhurst parish registers, with his wife Ann in the 1670s. Probably this is a relative of Thomas Berd who was baptised in 1577 and who appeared in Chapter 2 – possibly even a great- or great-great-grandson. On the other hand, Richard Trey who appears in the second column was definitely living in Bredhurst. His son, Thomas Trey or Tray, matriculated at Magdalen Hall, Oxford University in November 1674, aged eighteen, according to Foster's *Alumni Oxoniensis 1500–1714*, available online at British History (https://british-history.ac.uk/alumni-oxon/1500-1714); he is noted as being of Bredhurst. With six hearths, his house was one of the largest.

To discover more you would need to work with both the hearth tax and the parish registers of both places. However, this mixing of geographical place is unusual, and it is more normal to find a single list under an obvious place name. Hawkinge here is modern day Hucking, also an ancient part of Hollingborne manor (as was Bredhurst), although not actually contiguous to Bredhurst.

It may be generally assumed that those with fewer than three hearths were living a somewhat precarious economic life and were not comfortably off. Two hearths could suggest only two rooms, with heating downstairs and a simple structure of kitchen, plus parlour or other room, and an unheated upstairs (if there was any upstairs at all). Those with ten hearths (there are none here) can be considered to be very wealthy.[110]

The information that can be gathered from this simple list of households might at first glance to the genealogist seem to be very insufficient, particularly if your own family name does not appear. However, there is much useful indirect evidence that can be gleaned. The fact that there are only three houses with six hearths, and none with more than this, gives a clue as to the relative economic status of the locality. More are liable to pay the tax than are not chargeable; however, those not chargeable make up a third of the households, and these were the families who did not pay rates or had less than £10 of belongings. Both places seem to count twenty-one households or dwellings. Henry Staple, borsholder (head of the tithing) appears at the bottom of the list, but without appearing to be liable for any hearths himself. It is not clear whether he is signing off on the listing.

Demographers have long used lists of householders such as the hearth tax to estimate numbers in a place using a 'multiplier' based on what is known about the average numbers of people in a household for that time. For example, they have been able to use parish registers to find an average household size, based on evidence taken from several parishes. If the average household size taken from these complete listings is five, then any lists of houses or male householders where the whole population is not known, can simply be multiplied by five to give an estimate of population.

People in England at this date were not living in multi-generational households, and the death rate was high. Over the years there have been disagreements as to the exact multiplier to use; however, for the hearth tax it is commonly held that for rural areas a multiplier of 4.75 can be used with confidence.[111] Using this figure we see that the Bredhurst population can be estimated at about 100 people in 1664.

As parish registers become increasingly deficient from the later seventeenth century, due to nonconformity, the hearth tax gives an opportunity to provide at least an estimate of the families in the parish at this date. Those in the hearth tax who do not appear in the parish registers might therefore possibly be nonconformists. As the Bird family illustrates here, using several different types of record over the centuries makes it possible to speculate about the pattern of name change in a village, as well as the likelihood that the same surname means the same family line. Hearth-tax records are now also being used to map the population density of some counties.

For genealogy it is best to use the hearth-tax returns and the parish registers together; in this way you can build the most complete picture of the people resident in the parish for the time period. The more adventurous researcher could dive into other tax lists and records held in the E 179 database at The National Archives.

For Bredhurst there are twenty potentially useful records covering the period from 1428 up to 1678, and a very rare surviving list of assessments and defaulters from the 1678 poll tax. John Moore in his book *Counting People* (2013) has a discussion of multipliers to use in estimating population size, and gives a very useful case study of the population of Frampton Cotterell in Gloucestershire from 1086 to 1801, the methods of which could be used as the basis for any other rural population study.

Rate Books

If government taxes were not something that often affected the ordinary villager, local tax to pay for the upkeep of the poor, for the church and the roads, did impinge on their lives more regularly. Where they survive, the rate books for a parish are one of the best ways to establish householders' names, and even to spot the fluctuating fortunes of parishioners over a number of years because they contain lists of people (normally male) resident in a parish and village from year to year, together with the amount of rates paid, and often an assessment of the value of their property.

These records can also be used to pick up incomers and houses that fall vacant. Used in conjunction with other records they can prove that a person was resident at any one time. However, as the very poorest were exempt from paying rates, they can never be seen as a complete listing of male householders, and as it was only the head of the household who did pay rates, they do not cover married women, nor of course children. If there are surviving lists of people relying on the parish for maintenance, then using both together will, of course, provide a more complete list.

Each parish had the power to set their own rates (much as an English council can do today), and this was based on the rentable value of each property. This means that those who were liable for the rates were occupants of houses in the parish worth over a certain sum. Upkeep of the church was the main and original reason for raising money by rates. In 1555 the Highways Act allowed parishes to collect money for the upkeep of roads. The Commissions of Sewers looked after rivers, drainage and coastal areas, and also raised money from the rates. A sewer originally meant any artificial watercourse, such as a channel or ditch. Because money had to be raised from parishioners for the maintenance of local amenities of benefit to all – such as ditches, osier beds, bridges and roads – they are also a means of discovering information about those amenities and the costs of their upkeep.

As an example of what may be found, in the Surrey village of Beddington a rate was imposed in 1793 for highway maintenance, and the list of ratepayers shows the annual rental value of each property in pounds (house and any land) with the rate due, and in a further column the actual rate collected. Each collection is headed up by a statement of the purpose of the rate, and the period for which it is being collected: yearly from Michaelmas to Michaelmas in the case of Beddington's highway rate. Rental values for houses in 1793 Beddington vary from the very wealthy £300 per annum down to just £2 per annum. Finally, the list of ratepayers continues right down to those who paid only 2s with no rental value shown; perhaps these were people renting rooms only.[112]

Unfortunately there are relatively few rate books from the early eighteenth century; the main surviving ones appear to be from after 1744. Those for Bredhurst in Kent are sparse, starting with a surveyors' rate of 1776, and a churchwardens' rate and combined accounts in 1787. Those for Datchworth, Hertfordshire, only start in 1841. Those for Aysgarth in North Yorkshire survive from 1869, although there are also churchwardens' accounts from 1722. However, it is also worth searching in the vestry minutes, as they can hold lists of ratepayers in the absence of separate books.

Using the Early Census to Discover Whole Communities

All the problems of reconstructing a community more or less disappear by the time Victoria came to the throne in 1837. Along with many other political reforms of the first part of the nineteenth century, the start of civil registration (from July 1837), with the addition of the census from 1841, gives the family and local historian two sets of records, which can be easily combined to produce far more reliable information about each village, parish, township, town and city. These records should be very familiar to the family historian. Census returns are now widely available online, both on free websites and on subscription websites such as Ancestry.co.uk and Findmypast.co.uk.

A census has been taken in England every ten years since 1801. However, the census of 1841 is the first properly useful census from a genealogical point of view, as the enumerators' books giving the household details record the names of all the people in each household on the night of the census. They were stored centrally at the Home Office, thus encouraging their survival. Because the census was taken house by house along a route that was described by the enumerator on each return, it is easy for the family historian to use the census to reconstruct a whole village of people and to study in detail the whole community, including details of property. In urban districts the sheer number of people makes reconstructions of an area more difficult, but the average nineteenth-century English village can be dissected and analysed in many interesting ways.

Earlier census returns of 1801, 1811, 1821 and 1831 are far less easy to use for the purposes of retrieving information about individuals because usually no names are used; yet they survive in unexpected quantity, albeit patchily across the country. Fragments from the 1801–1831 census returns are held locally, and as well as including lists and counts of householders might also include, or be collected with, other inhabitant listings from earlier centuries. They give useful information about a community where they have survived.

For the serious family historian, if you can get away from obsessing that you must collect names, early census returns may provide many interesting clues and facts. Pre-1841 census fragments have so far been ignored by the genealogy data websites, and it is necessary to seek them out using the local record office catalogues and the helpful 'Gibson guide': *Local Census Listings, 1522–1930: Holdings in the British Isles (Second edition, 1994)* by Jeremy Gibson and Mervyn Medlycott.

However, even if the original counts and listings for the parish you are interested in do not survive, you can still find extremely useful information from the statistical analysis and population tables that were published by the census office as printed census reports prior to 1841. These reports were published fairly soon after each census was taken. Original printed copies of these may be found in the larger libraries and perhaps in the local archives. These, along with the reports from all later censuses, and the annual reports of the Registrar General, are also digitized and hosted as part of the UK Data Archive, from the University of Essex (http://www.histpop.org), known as 'Histpop'.

Histpop is an online resource of almost 200,000 pages of all the published population reports created by the Registrars General and its predecessors for England and Wales and for Scotland for the period 1801–1920, including all census reports for the period 1801–1937, along with related archival material and critical essays putting the figures into context. It is a very valuable resource. The information on Histpop is not to be found on commercial genealogy websites. Another website that hosts partial copies of the census reports is Vision of Britain (https://www.visionofbritain.org.uk/census/) and you may also find individual reports scanned from original copies held by libraries on https://www.archive.org.

These extracts from the 1801 census reports show the column headings and then statistics for four rural parishes in North Hertfordshire: Bennington, Datchworth, Digswell and Graveley.

1801	**Houses**			**Persons**	
	Inhabited	By how many Families occupied	Uninhabited	Male	Female
Bennington	92	103	4	244	243
Datchworth	81	81	2	207	208
Digswell	23	35	0	95	83
Graveley	39	54	0	129	131

1801	**Occupations**			**Total of Persons**
	Persons chiefly employed in Agriculture	Persons chiefly employed in Trade Manufactures or Handicrafts	All other Persons not comprised in the two preceding Classes	
Bennington	138	128	221	487
Datchworth	60	20	330	410
Digswell	39	12	127	178
Graveley	73	7	180	260

In 1801 in Bennington there were ninety-two houses, with 103 families in those houses (therefore eleven households are sharing accommodation with another household). Nevertheless, four houses were unoccupied. In total, the parish population consisted of 244 males and 243 females, giving a total number of 487 souls. Those employed on the land number 138, those in trade and handicrafts 128, leaving 221 not in those classes, some of whom would be children or the very elderly, as well as anyone who did not fit into the previous categories, such as servants and the clergy. The slightly smaller population of Datchworth appears to be just that bit better off, and no families are recorded as sharing a house. The much smaller Digswell and Graveley have a far higher proportion of shared houses.

The conclusion we might draw from this, using the evidence of multiple occupancy from the Eaves case in King's Bench from Chapter 5, is that the housing situation for the labouring family in Datchworth had improved between 1768 and 1801. Of course, this early census makes no comment on the condition or size of those houses, nor does it appear to include those who are in barns, outhouse or tents. It was only in the 1891 census that any attempt to count the number of rooms a household lived in (only if less than five) started to be made. By 1911 all the rooms in each house, or lived in by each household, were recorded.

In 1811, all four parishes had gained in population. Bennington lost two families, but Datchworth gained five new families and a total of thirty-seven more people, while the housing situation had rapidly deteriorated, as more people are now living in only seventy-two houses, thus nine houses have been removed. It would be interesting to investigate this further – boundary changes may have occurred, or is it possible that a landowner had cleared cottages away?

Digswell had grown by one family and Graveley by six families. The total population has grown in each village, thus the existing families have expanded as well as the new families moving in or being created from local couples marrying. In each place except for Datchworth, house building has occurred. The occupations were counted differently in 1811, so that now the families in each section were counted, rather than the numbers. There was also a new column for houses being built (not shown here):

1811	Houses			Persons	
	Inhabited	No. of Families	Uninhabited	Male	Female
Bennington	94	102	2	261	268
Datchworth	72	86	0	237	210
Digswell	35	36	0	88	99
Graveley	41	60	1	126	150

1811	Occupations by family			Total of Persons
	Agriculture	Trade Manufactures or Handicrafts	All others	
Bennington	81	16	4	529
Datchworth	75	9	2	447
Digswell	30	4	2	187
Graveley	49	4	7	276

And by 1821 more growth had occurred:

1821	Houses			Persons	
	Inhabited	No. of Families	Uninhabited	Male	Female
Bennington	110	129	0	347	311
Datchworth	99	99	0	254	240
Digswell	36	40	0	108	96
Graveley	60	66	2	158	158

1821	Occupations by family			Total of Persons
	Agriculture	Trade Manufactures or Handicrafts	All others	
Bennington	87	23	9	658
Datchworth	90	9	0	494
Digswell	33	2	5	204
Graveley	47	14	5	316

Datchworth has rectified its housing shortage, and increased total population by forty-seven, giving a total rate of expansion in the twenty years since 1801 of 20 per cent. Graveley, however, has absorbed a massive rise of just over 44 per cent in its population.

In 1831 the total acreage of a parish was added, but the other information was the same. Once again both Datchworth and Bennington's population growth was outstripping the supply of houses. In the case of Datchworth, a boundary change had included part of a neighbouring parish, although the housing stock only increased by four:

1831	**Houses**			**Persons**	
	Inhabited	No. of Families	Uninhabited	Male	Female
Bennington	120	129	2	337	294
Datchworth	103	115	0	292	301
Digswell	36	36	0	102	94
Graveley	82	82	0	165	166

1831	**Occupations by family**			**Total of Persons**
	Agriculture	Trade Manufactures or Handicrafts	All others	
Bennington	89	17	23	631
Datchworth	83	15	17	593
Digswell	31	2	3	196
Graveley	50	10	22	331

In 1841 the information the family historians crave was added: names and ages and some indication of place of birth, and whether they were born in the county of residence or not. However, researchers should not just forget about the statistical report summaries by place for the census years after 1831: they remain very useful for any study of a village, even if only to put an ancestor's life more into context.

The statistical information for the parish of Datchworth in 1841 records that within 1,930 acres 116 households with 581 people were residing. There was a total of 305 males and 276 females. Of these, 539 (93 per cent) of them were born in Hertfordshire and forty-two (7 per cent) were born outside Hertfordshire. Thus the population of the parish had grown 40 per cent in the period from 1801 to 1841.

The level of local detail brought out by the Registrar General's subsequent census reports can be exceptionally helpful to the genealogist, and can explain local variations in population, migration and movements. For example, in the 1861 report on Essex from Vol. 1, p.341, in the notes to the tables at the bottom of the page, the reader is informed that in the district of Ongar in Essex:

> The decrease of population in the parishes of Stanford-Rivers, Navestock, Stapleford-Tawney and Thoydon-Mount is attributed partly to the temporary absence of some of the principal families, and partly to the migration of labourers, owing to want of employment, etc...
>
> The decrease of population in Danbury parish is attributed to migration, partly owing to the introduction of steam thrashing...

Meanwhile again in the same 1861 report, the notes on Hertfordshire contain the following observations:

> The decrease of population in Heydon is attributed to emigration ...
>
> The decrease of population in Abington-in-the-Clay parish is attributed to the removal of cottages ...
>
> The decrease of population in Norton, William and Great Wymondly parishes is attributed partly to the dilapidated state of cottage property. Many of the cottages are said to have only one room fit for occupancy ...
>
> (Herts, p. 296)

There are many other examples of similar comments in other counties, which could be of direct help to someone researching people in these parishes for these years. In 1841, our understanding of life in Datchworth (wooded, and with plenty of manorial waste) is also helped by the information that the returns include '6 gypsies in tents'.

Geographical Structure of the Census

Since the widespread online indexing of the census, few genealogists ever get to grips with the structure of the census, because all we now tend to do is put names into an online index in order to find our families. In the past, different strategies were needed, and it was necessary to understand how it had all been organized based on registration districts. Then, the census had to be searched microfilm page by microfilm page, and when forced to do this, it gave an invaluable sense of the place. Locating someone in an index no longer gives us a feel for the place they lived in, particularly if all you then do is look at one census entry, rather than at a whole village or community – and this is particularly so if you have little or no knowledge of the local geography.

An understanding of the structural organization that lies behind the census remains very useful. This geographical structure forms the basis for the census referencing system used by The National Archives to describe, and put in order, the original books for all the census returns from 1841 to 1901 (the 1911 census differs). First comes the government department: Home Office for 1841 and 1851, and Registrar General for the following years. This is followed by a numerical code for the census year, then a number relating to the registration district, and finally a folio and page number.

Each enumerator walked and oversaw an area that was a subdivision of a civil registration district. Originally these were all meant to be of a standard size, with the area that an enumerator had to travel being no more than 15 miles; it did not relate to parish boundaries. The front page or front cover of the enumerator's books always described the geography of the district. The actual order of enumeration was totally up to the enumerator, so does not necessarily match with any descriptive list on the front cover; it was left up to him how he walked around the district. This results in some oddities: for example, the enumeration for some isolated farmsteads might be placed at the end or the beginning, as it took his fancy.[113]

At the start of each enumeration there is an enumerator's schedule, which describes the administrative area for each part of the enumeration. In 1841 it gives the hundred, something which is useful to note down, as you may need this later when searching in older records. It also gives the superintendent registrar's district, which is useful if you have people with very common names and you need to choose birth registrations from the civil registration indexes, as these will be the same. Anybody born in Datchworth would have been registered in the district of Hertford. Those born just a mile or two south of Datchworth in the village of Digswell remained in the hundred of Broadwater, but the registration district for births, marriages and deaths would be Hatfield and Welwyn. The parish of Gravely, also in the same hundred as both Datchworth and Digswell, but some way to the north, is in the superintendent registrar's district of Hitchin.

Thus it is useful to understand the complex administrative geography in order to help work out which civil registration events are most likely when trying to narrow down several candidates in the same small area of a county within the civil registration index. After the information about districts there is a number for the enumeration district, and then a short description. For Datchworth (part of), which is Enumeration District No. 5, it states that 'All that part of the Parish of Datchworth which lies to the South of Bridge Foot including Palletts Farm.' Thus you can be sure of what you will find in the pages following.

Datchworth parish is long, narrow and rectangular, with the village of Datchworth located centrally but drawn out over several small settlements. At each corner of the rectangle lies a completely separate hamlet: Bragbury End and Hooks Cross to the north, Bulls Green and Burnham Green to the south. It is, however, impossible to judge the parish layout from the enumeration. The 1851 census taking involved changes to the layout and the size of the enumeration areas. In the 1851 census, the civil parish of Datchworth includes both the old ecclesiastical parish, with its hamlets as well as some other places, and the enumerator has ended the first thirty-five entries with 'End of the Village of Datchworth'[114] – although the parish continues for another twenty pages with other hamlets and villages within the large civil parish. It is almost impossible to tell from this census where the enumerator started his journeys, and whether the families are in a logical order of households or not. At the bottom on the left-hand side the enumerator was supposed to fill in the number of houses. The total numbers in each house in what is called Datchworth Village (presumably the area round the green and crossroads) work out as thirty-five houses with an average of 4.5 people in each.

The enumeration then goes south to the outlying hamlet of Govers Green, and on to the villages of Bulls Green and Burnham Green, before suddenly reappearing in Datchworth at the Rectory; it then makes its way to the north via the village of 'Hollybush Cottages', showing what kind of confusion might exist in the enumerator's mind in a dispersed settlement. Then he veers off to an isolated part of the parish right to the north called Braggers End (now Bragbury End, and part of modern-day Stevenage) before the next hamlet, Hooks Cross; here he suddenly turns back to the middle of the parish and the houses around Pounds Green and the houses nearest to the church.

Right at the end of the circuit he has missed out several important farms, so he puts all these together, even though they are at opposite ends of the parish. By looking at the final pages you might be forgiven for thinking the farms were next to each other, but this is not so, so always take care to actually check on a map. Any stranger to the geography of Datchworth would have a great deal of difficulty in trying to reconstruct the parish layout from this enumeration, so it always pays to be familiar with a contemporary map.

Higgs, in *A Clearer Sense of the Census,* makes the useful-sounding suggestion (p.144) that an examination of the local newspapers on or after census night might provide more information about local conditions and the vagaries of the enumeration. I decided to put this to the test, to see whether the Hertfordshire villages we have been looking at were mentioned in the local newspapers of 1841 – but to no avail. A further search on the word 'census' over all the newspapers in the online British Newspaper Archive produced a lot of results, but narrowing that down to the weeks before and after the census did not seem to offer very much that would be helpful to someone studying a particular district. Some of the newspapers carried reports later in the year on the population counts (completed by August 1841 for a June enumeration, which is a testament to the hard work of the civil service). This type of search would still be worthwhile, as other places may have resulted in more commentary in the local press.

Population and the Census

Another reason for walking in the footsteps of the enumerator and looking at all the pages of the census for a village or small place, is that at least you can then be sure that no one has been missed by indexing errors. However, to save time, it is also possible to check the absolute numbers by looking at the census reports and then comparing the total population of a place with the numbers of people returned via an online index search. This will, of course, only work if you can search for everyone living in one place regardless of their name.

When looking more closely at Datchworth in the 1841 census, a search using the indexes of Ancestry.co.uk using the term 'Datchworth' for place of residence and leaving all other search boxes blank resulted in 575 results, or people resident in Datchworth on 6 June 1841, the night of the census. The formal returns counted 581 people in Datchworth. This means that Ancestry have managed to index everyone in the parish, bar the six gypsies living in tents. I suggest trying the same for villages or parishes you are interested in, as this comparison might prove instructive. What it does not tell us, however, is whether or not the names of those people have been indexed accurately: only a trawl through the whole village comparing the entries with the index will do that.

The 1851 census is of more use to the genealogist than that of 1841 as it includes extra information about relationship to head of household, and gives a place of birth for everyone listed (not just whether in the same county) – and addresses also start to become more detailed. Ages given are also more accurate, and not rounded down to the nearest five years, as they were in 1841.

In Datchworth in 1851 there was a total of 648 people, including two female servants from Warwickshire, who seem to be very out of place in Hertfordshire. What did they do on their rare half days off? With family probably so far away, whom could they visit?

Interestingly, of those who were obviously domestic servants rather than agricultural servants in Datchworth on the 1851 census, most of them were from outside the parish, and many of them from outside the county. Apart from the farmers, there is only the rector in the rectory to provide any hint of gentle folk; everyone else is either an agricultural labourer, a tradesman, or a victualler or shopkeeper. There was one unmarried schoolmistress, Hannah Baulk, age forty-one, born in Datchworth, and a police constable makes his first appearance. There is no impression of any great wealth in the parish at all. The main landowners at this date lived elsewhere.

In 1861 the population had dropped to 635 people in 140 households due to boundary changes; no one was living in a barn or a shed. There were more migrants from outside Hertfordshire, some of them married women: Mary Pennyfather from Colstfoot Farm was born in Yorkshire, Elizabeth Ephgrave at Bull's Green was from London, Emma Jackson was born in Rotherhithe; Richard Fenson, farmer at Burnham Green was from Bedfordshire, while William Brunton from Norfolk was a railway labourer. The publican and a farm worker at Burnham Green were from Bedfordshire.

In 'Datchworth Village', for the first time there is a hint of incoming middle class: a fundholder from Gloucestershire (but without live-in servants). There are two railway labourers, one from Norfolk, one from London, while the teachers at the school house are all outsiders, three born in London and one from Yorkshire (all young women, aged twenty-three, twenty, seventeen, and the youngest at fifteen a 'candidate for teacher'). The Rectory has live-in servants – from Cambridgeshire, Northamptonshire and two locals.

This seems to be testimony as to how the coming of the railway and increasing movement around England were affecting even very rural areas of the country. The population was rising, and the number of households and buildings was growing. We look at migration to and from the village in greater depth in the next chapter.

Datchworth population, 1801–1911, taken from the census

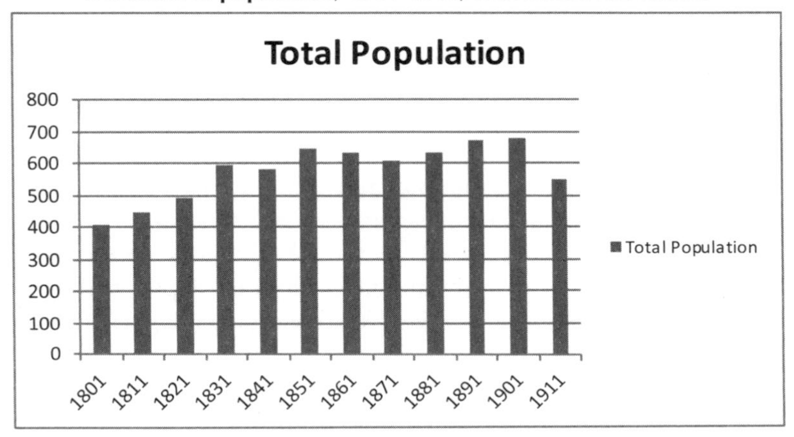

Migration away from Datchworth and those remaining in Datchworth 1851–1911

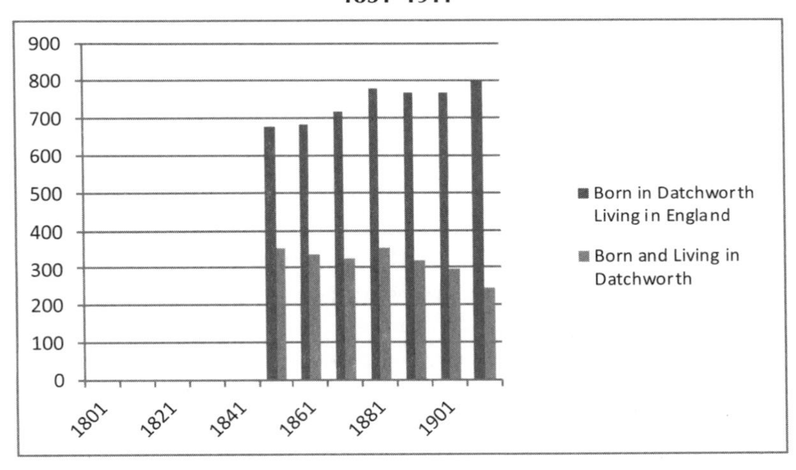

The chart above shows the numbers of people who were born in Datchworth who had migrated away from Hertfordshire into other parts of England at each census – that is, they were living elsewhere in England. The majority of those moving away from Datchworth into other counties spent at least some time in neighbouring Middlesex and London.

Who were the enumerators? In a village in many cases they could be your neighbour; thus in 1891 in Datchworth the enumerator was William Shippen, who also ran the post office and shop, and sold beer on Datchworth Green. Imagine having to give your information about age and place of birth to the person who also oversaw any post that you might send or receive. For some people no doubt the anonymity of the city was much to be preferred.

Using techniques such as this, and studying the population of a whole place, many genealogists have turned their family history into something of wider value to the local history community. Some have gone on to study one place in great depth; these are now known as one-place studies. As an example of what can be achieved, and to take inspiration for what you could do with your own village or the village of your ancestors, the One Place Studies website (https://www.one-place-studies.org/) features a number of articles on small places. The Bratton Clovelly study is a good example of how to use the census usefully, among other records, to bring the past back to life (https://www.one-place-studies.org/resources/in-depth-reports/in-depth-bratton-clovelly/).

Starting Points for the Researcher

To discover more about the population and people of villages or parishes that you are interested in you will need access to the England and Wales Census Returns, now very widely available online: this provides the opportunity either to browse a census return in its entirety, or to return results from the online database that shows all the people living in a place. For example, choose the 1851 census of England on Ancestry.co.uk, then simply fill in the location 'lived in' with your village, and leave all the other boxes blank in order to produce a list of results of everyone living there in 1851. If you can transfer the information into your own spreadsheet or build your own database you will achieve the best way of asking questions of this data; for example, you could find out how many people in your village were born outside the village, count the agricultural labourers, discover the average age, and so on.

You can then combine these results with information from the tithe returns to learn more about the landholdings. Find a contemporary map (preferably drawn at a large scale, such as the

Ordnance Survey's 6in series), and you will be able to plot 1851 census information on to a map.

For more information about the history of the census and insight into its administration, as well as how to interpret your findings, there are two excellent books: Edward Higgs, *A Clearer Sense of the Census* (Public Record Office Handbooks No. 28, HMSO, 1996); and aimed more broadly at the genealogist, Peter Christian and David Annal, *Census the Expert Guide* (The National Archives, 2008).

A detailed explanation of census geography is given on the Vision of Britain website (https://www.visionofbritain.org.uk/census/Cen_Guide/19).

Make it an aim to discover more about your own ancestors' villages from the early census as well. Use the Gibson Guide (*see* p.176 above), or search county record offices online and use The National Archives *Discovery* catalogues using terms such as '1801 census' to discover whether they have survived. You may also pick up other inhabitant lists and counts like this as well.

Find out about older lists of villagers and parishioners for your place of interest by looking at the E 179 database held by The National Archives. Do the same in the local archives catalogues by looking at any parish chest material (usually catalogued in the same series as the parish registers). Check the hearth tax digital online website for online transcriptions, and the British Record Society to see if your county has been covered by a printed edition of the hearth tax. You may be able to order this via an interlibrary loan, or find a second-hand copy. Anyone with Hertfordshire ancestors will be interested in getting hold of *Hertfordshire Population Statistics* 1563–1801 (Hertfordshire Record Society, 1st edition 1964, 2nd edition updated by Heather Falvey).

Don't forget online newspaper searches. It may be that by searching for terms such as 'census AND (village, parish or county name)' you will find reports about how the census was conducted in your own area. Another useful source of information for trades-people and gentry are local directories. Pigot's directories start in the 1830s, while Kelly's took over from the *London Post Office Directory* and was publishing county directories widely by the nineteenth century.

Other records that can be sought out would be lists of the local militia, as well as records of enclosure and tithe to add context to your community searches. Wills are not just good for individuals, but when all the wills from a village are read and used together, they can prove invaluable for building up a picture of relationships inside a community. Churchwardens' accounts and records of the overseers of the poor will also contain many names, and if estate papers exist from a large country estate, then tenant's lists are also invaluable. If as many records as possible are used in conjunction with the census and hearth tax, then a whole community can be brought back to life.

For an excellent introduction to the benefits of a one-place study refer to Janet Few, *Putting Your Ancestors in Their Place: A guide to One Place Studies* (The Family History Partnership, 2014).

And for a trove of articles on local populations, as well as many other aspects of local history, the journal *Local Population Studies* can be purchased, with back copies available for free at their website (http://www.localpopulationstudies.org.uk/).

8

Leaving the Village

The study of the migration of our ancestors over the centuries brings us many compelling and interesting stories. Which genealogist doesn't have a dead end in the tree somewhere due to movement from place to place? How much duller and less interesting would our ancestral journeys be if all people in the past could be traced back to one place, which they had always lived in, and so on backwards forever. The study of movement from place to place is one of paramount importance in the history of humanity as well as in our individual family stories. Tracing individuals over both time and space into eras and places where the records become more and more sparse can be both the most frustrating and the most exhilarating journey. It is only by considering and working on all the different aspects of genealogical and local historical method that a rich understanding of the past and our ancestors will be achieved.

When problem solving family-history conundrums due to movement, we need to combine local history of the parish and village with regional geography and history, as well as national or even international events that may have been factors in a move from place to place. We should examine occupations, surnames, local economic or employment opportunities, wars and natural disasters as well as the growth of transport networks. We might need to reconstruct whole communities, as well as fully explore all our family connections, both in kinship terms and through the networks of neighbours, friends, religious groups or trading connections.

In this chapter there are three main types of 'leaving the village' that I have in mind. The first is temporary absence from a rural home through seasonal work, together with the journeys within a region that an agricultural labourer was likely to make. The second is the ever-flowing movement of people from the countryside generally into the towns and cities over the whole of our period, which accelerated during the nineteenth century and into the twentieth. The final type is emigration to an entirely new life abroad, whether voluntary or forced, as with the transportation of criminals from the seventeenth to the nineteenth centuries.

People in the past moved around for many reasons. These reasons could have been personal, or local, or due to wider economics. Some people have always wanted to get away from the village, to leave, if only to return again, which is why as soon as transport of any kind became affordable or possible – by road, canal, rail, or the humble bicycle – mobility increased. People may have to move, but they also *want* to move.

The Big Picture

We have touched on the growth of populations and many aspects of life in the village over the centuries, and we now need to stand back and consider the movement of people in the widest possible historical context. At the start of our period a very high percentage of people lived in the countryside, and the population of the southern counties of England was greater than of those in the north. However, with such a low overall population of under 3 million, all countryside was very sparsely populated. Population tended to adapt itself to the carrying capacity of the land, or the amount of food being produced. There were still harvest failures, and plague and infectious diseases were ever present.

However, the population was growing, and there was a high proportion of children and younger people. By the end of the reign of Elizabeth I, the Great Poor Law had been enacted, and there was growing concern about the poor and the number of people on the move. Today this would be called subsistence migration.

Over the next 150 years, from the start of the seventeenth century to the mid-eighteenth century, there was a growth of trade and commerce, towns grew in size, and there was more and more industry in the countryside, giving much needed work to those who could not be supported by the land. At the same time, the old manorial system was on its knees and fast being dismantled.

Enclosure of common land and the consolidation of smaller fields was also growing. From the mid-eighteenth century through to the start of the twentieth century, the population expanded from around 7 million to over 30 million. The end of the Napoleonic wars saw the very large army and navy dismantled, with thousands of men finding themselves unemployed.

All those people had to go somewhere, and as labour was less and less needed on the land due to agricultural improvements and machinery, the only place was the towns and cities, where increasing amounts of trade both nationally and internationally gave rise to many jobs. At the same time, British colonization of other parts of the world started to take place, making Britain ever richer and providing ever more opportunity for economic growth, industry and commerce, as well as new places for the ordinary man to settle in.

All these trends accelerated during the nineteenth century. In addition, cottage employment for the women was taken over by the factories, and more and more villages that had no industry to complement their agriculture lost population to other places. Declines in the death rate and big improvements in health also provided a boost for the overall population. Transportation at the same time became cheaper and more abundant with the growth of railways and steam shipping.

Was Movement Restricted?

The manorial peasant may have been very largely tied to the land in his manor, with his movement restricted, but as we have seen, the manorial system was patchy throughout England, and even by the time of the Tudors it was already breaking down in many places. The fact is that throughout our period, many families moved around; even those that stayed rural tended to move around an area or district. It used to be believed that people in the past spent their whole lives in tight-knit communities. However, in the 1960s historians started to make investigations into parish registers on a wide scale, and these showed that both individuals and families disappeared from the registers, thus overturning the old ideas about geographical immobility. These findings were confirmed by historians working with other source material.[115]

The wealthy have always been very mobile, and the educated young gentleman was highly likely to move around as might be expected. Some professional occupations have also always required a certain amount of mobility, for example the vicar or curate moves from living to living, sometimes making many moves over his lifetime together with his family. Men joining customs and excise were also moved around the countryside with regularity. Of the gentry and yeomanry class, those not inheriting their father's land needed an occupation of some kind, and might be apprenticed into a trade in London, and then stay in the city.

Mostly the ordinary labourer did not move very far unless they were making a migration into London, in which case they did. Furthermore, people tended to move in short stages, even if they ended up a long way from the original starting point. The advice for genealogy researchers has always been to cast a research net over a 5- to 15-mile radius of the last known 'sighting', while bearing in mind the 'pull' of the bigger cities, particularly London.

To give an idea of the sheer scale of London in proportion to the rest of the country, it has been estimated that in the seventeenth century one-tenth of the population lived in London. Continuous inward migration mainly consisted of young servants and single labourers moving from the country into the city, and many of them travelled far further than 15 miles to reach London. Because the death rates were so high in the cities, particularly so in London, they needed a vast number of inward migrants simply to keep their populations stable, let alone growing. If you have siblings of an ancestor who seem to 'disappear', a move into a big city is more than just a possibility, it is very likely.

Because there was a long-term population rise (albeit with some periods of no or very low growth), and a constant drive to make agriculture more efficient and less labour intensive, this meant that over the long term there were always more people than there was available employment in agriculture. With less work in their immediate surroundings of the village and round about, the single young were constantly forced to migrate into towns and cities. The Elizabethan Poor Laws were in part enacted because of vagrancy and fears about roving gangs, as in the children's nursery rhyme 'Hark, hark the dogs do bark, beggars are coming to town'. Some people were vagrants, either due to misfortune or simply being literally rootless, others were probably simply on the move looking for work.

Parish officers did use the laws of settlement to restrict and even monitor movement, not just by the very poor, who were 'those likely to become chargeable', but by many others as well. When first enacted, the 1662 law was clear that as the vast majority of people did not rent or own property at £10 per annum, they could immediately be removed from any parish they moved to, if the parish did not want them there. In 1697 this changed, so that freeholders and copyholders could gain settlement in that place.

Once someone had moved into a parish as an independent adult it became very difficult to obtain settlement there unless they rented for more than £10 per annum, paid taxes in the parish, became a parish officer, or purchased a freehold or copyhold and resided there for forty days. In practical terms this meant that the only really viable way for the majority of people of obtaining settlement in a new parish from 1662 to 1697 was by paying the rates. If they could not fill this, or any other criterion, then they were at risk of being removed, regardless of whether they were in work or not.

In 1697 certificates of settlement were brought in, and forcible removal could not happen until there was actually a need for relief, rather than immediately. Then in 1698, the law changed again so that even if the holders of certificates did pay rates, they did not gain settlement. But did the parishes actually enforce these laws? Landau makes a convincing argument that they did. She quotes a very rare surviving minute book belonging to Justice Paul D'Aranda of Shoreham in Kent, who kept a diary of his work as a justice in 1708. All the settlement business brought to D'Aranda shows that the vestry or officers of Shoreham made efforts to ensure that all residents had settlement or a certificate, or were removed. Other examples given include Wimbledon in 1736, Walthamstow, Hungerford and Midhurst among others in southern counties. Mass investigations of everyone on a single day was common.[116]

Given these restrictions it is hard to imagine that anyone moved about at all. Yet move they did, as these investigations into settlement show. Painswick in Gloucester, an area of cloth industry and thus attractive to incomers, examined seventy incomers in the fifty years between 1695 and 1747. The town had only 186 families in 1700 (probably around 830 people). In Bromsgrove, Worcestershire, forty-three examinations were taken on one day in 1727. The date of examination should not be taken as meaning that the migrants were recently arrived, as certificates were often issued years afterwards. Single men, being the most wanted in terms of labour (and the most mobile) were rarely removed, examined or certificated. In 1795 the law changed yet again, and from hence forwards no person who was neither in need of relief nor an unmarried, pregnant woman could be forcibly removed.

More recent research has now shown that movement from the land into the towns, resulting in rural depopulations in certain places, took place earlier than was thought; for example, 2,900 people left the rural Wharfedale valley in Yorkshire between 1670 and 1743. Population growth in towns due to expanding urban work opportunities in the same period has also shown to be from inward migration, rather than an increase of births over deaths.[117]

There was also considerable movement from completely agricultural villages into those that presented more employment opportunity due to some industrialization, such as those in the textile areas. An example of this was Saddleworth on the border between Yorkshire and Lancashire, and with a high birth rate, where the fathers were almost exclusively employed in cloth manufacture rather than on the land.[118]

Genealogists and local historians such as Andrew Todd have argued that the open vestry parishes were more likely to see incomers settle down than the closed parishes, which were more likely to restrict incomers and evict the poor.[119] This must have been particularly so where there was one large landowner and no manorial waste to camp out on. A closed vestry was also more likely to be able to vote on cottage clearances, and to aim to consolidate tenancies. If the open parishes also had many trades as well as ways of making a living from the land, then their expansion would be assured, for example in areas of both farming as well as mining or quarrying. Closed parishes may also have suffered from a lack of workforce, meaning that any recruitment would have to come from labourers living in another parish and necessitating a long walk to work. Todd gives a useful summary of factors to look for in identifying the likelihood of somewhere being open or closed.[120]

Reasons for Moving

Reasons could range from the completely personal – for example, moving to escape an intolerable situation, or through some kind of shame or criminality – to the broadest national circumstances. Some people were pushed out of their villages due to lack of local work or housing, or family problems. On the other hand, both push and pull factors could be part of wider economic reasons, such as a rise in population, or broader opportunities with better wages in the cities or factories. Mobility depended on many factors: economics, status, and opportunities for betterment as well as religion and conflicts.

Those staying put were more likely to be occupiers of land they owned or had copyhold of, rather than rented or leased, and as long as agricultural depression didn't destroy their living, they might be expected to stay in one place. However, the agricultural labour force moved around more than might be expected. There were hiring fairs and gangs of workers traversing the countryside, and this mobility tended to be more about young, unmarried people. Once a labourer had married then he was likely to stay in one locality, perhaps in one village for the rest of his life, so long as employment was available. However, the small-scale farmer tenant moved around, particularly if he leased or rented his farm from year to year. These migrations could be within one region, such as the Yorkshire Dales, or very much further, as we shall see in the case of migrants to Datchworth on p.210.

As mentioned above, considerable numbers were prone to being moved off the land by the process of enclosure, as well as the demolition of cottages by a closed vestry who wished to keep the poor rate low. Not surprisingly, economic depression has played a big part in migration from place to place, and in particular from the countryside into the towns. This has been termed 'subsistence migration', and affected many thousands, if not millions of our ancestors, from the young people forced into cities, to whole families leaving Ireland for the English coal mines, walking from Liverpool to Newcastle, for example, and other industrial areas after the famine and exodus from Ireland of the 1840s. If you were without work or a way to make your living, then you had to move.

Throughout the ages there were many people 'on the tramp', and parish registers on popular routes testify to the many 'strangers' who died while on the move from place to place. Parishes sited on popular routes into cities or near dockyards, or other places attractive to the unemployed, saw plenty of people move through. Gillingham in Kent, near the naval dockyards, is one example, with the ratepayers having to bear the cost of burial of numerous 'strangers' on the move for work.

As well as known national agricultural depressions, such as that of 1730–1750, there were also regional depressions and more local harvest failures. Any of these could be reasons for a move into a town and away from work in the fields. During the 1870s and 1880s England was again in the grip of a major agricultural crisis, known as the 'Great Depression'. Harvest failure and lower yields were caused by a string of wet summers, which also promoted illness and death in sheep and cattle. This was followed by drought in 1885 and 1887.

Meanwhile, heavy and long-lasting snow and frost during the winters in some regions brought a different kind of misery. Prices would normally have risen to compensate for this; however, late Victorian Britain was now connected to the rest of the world by steamship and rail, and cheap imports of food and wool kept a downward pressure on prices. This caused many small farmers to give up trying to make a living on the land, and to move to the towns. Vacant farms were advertised, and failed to find tenants.[121] In Hertfordshire, notices were put in the Scottish papers to entice Scottish farmers southwards – and down they did come. Descendants of some of those families are still farming and managing the land today.

On a more individual note, it is notable and sad that a large number of settlement examinations and removals concerned women who were widowed or deserted by their husbands. If there were legal disputes as to these women's settlement once they were no longer with their husbands, then these cases often ended up in the sessions courts. James Eaves of Datchworth spent time working away from his wife and children, but seems to have returned to them. However, there were men who abandoned their wives and children, and set out for a new life. In this case, the parish would have to step in with help for the families, so the abandonment would be deplored. In these cases the overseers advertised in the papers and offered rewards for the capture and return of the runaway men! Thus an advert appeared in the *Kentish Gazette* of 28 October 1769, placed by the parish of Chiddingstone seeking information:

> Run away from their FAMILIES, leaving them chargeable to the Parish of Chiddingstone in Kent:
>
> WILIAM EARLE, Labourer, aged about 24 Years, is of a light Complexion, and about Five Feet Four Inches high, wears his own Hair, and goes a little stooping.
>
> HENRY COCKRELL, Cooper, but often workd as a Labourer, about Five Feet Eight Inches high, 45 Years of Age; has short curled Hair, and is of a fair Complexion; he is somewhat round shoulder'd, and in walking turns his Feet pretty much outward- He is famous at making Spinning-Wheels with Two Carriers.
>
> THOMAS EASTWOOD, Carpenter, aged full Thirty Years, of a Dark Complexion, with Black curl'd Hair, about Five Feet Nine Inches high, and is rather thin; he had with him, at going off, a Son, now about 15 or 16 Years of Age.
>
> Whoever will give Information of the said Persons (or either of them) to the said Parish, shall have Two Guineas Reward for each of them, on their being apprehended. To be paid by us, JOHN BOAKES, Churchwarden, WILLIAM MEDHURST, Overseer.

One has to wonder whether their families actually wanted these men returned to them, and what the relationship might be like if they were found and returned!

Seasonal Mobility

Among the agricultural labour force there was a great deal of temporary movement, for example in droving animals to market. Countryside people may have taken their flocks of geese or herds of pigs into the nearest large city for sale, or into other country districts. Journeys like this could be surprisingly long; I once came across a case in Chancery from the seventeenth century, which involved two shepherds who had walked their sheep from Wales over to East Anglia. People were hardy, and long journeys by foot were common. There are many instances in diaries and other first-hand accounts of people walking miles to church on a Sunday and back again, and thinking not much of it.

Armstrong (1988) gives plenty of examples of agricultural workers walking long distances for seasonal employment, particularly at harvest time. Scotsmen in late eighteenth-century Norfolk who walked there and back for the good wages, people from North Wales who walked to the grain harvests in Herefordshire, from the Yorkshire Dales into the East Riding of Yorkshire, and those who went south and east from Wiltshire between the heavy and lighter soils, which had crops ripening at different times.[122]

There are also many examples of those working in manufacturing industries going out to the countryside to help with harvest work because of the raised rate of harvest pay. The exodus from the East End of London into the hop fields of Kent is one of the best-known examples, however, there were many other local examples of similar seasonal flow of labour. There are implications for family history in this. Did an ancestor meet a local sweetheart on such a journey, did someone die in a district away from home during harvest? In Chapter 5, the example of the workers in Datchworth in the 1760s moving around to chase the harvest can probably be extrapolated to almost all villages in arable areas.

It is widely supposed that whole families were missed from each Victorian census due to people sleeping in hedgerows and in barns, and numerous other unenumerated places. It is fairly well known that no attempt was made in the 1841 census to enumerate any of the agricultural labourers on the move, and as the census was taken in June, there must have been many people excluded. Edward Higgs gives more information about this in his book *A Clearer Sense of the Census* (PRO, 1996). But this was not just a feature of the nineteenth century: throughout the whole of our period it was common for adolescents and unmarried young adults to spend a part of their lives on the move or away from home.

Some of the examples that have appeared in previous chapters shed light on the subject of movement from the point of view of contemporaries, and are illuminating in what they might teach us generally about movement around the country. Often the lesson is to cast our net wide if we are to find all the missing people from our tree. Thus, in the 1848 newspaper report on p.144 we see the case of Sarah Ferminger from Bredhurst, whose husband was at work at Cobham, charcoal burning, and who was brought up charged with stealing a child's frock from the shop door of Mr Clift, pawn-broker, Chatham. Aside from the poverty this probably speaks of, it implies more. There was no work for charcoal burning locally, so her husband was forced to be at 50 miles distance, living on the very edge of subsistence, so a second-hand child's frock might seem like a reasonable theft.

An investigation of the family using the 1851 census brings more information about them in Bredhurst: Francis Ferminger, charcoal burner, aged fifty-five, born Bexley? in Kent; Sarah his wife, aged thirty-nine, born St Margaret's, Kent, with sons Joseph aged fourteen, born in London, and Francis, aged twelve, born in Bredhurst; Sarah aged eight, born in Bredhurst (the only child at school), and William aged four at home, born Bredhurst. By 1861, Francis the elder's place of birth is shown as Bromley, Kent, while son Francis has gone to sea and Sarah has died.[123] The 1851 census shows that the family had spent time in the London area, very probably on the hunt for work, and the baptism of Joseph can be found in Walworth, St Peter, recorded on 9 October 1836, his father being shown as a charcoal burner.[124]

Therefore, we can see that Francis Ferminger, born in Bromley or Bexley who married a woman from St Margaret's, came to live in Bredhurst. However, the charcoal burning in Bredhurst did not keep him in full employment there, so that in 1836 he was in Walworth in Surrey, and in 1848 in Cobham. The census returns probably hide far more movement of Francis around the same areas outside the census years, in the search for work.

How Did They Travel?

From the earliest times, rural people were restricted by the lack of roads, and the bad state of the existing roads in wet weather.

Outside cities and towns, main routes were not paved, and in badly drained or clay districts they would become totally impassable, with mud and ruts. Travel for the poor was on foot, or by relying on hitching lifts; for the better off by horse, and for the wealthy by coach – but even the wealthy could be stuck at home in the countryside during periods of bad weather when the local roads were impassable.

Rivers provided one answer, and it is for good reason that thriving towns and cities had navigable rivers providing ways in and out. Travel up and down the coast was also possible for mariners, and there were routes and trading links and ferry services between the many small ports. Coastal and riverine transport was thus extremely important, and there were constant attempts to make new navigations further inland on the smaller rivers.

However, travel problems for everyone began to lift during our period. In certain areas, such as Lancashire where limestone was literally just lying around, roads were easily laid, but in the clayey south, where there was no natural stone, travel by road remained difficult, and the importation of stone for roads was expensive. Local turnpike trusts were set up by individual Acts of Parliament from the 1690s, and increasingly through the eighteenth century and into the first half of the nineteenth, to allow tolls to pay for road maintenance. The tolls were paid by coaches and wagoners, as deep wheel ruts did the most damage to road surfaces. However, until the nineteenth century many roads were unusable for wheeled transport for much of the winter, even after the turnpikes were brought in, and packhorses in some areas were the only way of getting goods to market.

The technology for making a consistently good durable road surface suitable for taking heavily laden horses and carts was in its infancy. However, the eighteenth century did see new, fast coaches for those who could afford them, and it was perfectly possible to travel by coach from London to Bath within twenty-four hours. In the early nineteenth century engineers began to work on the problem of the road surface itself, as well as the design of wheels.

It is a good idea for researchers to find out whether their villages and regions of interest had access to turnpike roads, and how this would have impacted on their ancestors. For example, at least sixty-three separate trusts have been identified in Sussex, thirteen in Hertfordshire, seventeen for the whole of North Yorkshire, and at least sixty-two in Kent.[125] Look at the carrier departures from the big cities, and where they stopped off by finding newspaper adverts for them. Pubs that were once coaching inns may also give insight into old routes and stopping-off points.

From the 1750s onwards canals were built in an increasing canal 'mania', until in the 1820s no place in England south of Durham was more than 15 miles from water transport. Canals transformed the transportation of goods, but at a relatively slow pace. For passenger traffic and goods that needed to be somewhere quickly, the truly large revolution in transport was the iron railway track and the steam locomotive. Railways started being laid in earnest in the 1830s and 1840s, continuing throughout the nineteenth century. It was the railway that really changed the rural ways of life, bringing much bigger markets nearer to the countryside, but also enabling people to get to the cities easily, or indeed to just about anywhere in Britain.

Thus from the 1690s to the 1840s Britain passed from separate localities served by a variety of poor transport to a service that was just about adequate, to the start of what would soon develop into a fully functioning integrated transport network.[126] This was a revolution in the lives of our ancestors, and it is no surprise that the huge growth of towns and city population and subsequent rural depopulation in the nineteenth century is closely linked to the railway network's expansion.

Road networks in Hertfordshire tended to run along a north–south axis, and roads going across the county east to west were in effect minor ones; thus travel by road, even today, is dictated by a north–south pattern. During the nineteenth century Hertfordshire was a corridor for the new transport links by canal and then rail out of London in particular.

In the three examples of Datchworth, Hertfordshire, Bredhurst in Kent and Abbotside in North Yorks it is easy to see which the easiest place for travel was. Bredhurst is just 4 miles from Chatham, and the main routes into London by road and by water. Datchworth church is only 1 mile from the A1, the old Great North Road from London to York, although not near any river or water transport. Abbotside, however, is by contrast much more remote. To go from one of its hamlets to the nearest main road, the same A1, this time the section going north from York is a journey of about 30 miles, on hilly, bendy and slow roads.

Leaving England For a New World

Emigration away from England in large numbers started in the seventeenth century; the first big destination was Ulster, then the Americas and the Caribbean.[127] English emigrants to Ulster, although fewer than the Scottish, were in significant numbers during the Plantation of Ulster, when land was granted to settlers cheaply. Two main periods of movement occurred, firstly in the first part of the seventeenth century, and then again after the 1660s. Landholders in Ireland became mainly English gentry and aristocrats, but with a class underneath of yeoman tenant farmers from Scotland and England.

At the same time, a similar pattern of migration to the Americas from the very start of the seventeenth century saw at first single male settlers, followed by women and servants. Some of the early movement to New England consisted of theologically minded pilgrims, such as Quakers, wishing to set up new communities in a fresh place so they could apply their beliefs to a new society. Soon emigrants to the Americas and the Caribbean included many indentured servants: people who contracted to work on arrival for five or seven years in exchange for a free passage. About 80 per cent of English migrants to the Americas in the seventeenth century took this route. At the same time increasing numbers of transported criminals were also being sent. After 1688, the Headright System in Virginia offered 50 acres of free land to anyone who could pay for their own transport, which encouraged many people with the monetary means searching for a new life either for economic or religious reasons.

For others there was less pull from the promise of freedom and land, but more likely a severe push as a result of losing their home. The process of enclosure that was taking place throughout the eighteenth century turned some off their land, and the demolition of cottages by closed vestries removed the landless poor from others. Those who did not want to try their luck in London or a nearby town turned to the Americas. The poem by Oliver Goldsmith called *The Deserted Village*, written in 1770, is a poem of social protest about these forced removals, the greed of the rich, and the emigration of the village to America:

> I see the rural virtues leave the land.
> Down where yon anchoring vessel spreads the sail,
> That idly waiting flaps with every gale,
> Downward they move a melancholy band,
> Pass from the shore, and darken all the strand.

The first census of the USA was taken in 1790, and of the 3.9 million counted, about 60 per cent are calculated to be of English origin, although as this was based on surname, rather than a question of origin in the census, it is a very crude calculation.[128] More than a million British people emigrated in the first part of the nineteenth century to British North America, and around 10 million people left Britain permanently to settle abroad in the period 1815–1930. Destinations included America, Canada, Australia, New Zealand and South Africa. However, many people who migrated long distances, such as to America, in the period 1861–1913 did not stay but came home again.[129]

Local newspapers can once again provide an insight into how people came to hear about opportunities abroad. In the 1830s and 1840s they are full of information about emigration to the colonies and North America, with direct advertisement as well as 'advice'. Every area seeking for settlers in the Americas as well as Australia and New Zealand had a British agent responsible for attracting immigrants and facilitating passages. For example, the *Worcester Journal* ran the following advertisement on 9 December, 1830:

> EMIGRATION to the TOWN of GAMBIER, and
> FERTILE SETTLEMENT of OHIO, NORTH AMERICA
>
> CAPITALISTS, AGRICULTURALISTS, STUDENTS, MECHANICS and others who are desirous of EMIGRATING to this highly-favoured SETTLEMENT, may receive

> information of the superior advantage which it possesses, and make arrangements for the occupation of Land, and purchase of the same, in any quantities, at the rate of £1 British per acre, on application to the appointed AGENT, Charles GALINDO, Merchant, Liverpool, or to any of his Country Agents, C.G. is in want of Agents for the principal Towns of Worcester, Stafford and Salop.

Advice such as this in the *Preston Chronicle* on 26 March 1842, extolling how wonderful Ohio was and how suited to farming, makes it all seem easy:

> The emigrant on landing at any of the towns on the Ohio river, if he has a family, had better engage a lodging for his family immediately, or go into some cheap boarding-house. His next object will be, if he intends to farm, or to labour on a farm, to get into the country as soon as he can; for he will there find everything much cheaper, and have a better opportunity of becoming acquainted with the quality and the local advantages of the land. Should the emigrant be possessed of a few pounds, I would advise him to be in no hurry in making a choice of land, He had better hire a small farm for a season than make too hasty a purchase. By so doing, he will be better able to know the quality and eligibility of the land. The smallest quantity of land sold by the government is forty acres; this can be purchased for around £10 6s. Those who have the means, will find it to their advantage to purchase improved farms. They can be purchased generally for less than the improvements cost. Make no purchase but what you can pay for.

Transportation

Some people were transgressors of the law, and thus forcibly removed from their home, taken into local prisons, normally the county jail, and then transported and banished from Britain. Transportation started in the reign of Charles I – the first one is said to have been in 1617 using the 1597 legislation against rogues and vagabonds. Of course, this was a useful way to escape the expense of putting up prisoners at the local jail, but it was not until further legislation in 1718 that the practice really began to grow. Transportation was given as a punishment for offences that were not capital, and mainly consisted of larceny; many were women and many were very young. At first, those transported went to the new colonies and plantations of the Americas. From the *Derby Mercury* 28 September 1744:

> Yesterday upwards of 70 Transports, who were confin'd in York-Castle, Nottingham, Leicester, Horsham, Chelmsford, and other Country Jails, were brought to Town in Waggons, and Lodg'd in the New Jail, Southwark. And This Morning the above Transports with the Felons from Newgate, were convey'd from that Jail to Black Friars and put into a close Lighter, which carried them on Board a Vessel belonging to Andrew Read, Esq; Merchant, bound to Rappahannock River in Virginia; and it is very remarkable, that in the whole Draught of Transports, which consists of 118, there are 85 Females, and but seven of them more than 18 Years of Age.

This route to America was stopped by the American wars and independence in 1776. Somewhere new had to be found, and that place was, of course, Australia. The nineteenth century saw a rise in the numbers of people convicted of small crimes and then transported to Australia. Several factors were responsible for the rise in those turning to crime. In 1815 after the triumph of Waterloo and the British over Napoleon and his forces, thousands of soldiers were dumped out of the military forces. Many of these men, some of whom were discharged far from home, turned to begging and became a common sight in the streets of towns and cities.

Meanwhile the use of new machinery in the fields caused rural unemployment to rise. In 1834 came the disruption of the end of the old system of Poor Law, with outside relief and payment by each parish to 'their' poor. In times of unemployment the rural landless poor man now had only three stark options; either to steal to feed his children and himself, or take the whole family into the workhouse, or leave the village for the nearest city in order to seek new employment.

In the 1830s the swing riots and other disturbances were a manifestation of the rural economic discontent as farm wages fell and unemployment rose in the south of England. The 'swing riots' were a widespread uprising by agricultural workers, beginning with the destruction of threshing machines in the Elham Valley area of East Kent in the summer of 1830. Very quickly over the next few weeks over 100 threshing machines in Kent had been destroyed. By early December agitation had spread throughout southern England and East Anglia. Attacking threshing machines was only one aspect of the labourers' discontent: they demanded wage rises, and destroyed workhouses, tithe barns, set hayricks alight, attacked the clergy and farmers and even sheep and cattle, and took part in generally riotous and threatening behaviour.

The source of their anger was threefold: the tithe system, the Poor Law, and the farmers who had lowered wages at the same time as introducing new machinery. Threatening letters were sent to the press, and to farmers from a fictitious Captain Swing, hence the swing riots – the swing being a reference to the flail that swung on a stick that was used in hand threshing. The swing riots were mainly a southern phenomenon, as labourers in the north had more opportunity to change employment. As a result of arrests made, some 1,976 prisoners were tried in over thirty-four counties, although the vast majority were from Berkshire, Hampshire, Kent, Sussex and Wiltshire. Local newspapers are a good source for descriptions of these, and those captured and convicted by the authorities were often transported and sometimes hung.

The assize courts throughout our period worked on a system of large regional circuits, which meant that two judges travelled around a region in a set pattern. The assize town was not necessarily the county town. In Sussex the roads were so notoriously bad that the judges would only venture into the northernmost tip of Sussex, near Surrey, and the assize was held at Horsham and East Grinstead, rather than automatically at Lewes. Below the assize courts were the quarter sessions, where smaller, less difficult cases to judge were heard by JPs.

Both the assize and quarter sessions could condemn prisoners to transportation for a period of years or for life. Very often an original sentence of death was commuted to transportation. So many people were tried at each session, and the judges were in such a hurry to get the cases heard over a one- or two-day period, that even with a jury system, there must have been very many miscarriages of justice.

No legal defence existed for the ordinary man. Witness depositions could have been rigged, but even if they were not, they were taken and presented in a somewhat formulaic manner. In any event there was no national professional police force until 1856 to investigate crime and take statements. Each parish had to rely on unpaid constables who were basically volunteers. After conviction the local jail held the convicts before they were taken by cart to London and Kent and the River Medway, to the hulks ready for a ship going to Australia.

Unfortunately, assize indictments are not good indicators for where a felon originated from. Amanda Bevan in her book *Tracing your Ancestors in The National Archives* says that although the indictments appear to show the parish and occupation of the accused, the information is fictitious. Men are almost always described as labourers even if they were skilled artisans, and the parish is the place where the crime was committed, not where he or she was living or was born.[130] The information from this comes from a study made into law in Kent in 1602, and it is not known whether the later indictments are also so deficient.

Migration as Evidenced by the Census

In the previous chapter we looked at what the census returns told us about Datchworth and its people. We also saw examples from the census reports, which gave insights into local population movements. One of the most interesting aspects of an in-depth study of one place is what it can tell us about migration to and from that place. Taking each census return in its turn, incomers to the village and emigrants can be counted and compared and even plotted on a map. By paying attention to where children are reported to be born on the census, as well as where births are registered, you will gain an insight into movement around the country for one family, which can also be easily plotted on a map. Taking several families together, or all families, would show the likely steps that were taken by the people who ended up in the village or local town.

There is a startling change in Datchworth residents in the years from 1851 to 1911. In 1851, of all the 137 heads of household, only five were originally from outside the parish. By 1911, the farmers were from Scotland: the Gaddie family who settled at Hawkins Hall were from Orkney, while the Little family at Moat Farm were from the Scottish borders, via Durham. Other males living in Datchworth and born outside Hertfordshire were from Berkshire, London, Cambridgeshire, Bedfordshire, Suffolk and Middlesex, while females were born in a far greater variety of places, including Surrey, Lincolnshire, Essex, Oxfordshire, Cornwall and Glamorgan.

By contrast, Bredhurst in 1851 had a smaller number of people than Datchworth with only 113 in total, of whom fifty-eight were born in Bredhurst, while all the others were born elsewhere in Kent, with the exception of one born in Surrey, one in London, one in Berkshire, and one retired Chelsea pensioner born in Ireland. Of the incomers who were born in Kent, most were from the same Medway area. In 1911 in Bredhurst, the situation was still remarkably static when compared with the much more mobile population of Datchworth. From a total population of 392, 365 were born in Kent and 107 of them were born in Bredhurst, with only twenty-seven born outside Kent. Of the outsiders, the highest number were incomers from London and Surrey; other places of birth included Devon, the Isle of Wight, Oxfordshire, Essex, Middlesex and Cambridgeshire.

When looking only at the heads of household and their occupations as well as their place of birth, those working on the land as farmers and labourers in farming and the woodland crafts, including dealing in wood, were almost all Kent born. Those born in Bredhurst and staying in Bredhurst tended to have more lowly occupations. The incomers from outside Kent were a shopkeeper, a civil servant, a dairy farmer, a traction-engine worker, a hoop maker and a wood cutter.

In 1851 for the township of High Abbotside in the Yorkshire Dales, which includes several separate settlements and 608 people in total, only thirty-two were born outside the Yorkshire Dales. Most of those were born in Westmorland, the furthest was born in London, two were born in other parts of Yorkshire, and one in Lincolnshire, one in Lancashire and one in Cambridgeshire. However, when this was broken down into just the heads of households, only the curate of the hamlet of Lunds stood out, as he was born in Cambridgeshire, and only five other heads, all of them farmers, were from outside the Dales, all of them born in next-door Westmorland.

The census can also be used to find out where people born in one area ended up. Using the example of Bredhurst, on the 1911 census there were seventy-three people recorded as being born in Bredhurst, but living outside Bredhurst by the time of the census. Where did they end up? Again, the vast majority were living in other places in Kent, mainly in the same Medway area. The majority were in occupations that were still farm related, however, there was migration to, and occupations in the brick-making areas and the paper mills of Milton near Sittingbourne, as well as engineering jobs in Rochester. Only seven people had left Kent altogether: they had gone to Sussex, Essex and London, and the furthest was a clerk in Holy Orders in Herefordshire. All the occupations of those leaving Kent were outside farming, and included shop keeper, house painter, antique dealer and carpenter.

We might expect that the Yorkshire Dales, with its special topography and hill-farming conditions, would lead to a great deal of homogeneity among the farmers in 1851. What is perhaps more surprising is the remarkable homogeneity among the Kent folk in the Medway parish of Bredhurst, both in 1851 and in 1911. Datchworth in Hertfordshire, near to London and with excellent transport links on the other hand, was changing very rapidly, with a far greater mixing of its population.

Hypotheses for Individual Migrants

Migration and movement from place to place is a fascinating part of historical studies, but it is often simply frustrating for the genealogist, as disappearance from a parish can provide difficult research blocks as we proceed backwards. None of these statistics on their own are going to help the genealogist discover exactly where their ancestor arrived from or disappeared to.

However, statistics do help to build up vitally important background context to the decisions people may have made, and they suggest avenues to explore further.

In cases where people have moved from place to place, or simply appear as if by magic in one place – as so often happens in the case of men marrying in their wife's parish without any hint of where they are 'from' – then this is often where a research block appears. In such cases you will have to build a hypothesis based on what you already know about the possible migrant from his life and the place and time in which he first appears, and then research your hypothesis to see whether it fits. You may need to do this several times as you eliminate likely starting places.

It is vitally important that you draw out all the details already known for certain, with specific places and dates. Gather every possible bit of evidence for this person, however small, and produce a timeline to help clarify your thinking before you start researching an origin.

Your hypothesis will be based around the known facts concerning the individual, which could include occupation, dates, name, parish of marriage, names of their children. For example, an agricultural labourer who appears in a village parish in the late seventeenth or early eighteenth century is most likely to have come from within a day's walk. Therefore, the first searches should concentrate on parishes within a day's walk, bearing in mind that topography may have played a part, so consider roads in and out, and other transport routes such as rivers, canals and the sea. As people did walk long distances and think nothing of it, this might mean extending a search outwards from the place of arrival for 20 or 30 miles, although you should start within a 15-mile radius. What does a survey of the records of the surrounding parishes within a 15-mile radius tell you? If there are any parish registers that are not online, or indexed, then prioritize those.

In these cases that are not obviously solved by parish record indexes, or by the records of settlement, then a far more complex set of hypotheses and actions has to be brought into play. First, make a study of the place he or she arrived in, placed into its historical context. Thus for a labourer who appears in a town, it would be necessary to find out what was happening in the town around the date he arrived – for instance, what were the opportunities for employment? What were the routes in at that time, and is it possible to find out from which direction most other migrants had come? How old might they have been when they moved? Could this person have made a number of short jumps from an original place?

How would this person have arrived in the area? Where did they settle in later life, and among whom? Are they in a community of people who all work in the same industry or come from the same place? What were the possible 'pull' factors for the area? Are there other migrants into that place, is it possible to find out where they are from? Does the surname tell you anything about likely origins? For example, is it a name mainly found in one part of the country? Surname surveys for less common names can be surprisingly effective in giving useful evidence of possible original starting points.

Were there any economic factors (regionally or nationally) that might have come into play at this time, such as harvest failures, or economic depression? What enclosures were happening in the locality? Or could this person be a discharged soldier or a deserter from the Napoleonic wars?

Consider whether the problem is not the case of a single man moving, but could in fact be a whole family moving together: perhaps your ancestor came into a new area as a child, not an adult. Possibly they were baptised further away, but it was their parents who were the immigrants.

If the mystery involves someone who is educated or more obviously well-to-do than the average agricultural labourer, then the net and the hypotheses will be far wider. In these cases, it is more likely that occupational records will help.

Starting Points for the Researcher

There are few records that will confirm for certain that migration from one place to another has taken place. The most obvious records are settlement certificates, settlement examinations and removal orders created by the Poor Law system, which should certainly be sought out in the parish Poor Law records held at the county record office. Of these, the most illuminating are normally the examinations.

Local newspapers are also a good place to hunt for issues relating to settlement laws among the reports of petty sessions and quarter sessions. If the surname is a common one, often an online newspaper search would bring too many results, therefore try searching for the surname, plus 'sessions', plus the likely county.

Newspapers are also a good source for advertisements for jobs, farm tenancies, or for the sale of businesses in the place of arrival. In these cases you may need to read the local newspapers around a certain date in order to pick up clues. Advertisements for land opportunities abroad can be very instructive, and newspapers may also help you pick up which market towns had hiring fairs.

Most other records will hold the information not as evidence of movement *per se*, but indirectly, due to recording the place of birth. Thus any apprenticeship indentures that exist (such as those for the City of London livery companies) will help pinpoint the place of origin of incoming apprentices. Occupational and university records may help – for example, anyone who was a clergyman needed a degree from Oxford or Cambridge, and alumni lists are available online that often give good detail of family origins.

Records of the humble soldier may not always list his place of birth, however, if you can find his recruitment place, then you can infer that as a likely starting hypothesis. If your own ancestor did not have any of these occupations, then perhaps a brother did, so searching down information for all siblings can provide evidence of a parish of origin.

Contemporary maps are a vital tool in determining likely transport routes. Don't expect the road system to be the same as for modern roads, as there are simply many, many more roads today. As far as your ancestor was concerned, find out where the roads, rivers, canals or railway were situated. How far could he or she likely travel in a day? Locate the nearest market town or local place of industry or significance.

Doing a surname survey may help you to pinpoint the likely origin of a surname, and from there a possible direction of travel. The Guild of One Name Studies (https://one-name.org) is a good place to learn more about surnames, and what their study can reveal. Membership is very good value, and you will find yourself in good genealogical company.

Famine and mortality crises can be explored by anyone using a selection of years in the parish registers of a single parish, or even better by comparing several parishes in a region. Are there years when burials were abnormally high? Can known epidemics be discounted? What was happening with food prices at the same time? Do past weather events explain any movements? Local history and wide background reading will help you to build up a picture that could prove informative.

If the migrant is found in a country town, then movement into the town is most likely to have been from the sphere of influence of that town – so what are the main routes into town? Concentrate your first searches in parishes up to 15 miles away along the most obvious routes. When those have all been searched, then consider widening the search.

The census reports at Histpop and Vision of Britain have much valuable information about migration around Britain, and also the numbers of emigrants to other countries.

As with other types of research block, the only truly reliable method of solving mysteries comes from full family reconstruction, working with as many documentary sources together as possible, using all available records, exploring all angles, and building many collateral or sideways trees in order to proceed further back on the main line. A very helpful book to get you started on this is Andrew Todd's *Family History Nuts and Bolts* (2015).[131] My book *Genealogy: Essential Research Methods* (2012) will also help you problem solve.

Conclusion

As we end our research journey with a deep consideration of communities, populations and migrations, it may seem as if we have come a long way from the baptism of new-born Thomas Berd recorded in the parish registers in Bredhurst in 1577 in Chapter 2. Many genealogists will agree that an individual small event – one person in one place at a certain date – can spark the most interesting diversions into how and where an ancestor lived and worked.

While we might never be able to answer some questions – such as how they felt, or why they moved here or there – it is only by fully placing them into a framework and the context of their neighbours and day-to-day life that we are ever going to come close to discovering more about them.

All the records discussed in this book can be used to find individuals, as well as to discover and reconstruct whole villages and communities. By seeking out and reading probate inventories for everyone from a place, to reading the whole of a parish register rather than just the entries that directly concern your own family, you can build an instructive picture of a place. Use the census for more than just your own family, and you will discover a statistical tool that may also shed direct light on your family and their circumstances. Use both manorial rental rolls and find out about customs, to make great sense of life as it was really lived. Use parish registers, and don't forget to also find out about glebe terriers, tithe and enclosure.

Above all, never forget the sheer complexity of the great patchwork quilt that is the historic past: consider the ways in which places differ from each other, also that there is no such thing as a typical village dweller, any more than there is a typical village – there are only your ancestors living in their village.

APPENDIX
Dates of Interest

1066 – William the Conqueror
1072 – Church courts created
1086 – Domesday Book
1167 – Very first known churchwardens' accounts
1509 – Accession of Henry VIII
1532 – Break with Rome and English Reformation starts
1535 – Henry VIII surveys church livings
1536–41 – Dissolution of the Monastries
1536 – Parishes to provide for the 'impotent' poor
1538 – Parish registers start
1547 – Accession of Edward VI
1550 – Population of England estimated to be around 2.8 million
1553 – Accession of Queen Mary, England returns to Catholicism
1554 – Reign of Philip and Mary starts
1555 – Repair of highways to be the responsibility of the parish
1558 – Accession of Elizabeth I, Protestantism reinstated
1559 – Act of Uniformity, punishment of recusants and nonconformists
1566 – Churchwardens required to destroy vermin by statute
1571 – Survey of church land leads to glebe terriers. Statute to enforce wearing of woollen caps on Sunday
1572 – Parishes to appoint overseers of the poor
1578 – Spanish Armada
1590 – Terms of reference for quarter sessions laid down
1597 – Parish overseers to be appointed by JPs, first transportation of criminals
1598 – The Canterbury Commission, parish registers to be on parchment, thus starting a copying-out of previous entries; formal bishops' transcripts start
1600s – Slow decline starts of the courts leet and court baron; only 27 per cent of land still common land

1601 – Great Poor Law Act, payment of parish rates becomes compulsory
1603 – Accession of James I
1609 – Official start of the Plantation of Ulster
1620 – The *Mayflower* sails for America
1625 – Accession of Charles I
1641–42 – Protestation returns
1642 – English Civil War starts
1650 – Church relaxes baptism to fourteen days after birth
1653–1660 – The Commonwealth period, gaps in records
1660 – Restoration of Monarchy with Charles II, final sweeping away of the old feudalism, no new copyholds to be created
1662 – Act of Settlement and Removal, first hearth tax
1665 – Widespread plague
1676 – Compton Census, the ecclesiastical census
1685 – Accession of James II
1689 – Accession of William and Mary
1689 – The vestry given the right to make byelaws, final hearth tax
1691 – Amending Act to the Great Poor Law
1694 – Accession of William III
1702 – Accession of Anne
1714 – Accession of George I
1723 – Knatchbull's Act: parishes to provide workhouses
1727 – Accession of George II
1730 – Agricultural depression starts, lasts until 1750
1733 – All legal documents from now on to be in English, not Latin
1738 – Wesleyan revival
1750s – Canal mania
1750 – Agrarian and industrial revolutions accelerate
1750 – Enclosure of common land accelerates
1753 – Hardwicke's Marriage Act
1760 – Accession of George III
1770s – Increasing popularity of parliamentary enclosure of common land and smaller fields
1770s – Acceleration of new local newspapers being published
1776 – Transportation to America ends with loss of America colonies, Australia sought as alternative
1780 – Sunday Schools start to appear
1781 – Population of England estimated at 7.2 million
1795 – Removal curtailed to only those chargeable to a parish

1795 – Speenhamland system of subsidy for paupers' wages from parish rates
1801 – The first census year: already one-third of the population living in a town, total population 8.6 million
1803 – Napoleonic Wars, military expansion
1811 – Census year
1813 – Rose's Act introduced, printed forms for baptisms and burials
1815 – End of Napoleonic Wars, military contraction
1820 – Accession of George IV
1821 – Census year
1825 – Railways start
1830 – Accession of William IV, swing riots start
1831 – Census year
1831 – Samuel Lewis publishes his first topographical dictionary
1834 – New Poor Law
1836 – Great Tithe Act
1837 – Accession of Victoria
1837 – Civil registration begins
1840s – Railway building accelerates
1841 – Census year
1851 – Census year, more than 50 per cent of the English living in towns and cities
1852 – Copyhold Act, copyholders could demand enfranchisement
1858 – Probate becomes civil, no longer under jurisdiction of the church
1861 – Census year
1870s – Great Depression
1870 – National Education Act
1871 – Census year, population 21.5 million
1873 – Return of Owners of Land, reissued 1883
1880 – Compulsory education
1881 – Census year
1888 – Local Government Act removes the quarter sessions
1891 – Census year, primary education becomes free
1891 – Tithe Act
1899 – Foundation of the Victoria County History
1901 – Census year, population 30.8 million
1901 – Accession of Edward VII
1910 – Survey of land, known as the Lloyd George Survey
1911 – Census year
1922 – Copyhold Act

Sources

Parliamentary Papers

Commission on Employment of Children, Young Persons and Women in Agriculture (1867), Tremenheere, H. Seymour. (186870). *Report(s: with appendices)*. London: printed by G.E. Eyre and W. Spotteswoode, for H.M. Stationery Office, London 1868–70, 7 vols. https://catalog.hathitrust.org/Record/100697059

Home Office (1835) *Education enquiry: Abstract of the answers and returns made pursuant to an address of the House of commons, dated 24th May 1833. England [and Wales]*. 3 Vols. (London, 1835) https://catalog.hathitrust.org/Record/001882253

1801, Census Report, Enumeration Abstract, Hertford, pp.137–141

1811, Census Report, Enumeration Abstract, Hertford, pp.130–133

1821, Census Report, Enumeration Abstract, Hertford, pp.128–132

1831, Census Report, Enumeration Abstract, Part 1, Hertford, pp.244–251

1841, Census Report, Enumeration Abstract, England, Hertford, pp.119–123

1861, Census Report, Population Tables, Vol 1. Division IV, Eastern, Essex, p.341

1861, Census Report, Population Tables, Vol 1. Division III, South Midland, Herts, p.296

online at: http://www.histpop.org

Manuscript Sources

The National Archives

King's Bench affidavits: KB 1/17/6

King's Bench rule books: KB 21/40

Tithe maps: IR 30/17/48

Tithe apportionments: IR 29/8/12

Tithe files: IR 18/3526

Criminal registers England and Wales: HO27/50 p.338

Census of England and Wales:
1841 Datchworth, HO 107/436/6
1851 Datchworth, HO 107/1711
1861 Datchworth, RG 9/822
1891 Datchworth, RG 12/1109
1911 Datchworth, RG 14/7617
1851 Bredhurst, HO 107/1618/72 p.3
1861 Bredhurst, RG9/504/55 p.3
1911 Bredhurst, RG 14/4163
1851 High Abbotside, HO 107/2380
1911 High Abbotside, RG 14/29448

Cheshire Record Office
Cheshire tithe maps online: https://maps.cheshireeast.gov.uk/tithemaps/

Cumbria Archive Centre, Carlisle
Kendal Court Book 1736–1747, D/Lons/L5/2/11/117

East Sussex Record Office
East Blatchington, St Peter, Composite Register, PAR 248/1/1
Rotherfield, St Denys, Composite Register PAR 465/1/1
Baptisms PAR 465/1/2, Marriages PAR 465/1/3, Burials PAR 465/1/5
Overseers of the poor, monthly relief request books: PAR 465/7/7
ditto: PAR 465/7/10
Overseers of the Poor, ledgers concerning paupers: PAR 465/8/7
Uckfield Union Indoor Relief, G11/19/8

Essex Record Office
Earl's Colne, settlement examinations DP/209/13/4, transcribed and from https://wwwe.lib.cam.ac.uk/earls_colne/poor/12201932.htm, accessed on 18 August 2020

Hertfordshire Archives
Catalogue: http://calm.hertfordshire.gov.uk
Datchworth Vestry Book: DP/33/8/1
Datchworth Overseers Accounts: DP/33/12/2
Datchworth Parish Registers: Composite Register DP 33/1/2, accessed at Findmypast: https://www.findmypast.co.uk/

Kent Archaeological Society
Tithe apportionment, Bredhurst:
https://www.kentarchaeology.org.uk/research/tithes/bredhurst (accessed 17 September 2020)

Lichfield Record Office

Will and inventory of John Beachcroft, Consistory Court 2 May 1579 Ref: 168

London Metropolitan Archives

Walworth, St Peter, Ref: *p92/pet1/006,* Ancestry.com. *London, England, Church of England Births and Baptisms, 1813–1917* (database on-line, accessed 28 September 2020)

Rate books: London Borough of Sutton, Beddington Highway Rate 1793–1802 Ancestry.com. Sutton, Surrey, England, Tax Collection Rate Books, 1783–1914 (database online)

Medway Archives

Bredhurst, St Peter, Composite Register, 1546–1701[1789] Ref: P44/1/1 & Composite Register 1706–1791 P44/1/2. Accessed via City Ark online 28 September 2020 https://cityark.medway.gov.uk/Details/archive/110000345

Warwickshire Archives

Coughton, Churchwardens Accounts, 1729

Online at https://www.ourwarwickshire.org.uk/content/article/churchwardens-account-book-coughton-1729

Newspapers

Derby Mercury, 28 September 1744, 3 February 1769, 9 June 1769

Hastings and St Leonard Observer, 31 May 1884

Ipswich Journal, 18 April 1747

Kentish Gazette, 23 May 1786, 22 February 1769, 14 August 1838

Preston Chronicle, 26 March 1842

Sussex Advertiser, February 1758, November 1830, 20 April 1835

West Kent Guardian, 2 April 1836, 29 July 1848

Worcester Journal, 9 December 1830

Yorkshire Gazette, 20 October 1838

Articles, Books

Arkell, Tom, Evans, Nesta and Goose, Nigel *When Death Us Do Part, understanding and interpreting the probate records of early modern England* (Leopards Head Press, 2000).

Armstrong, Alan *Farmworkers, A Social and Economic History 1770–1980* (Batsford, 1988).

Baggs, A.P. and Siraut, M.C. 'Over Stowey: Economic History', in *A History of the County of Somerset: Volume 6, Andersfield, Cannington, and North Petherton Hundreds (Bridgwater and Neighbouring Parishes)*, ed. R.W. Dunning and C.R. Elrington (London, 1992), pp.165–168.

British History Online http://www.british-history.ac.uk/vch/som/vol6/pp165–168 (accessed 22 June 2020).

Beech, Geraldine and Mitchell, Rose eds., *Maps for the Family and Local History: The Records of the Tithe, Valuation Office, and National Farm Surveys of England and Wales, 1836–1943* (Dundurn, 2nd Revised edition 2004)

Bevan, Amanda *Tracing your Ancestors in The National Archives* (The National Archives, 7th edition, 2006).

Bindoff, S.T. *Tudor England* (The Pelican History of England, 1950).

Brigg, William *The Hertfordshire Genealogist and Antiquary* (3 vols, 1895–1898) Kimpton, Vol. 3, p.120 https://archive.org/stream/hertsgenealogist03brig (accessed 17 December 2018).

Broad, John 'Housing the Rural Poor in Southern England, 1650–1850', *The Agricultural History Review* Vol. 48 No. 2 (2000) pp.151–170.

Cantor, Leonard *The Changing English Countryside 1400–1700* (Routledge & Kegan Paul Ltd, 1987).

Carter, Paul and Thompson, Kate *Sources for Local Historians* (Phillimore, 2005).

Clark, Gregory and Antony 'Common Rights to Land in England 1475–1839', *Journal of Economic History* Vol. 61 (2001) pp.1009–1036.

Christian, Peter and Annal, David, *Census the Expert Guide* (The National Archives, 2008)

Cobbett, William, *Rural Rides* (1st published 1830, Penguin Classics, 2001)

Cockett, Roger A.C. *The Early History of Bredhurst Manor*, Kent Archaeological Society website http://www.kentarchaeology.org.uk/Research/01/BRH/02.htm (accessed 31 December 2018).

Cockin, Tim C. H., *The Parish Atlas of England* (Malthouse Press, 2017)

Collinge, J.M. (ed.) *Office-Holders in Modern Britain: Volume 9, Officials of Royal Commissions of Inquiry 1815–1870* (London: University of London, 1984). *British History Online.* 25 September 2020. http://www.british-history.ac.uk/office-holders/vol9.

Coward, Barry *Social Change and Continuity in Early Modern England 1550–1750* (Longman, 1988).

Cox, J.C. *The Parish Registers of England* (Methuen, 1910).

Crompton, Catherine A. 'An exploration of the craft and trade structure of two Hertfordshire villages, 1851–1891: an application of nominal record linkage to directories and census enumerators' books, *The Local Historian* Vol. 28, No. 3, August 1998.

Darby, H.C. 'The Age of the Improver: 1600–1800' in *A New Historical Geography of England after 1600* (Cambridge University Press, 1976) p.21, p.56.

Ecton, J. and Bacon, J. (1786) *Liber regis, vel, Thesaurus rerum ecclesiasticarum: with an appendix, containing proper directions and precedents relating to presentations, institutions, inductions, dispensations, &c.* London: Printed for the author by John Nichols and sold by J.F. and

C. Rivington (etc). The Hathi Trust: http://catalog.hathitrust.org/Record/000704611 (accessed 17 September 2020).

Edwards, Peter *Rural Life, Guide to Local Records* (Batsford, 1993).

Elton, G.R. *England 1200–1640* (Hodder & Stoughton, 1969).

Evans, Francis T. 'Roads, Railways and Canals, Technical Choices in 19th Century Britain' in *Technology and Culture* (Vol. 22, 1981).

Evans, George Ewart *Ask the Fellows Who Cut the Hay*, (1st published 1965, Faber & Faber, 2018)

Falvey, Heather ed., *Hertfordshire Population Statistics 1563 to 1801* (2nd edition) First edition by Lionel Munby (1964); updated by Heather Falvey, (Hertfordshire Record Society, 2019)

Few, Janet *Putting Your Ancestors in their Place: A Guide to One-Place Studies* (The Family History Partnership, 2014)

Foster's *Alumni Oxoniensis 1500–1714*. Online at British History: https://www.british-history.ac.uk/alumni-oxon/1500-1714.

Goose, Nigel 'Farm Service in Southern England in the mid Nineteenth Century', *Local Population Studies*, No. 72, Spring 2004.

Gottlieb, Beatrice *The Family in the Western World from the Black Death to the Industrial Age* (Oxford University Press, 1993).

Gray, I.E. and Gaydon, A.T. *Gloucestershire Quarter Sessions Archives 1660–1889* (Gloucester County Council, 1958).

Grey, Edwin *Cottage Life in a Hertfordshire Village* (Harpenden and District Local History Society, 1977)

Hardy, William John *Hertford County Records, Notes and Extracts from the Sessions Rolls 1581–1698* Vol. 1 (Hertfordshire County Council, 1905) p.101 (accessed online 25 September 2020: https://catalog.hathitrust.org/Record/000275228).

Harrington, Duncan (ed.) *Kent Hearth tax – Lady Day 1664* (British Record Society and Kent Archaeological Society, 2000).

Harvey, P.D.A. *Manorial Records* (British Records Association, Archives and the User No 5, rev. ed. 1999).

Hasted, Edward 'Parishes: Bredhurst' in *The History and Topographical Survey of the County of Kent: Volume 5* (Canterbury: W. Bristow, 1798), pp.585–590. *British History Online*, accessed 28 September 2020, http://www.british-history.ac.uk/survey-kent/vol5/pp585-590.

Hastings, R.P. *Essays in North Riding History 1780–1850* (North Yorkshire County Record Office Publications No. 28, 1981).

Hawkings, David T., *Pauper Ancestors: A Guide to the Records created by the Poor Laws in England and Wales* (The History Press, 2011)

Herber, Mark D. *Ancestral Trails* (Sutton, reprint 1998).

Hey, David *Family History and Local History in England* (Longman, 1987)

Hey, David *Journeys in Family History* (National Archives Books, 2004).

Hey, David (ed.) *The Oxford Companion to Family and Local History* (Oxford University Press, 2nd ed. 2008).

Higginbottam, Peter *The New Poor Law* from http://www.workhouses.org.uk/poorlaws/newpoorlaw.shtml (accessed 15 July 2019).

Higgs, Edward *A Clearer Sense of the Census* (Public Record Office Handbook, London HMSO, 1996).

Hind, Robert J. 'Elementary Schools in Nineteenth-Century England: Their Social and Historiographical Contexts' *Historical Reflections / Réflexions Historiques*, vol. 11, no. 2, 1984, pp.189–205. *JSTOR*, www.jstor.org/stable/41298830.

Hone, Nathaniel J. *The Manor and Manorial Records* (Methuen, 1908)

Howell, Roger '7. Hearth Tax Returns' *History* 49, no. 165 (1964): pp.42–45. www.jstor.org/stable/24404528.

Humphery-Smith, Cecil R. ed., *The Phillimore Atlas and Index of Parish Registers* (Phillimore, 3rd revised edition, 2002)

Jones, Anthea *A Thousand years of the English Parish* (Windrush Press, 2000).

Kain, Roger J.P. 'The Tithe Commutation Surveys in Kent' *Archaeologia Cantiana* Vol. 89, 1974 p.101.

Knödel, Natalie, University of Durham, April 1995, online document accessed 28 September 2020, http://users.ox.ac.uk/~mikef/church.html.

Landau, Norma 'Who Was Subjected to the Laws of Settlement? Procedure under the Settlement Laws in Eighteenth-Century England' *The Agricultural History Review*, Vol. 43, No. 2, 1995.

Laslett, Peter *The World We Have Lost, England Before the Industrial Age* (New York, 3rd revised edition, 1984).

Lee, Laurie *Cider with Rosie* (1st published 1959, Vintage Classics, 2002)

Lewis, Samuel *A Topographical Dictionary of England*, 1848.

Long, Moria H. 'A Study of Occupations in Yorkshire Parish Registers in the Eighteenth and Early Nineteenth centuries' in *Local Population Studies*, 71 (Autumn, 2003).

Lord, Evelyn 'Communities of Common Interest; the Social Landscape of South East Surrey 1750–1850' in *Societies, Cultures and Kinship 1580–1850* ed. Charles Phythian-Adams (Leicester University Press, 1993).

Marshall, Lydia M. 'The Levying of the Hearth Tax, 1662–1688' *The English Historical Review* 51, no. 204 (1936): pp.628–46. www.jstor.org/stable/554438.

Martin, David and Barbara *Old Farm Buildings in Eastern Sussex, 1450–1750* (The Rape of Hastings Architectural Survey, Hastings Area Archaeological Papers, 1982).

Mills, Dennis and Joan 'Farms, farmers and farm workers in the nineteenth-century census enumerators' books: a Lincolnshire case study' in *The Local Historian*, Vol. 27, No. 3 August 1997.

Moore, John S. *Counting People, A DIY Manual for Local and Family Historians* (Oxbow Books, 2013).

Osborn, Helen *Genealogy: Essential Research Methods* (Robert Hale, 2012)

Oxley, Geoffrey W. *Poor Relief in England and Wales 1601–1834* (David & Charles, 1974).

Palmer, John, transcription of *Wirksworth Churchwarden's Accounts 1658–1627* http://www.wirksworth.org.uk/CWA.htm (accessed 17 September 2020).

Phythian-Adams, Charles (ed.) *Societies, Cultures and Kinship, 1580–1850* (Leicester University Press, 1993).

Pickles, M.F. 'Labour Migration: Yorkshire c. 1670 to 1743' in *Local Population Studies 57* (1996) 30.49.

Plomer, William (ed.), *Kilvert's Diary 1870–1879 – Selections from The Diary of The Rev. Francis Kilvert* (Penguin, 1977).

Poole, Anthony 'Baptismal Delay; Some Implications from the Parish registers of Cranbrook and Surrounding Parishes in the Kentish Weald', *Local Population Studies* 65 (2000) pp.9–28.

Porter, Roy *English Society in the Eighteenth Century* (Penguin, revised edition, 1990).

Powell, W.R. (ed.) 'High Laver: Parish government and poor relief' in *A History of the County of Essex: Volume 4, Ongar Hundred* (London, 1956), pp.95–96 http://www.british-history.ac.uk/vch/essex/vol4/pp95-96 (accessed 20 October 2015).

Probert, Rebecca *Divorced, Bigamist, Bereaved?* (Takeaway Publishing, 2015)

Probert, Rebecca *Marriage Law for Genealogists* (Takeaway Publishing, 2016)

Pryor, Francis *Britain in the Middle Ages* (Harper Perennial, 2007).

Purvis, Thomas L. 'The European Ancestry of the United States Population, 1790: A Symposium' *The William and Mary Quarterly* 41, no. 1 (1984): 85–101. (Accessed 18 September 2020. doi:10.2307/1919209).

Raymond, Stuart A. *Tracing Your Ancestors' Parish Records, a Guide for Family and Local Historians* (Pen & Sword, 2015).

Razzell, Peter 'Evaluating the same-name technique as a way of measuring burial register reliability in England' in *Local Population Studies*, No. 64 Spring 2000 pp.8–22.

Robinson, Maude *A South Down Farm in the 1860s* (Country Books 2004 reprint, original J.M. Dent, 1938).

Roth, Randolph 'Homicide in Early Modern England 1549–1800: The Need for a Quantitative Synthesis' in *Crime, History & Societies* 5, no. 2 (2001): 33–67. Accessed 21 September 2020: http://www.jstor.org/stable/42709842.

Samuel, Raphael 'Quarry roughs: life and labour in Headington Quarry, 1860–1920. An essay in oral history' in *Village Life and Labour*, ed. Raphael Samuel, History Workshop Series (Routledge & Kegan Paul, London 1975).

Samuel, Raphael ed., *Village Life and Labour* (History Workshop Series, Routledge & Kegan Paul Ltd, 1975)

Saxby, Michael J. 'Age at Baptism in the Parish of St Nicholas, Pevensey, 1761–1800' in *Local Population Studies* No. 61 (Autumn 1998).

Sayles, G.O. *Medieval Foundations of England* (Methuen, 1950).

Stamp, L. Dudley 'The Common Lands and Village Greens of England and Wales' in *The Geographical Journal* Vol. 130, No. 4 (December 1964) pp.457–468.

Steel, Don J. *National Index of Parish Registers Volume 1, General Sources of Births, Marriages and Deaths before 1837* (Society of Genealogists, 3rd edition, 1980).

Tate, W.E. ed., *A Domesday of English Parliamentary Enclosure Acts and Awards* (University of Reading, 1978)

Tate, W.E. *The Parish Chest* (Phillimore, 3rd edition, 1983).

The Readers Digest: https://www.sabre-roads.org.uk, accessed 24 August 2020.

Thirsk, Joan 'The Content and Sources of English Agrarian History after 1500', *Agricultural History Review* Vol. 3, No. 2, 1955 pp.66–79.

Thompson, Flora *Lark Rise to Candleford*, (1st published 1939, Penguin Modern Classics, 2008)

Tiller, Kate *English Local History, an Introduction* (Sutton, revised edition, 2002).

Todd, Andrew *Family History Nuts and Bolts, Problem-Solving through Family Reconstitution Techniques* (3rd edition, Allen & Todd, 2015).

Walker, Jane (ed.) *Datchworth Tithe Accounts 1711–1747* (Hertfordshire Record Publications Volume 25, 2009).

Waller, Ian H. *My Ancestor was an Agricultural Labourer* (Society of Genealogists Enterprises, 2007).

West, John *Village Records* (Macmillan, 1962).

West Sussex Record Office, Billingshurst Churchwardens' Accounts Ref: Par/21/9: Catalogue description, online at https://discovery.nationalarchives.gov.uk (accessed 17 September 2020).

West Sussex Record Office, West Dean Churchwardens' Accounts Par/65/12/1 Catalogue description, online at https://discovery.nationalarchives.gov.uk (accessed 17 September 2020).

Winchester, Angus 'Parish Township and Tithing' in *The Local Historian* Vol. 27, No. 1, February 1997.

Wood, Michael *The Story of England* (Penguin Books, 2010).

Wrightson, Keith *Earthly Necessities, Economic Lives in Early Modern Britain, 1470–1750* (Penguin Books, 2002).

Wrigley, E.A., Davies, R.S., Oeppen, J.E. and Schofield, R.S. *English Population History from Family Reconstitution* (Cambridge University Press, 1997).

Yates, E.M. 'The Evolution of the English Village', *The Geographical Journal* Vol. 148, No. 2 (July 1982) pp.182–202.

Young, The Rev. Arthur *General View of the Agriculture of the County of Sussex* (1813, David & Charles Reprints edition, 1970).

Notes and References

1 John West, *Village Records* (Macmillan, 1962).

2 Peter Edwards, *Rural Life, Guide to Local Records* (Batsford, 1993).

3 Samuel Lewis's *A Topographical Dictionary of England* is available in a number of different editions; 1831 and 1848 are commonly available online.

4 Kate Tiller, *English Local History, an Introduction* (Sutton, rev. ed., 2002) p.58.

5 S.T. Bindoff, 'Tudor England', *The Pelican History of England* (1950).

6 E.A. Wrigley, R.S. Davies, J.E. Oeppen and R.S. Schofield, *English Population History from Family Reconstitution* (CUP, 1997), p.614.

7 Michael Wood, *The Story of England* (Penguin, 2010) p.258.

8 Leonard Cantor, *The Changing English Countryside 1400–1700* (Routledge & Kegan Paul Ltd, 1987).

9 Barry Coward, *Social Change and Continuity in Early Modern England 1550–1750*, (Longman, 1988) pp.53–4.

10 'Brede–Brent-Tor', in *A Topographical Dictionary of England*, ed. Samuel Lewis (London: S. Lewis, 1848), pp.353–357. *British History Online*, accessed 28 September 2020, http://www.british-history.ac.uk/topographical-dict/england/pp.353–357.

11 'Datchworth–Dean, West', in *A Topographical Dictionary of England*, ed. Samuel Lewis (London: S Lewis, 1848), pp.15–23. *British History Online*, accessed 28 September 2020, http://www.british-history.ac.uk/topographical-dict/england/pp.15–23.

12 'Abbas-Combe–Aberystwith', in *A Topographical Dictionary of England*, ed. Samuel Lewis (London: S. Lewis, 1848), pp.1–5. *British History Online*, accessed September 28, 2020, http://www.british-history.ac.uk/topographical-dict/england/pp.1–5.

13 Edward Hasted, 'Parishes: Bredhurst', in *The History and Topographical Survey of the County of Kent: Volume 5* (Canterbury: W. Bristow, 1798), pp.585–590. *British History Online*, accessed 28 September 2020, http://www.british-history.ac.uk/survey-kent/vol5/pp.585–590.

14 Natalie Knödel, University of Durham. April 1995, online document accessed 28 September 2020 http://users.ox.ac.uk/~mikef/church.html_

15 Medway Archives: Bredhurst, St Peter, Composite Register, 1546–1701[1789] Ref: P44/1/1 Accessed via City Ark online 28/09/20 https://cityark.medway.gov.uk/Details/archive/110000345

16 Don J. Steel (1980), *National Index of Parish Registers Volume 1* 'General Sources of Births Marriages and Deaths before 1837' (Society of Genealogists, 3rd edition 1976, reprinted 1980).

17 Don J. Steel (1980).

18 J.C. Cox, *The Parish Registers of England* (1910).

19 Peter Razzell, 'Evaluating the same-name technique as a way of measuring burial register reliability in England' (*Local Population Studies,* No. 64 Spring 2000 pp.8–22.

20 Razzell (2000).

21 Bredhurst is odd, being in the Rochester archdeaconry and yet ruled by the Consistory Court of Canterbury; therefore both courts might have to be searched for records.

22 Don J. Steel (1980), p.167 ff.

23 Peter Laslett, *The World We Have Lost, England Before the Industrial Age* (New York, 3rd revised edition, 1984) p.112.

24 Michael J. Saxby, 'Age at Baptism in the Parish of St Nicholas, Pevensey 1761–1800' in *Local Population Studies* No. 61 (Autumn 1998).

25 Anthony Poole, Baptismal Delay; Some Implications from the Parish registers of Cranbrook and Surrounding Parishes in the Kentish Weald, *Local Population Studies* 65 (2000) pp.9–28.

26 *Bredhurst, St Peter, Composite Register*, 1546–1701 [1789].

27 Laslett (1984) p.116.

28 Medway Archives, *Bredhurst Composite Register*, 1706–1791 P44/1/2, accessed via City Ark cityark.medway.gov.uk, date 22/09/20.

29 East Sussex Record Office, *East Blatchington, St Peter, Composite Register*: PAR 248/1/1.

30 Medway Archives, *Bredhurst Parish Register*'s description: https://cityark.medway.gov.uk/Details/archive/110000345

31 *See*, for example, David Hey (ed.), *Oxford Companion to Family History* p.72, and the work of Charles Phythian-Adams.

32 G.O. Sayles, *Medieval Foundations of England* (Methuen, 1950) p.244 ff.

33 Inheritance by the youngest may be because it was believed that the youngest would be the most likely to need support, or to be destitute if not given support. It was a Saxon custom and therefore found in places where Saxon influence was still strong after the Norman Conquest.

34 Roger A.C. Cockett, *The Early History of Bredhurst Manor*, 2012, on the Kent Archaeological Society website https://www.kentarchaeology.org.uk/Research/01/BRH/02.htm (accessed 22 September 2020).

35 Cumbria Archive Centre: Kendal Court Book 1736–1747, D/Lons/L5/2/11/117.

36 Possibly a local word.

37 A fee customary to this manor.

38 L. Dudley Stamp, 'The Common Lands and Village Greens of England and Wales', *The Geographical Journal*, Vol. 130, No. 4 (Dec. 1964), pp.457–468.

39 Gregory and Antony Clark, 'Common Rights to Land in England 1475–1839', *Journal of Economic History* Vol. 61 (2001), pp.1009–1036.

40 Lichfield Record Office, Consistory Court, 2 May 1579, Will and Inventory, Ref: 168.

41 E.M. Yates, 'The Evolution of the English Village' *Royal Geographical Society* Vol. 148, No. 2, July 1982, pp.182–202.

42 *Yorkshire Gazette*, 20 October 1838.

43 Ecton, J. and Bacon, J. (1786). *Liber regis, vel, Thesaurus rerum ecclesiasticarum: with an appendix, containing proper directions and precedents relating to presentations, institutions, inductions, dispensations, &c.* London\: printed for the author by John Nichols and sold by J. F. and C. Rivington [etc.]. The Hathi Trust: http://catalog.hathitrust.org/Record/000704611 (accessed 17 September 2020).

44 Anthea Jones, *A Thousand Years of the English Parish* (Windrush, 2000) p.152.

45 W.E. Tate, *The Parish Chest* (Phillimore, 3rd edition, 1983) p.126; and Jane Walker (ed.), *Datchworth Tithe Accounts 1711–1747*, Hertfordshire Record Publications Volume 25, 2009, p.xxxvii.

46 Hertfordshire Archives Catalogue: http://calm.hertfordshire.gov.uk

47 William Brigg, ed., *The Hertfordshire Genealogist and Antiquary* (3 vols, 1895–1898), Kimpton, Vol. 3, p.120 https://archive.org/stream/hertsgenealogist03brig (accessed 17 December 2018).

48 Brigg, *King's Langley*, Vol. 3, p.184.

49 Walker (2009).

50 Tate (1983) p.137–8.

51 The National Archives, Tithe Maps: IR 30/17/48.

52 TNA: IR 18/3526.

53 Jones (2000), p.159.

54 Kent Archaeological Society: https://www.kentarchaeology.org.uk/research/tithes/bredhurst (accessed 17 September 2020).

55 Roger J.P. Kain, 'The Tithe Commutation Surveys in Kent', *Archaeologia Cantiana*, Vol. 89, 1974, p.101.

56 TNA: IR 29/8/12 accessed via *The Genealogist.*

57 Kilvert's diary 1870–1879, *Selections from the Diary of The Rev. Francis Kilvert*, ed. William Plomer (one vol. edition, Penguin, 1977) p.34.

58 Tate (1983), p.140.

59 Walker (2009).

60 West Sussex Record Office, *Billingshurst Churchwarden's Accounts* Ref: Par/21/9: Catalogue description, online at https://discovery.nationalarchives.gov.uk (accessed 17 September 2020).

61 John Palmer, transcription of Wirksworth Churchwarden's Accounts 1658–1627 http://www.wirksworth.org.uk/CWA.htm (accessed 17 September 2020).

62 'High Laver: Parish government and poor relief', in *A History of the County of Essex: Volume 4, Ongar Hundred*, ed. W.R. Powell (London, 1956), pp.95–96 http://www.british-history.ac.uk/vch/essex/vol4/pp95-96 (accessed 20 October 2015).

63 Walker, (2009).

64 West Sussex Record Office, Catalogue, West Dean, Par/65/12/1.

65 Randolph Roth, 'Homicide in Early Modern England 1549–1800; the need for a Quantitative Synthesis', *Crime History and Societies*, 2001, Vol. 5, No. 2, p.33 https://www.jstor.org/stable/42709842 (accessed 20 September 2020).

66 Laslett (1984), p. 129.

67 *Sussex Advertiser*, February 1758.

68 Essex Record Office, *Earl's Colne Settlement Examinations*, DP/209/13/4, transcribed and from the https://wwwe.lib.cam.ac.uk/earls_colne/poor/12201932.htm, accessed on 18 August 2020.

69 I.E. Gray and A.T. Gaydon, *Gloucestershire Quarter Sessions Archives 1660–1889* (Gloucester County Council, 1958).

70 TNA, King's Bench, KB 1/17/6.

71 *Derby Mercury*, Friday 3 February 1769.

72 *Derby Mercury*, 9 June 1769.

73 William John Hardy, *Hertford County Records, Notes and Extracts from the Sessions Rolls 1581–1698* Vol. 1 (Hertfordshire County Council, 1905) p.101 (accessed online 25 September 2020) https://catalog.hathitrust.org/Record/000275228).

74 ESRO, Rotherfield Parish Registers PAR 465.

75 Rev. Arthur Young, *General View of the Agriculture of the County of Sussex* (1813, David & Charles Reprints edition, 1970) pp.436–7.

76 Young (1813), p.22.

77 *Sussex Advertiser*, November 1830.

78 ESRO: PAR465/7/7.

79 ESRO: PAR465/7/10.

80 *Sussex Advertiser*, 20 April 1835, TNA: Home Office: HO 27/50 p338.

81 ESRO: PAR465/8/7.

82 ESRO: *Uckfield Union Indoor Relief*, G11/19/8.

83 *Hastings and St Leonard Observer*, 31 May 1884.

84 *West Kent Guardian*, 29 July 1848.

85 Catherine A. Crompton, 'An exploration of the craft and trade structure of two Hertfordshire villages, 1851–1891': an application of nominal record linkage to directories and census enumerators' books, *The Local Historian*, Vol. 28, No. 3, August 1998.

86 Evelyn Lord, *Communities of common Interest; the social Landscape of South East Surrey 1750–1850* in *Societies Cultures and Kinship 1580–1850*, ed. Charles Phythian-Adams (Leicester University Press, 1993).

87 Crompton (1998).

88 Denis and Joan Mills, 'Farms, farmers and far works in the nineteenth-century census enumerators' books: a Lincolnshire case study', in *The Local Historian* Vol. 27. No. 3 (August 1997).

89 Poole (2000).

90 Victoria County History of Somerset: A.P. Baggs and M.C. Siraut, 'Over Stowey: Economic History' in *A History of the County of Somerset: Volume 6, Andersfield, Cannington, and North Petherton Hundreds (Bridgwater and Neighbouring Parishes)*, ed. R.W. Dunning and C.R. Elrington (London 1992) pp.165-168. *British History Online* http://www.british-history.ac.uk/vch/som/vol6/pp165-168 (accessed 22 June 2020).

91 Raphael Samuel, 'Quarry roughs: life and labour in Headington Quarry, 1860–1920'. An essay in oral history, in *Village Life and Labour*, ed. Raphael Samuel, History Workshop Series (Routledge & Kegan Paul, London 1975).

92 Mills (1997)

93 Edward Higgs, *A Clearer Sense of the Census* (Public Record Office Handbook, London HMSO, 1996), p.105.

94 Peter H. Lindert, 'English Occupations 1670–1811', *The Journal of Economic History* Vol. 40, No. 4 (December 1980), pp.685–712.

95 Maude Robinson, *A Southdown Farm in the 1860s* (Country Books edition, 2004, first pub. J.M. Dent, 1938) p.14.

96 Edwin Grey, *Cottage Life in a Hertfordshire Village* (St Albans, 1935, reprinted 1974) p.57, 59–62.

97 Robinson (2004), p.14.

98 Robinson (2004), p.24.

99 *Kentish Gazette*, Tuesday 23 May 1786.

100 Alan Armstrong, *Farmworkers, A Social and Economic History 1770–1980* (Batsford, 1988) p.28.

101 Yates (1982).

102 Robert J. Hind, 'Elementary Schools in Nineteenth-Century England: Their Social and Historiographical Contexts' *Historical Reflections/ Réflexions Historiques*, vol. 11, no. 2, 1984, pp.189–205. JSTOR, www.jstor.org/stable/41298830.

103 Great Britain. Home Office. (1835). *Education enquiry: Abstract of the answers and returns made pursuant to an address of the House of Commons, dated 24th May 1833. England [and Wales].* 3 Vols. (London, 1835) https://catalog.hathitrust.org/Record/001882253

104 *Abstract of Education Enquiry Returns*, 1833, Yorkshire North Riding, Vol. 3, p.1111.

105 Robinson (2004), p.63.

106 Lindert (1980).

107 *Office-Holders in Modern Britain: Volume 9, Officials of Royal Commissions of Inquiry 1815–1870*. Ed. J.M. Collinge, London: University of London, 1984. *British History Online*. Web. 25 September 2020. http://www.british-history.ac.uk/office-holders/vol9.

108 Lydia M. Marshall, 'The Levying of the Hearth Tax, 1662–1688' *The English Historical Review* 51, no. 204 (1936): 628-46. www.jstor.org/ stable/554438.

109 Duncan Harrington (ed.) *Kent Hearth Tax – Lady Day 1664* (British Record Society and Kent Archaeological Society, 2000).

110 Roger Howell '7. HEARTH TAX RETURNS' *History* 49, no. 165 (1964): 42–45. www.jstor.org/stable/24404528.

111 John S. Moore, *Counting People, A DIY Manual for Local and Family Historians* (Oxbow Books, 2013).

112 Ancestry.com. *Sutton, Surrey, England, Tax Collection Rate Books, 1783–1914* (database on-line). Provo, UT, USA: Ancestry.com Operations, Inc., 2016. Original data: rate books. London Borough of Sutton, Sutton, England, Beddington Highway Rate 1793–1802.

113 Higgs (1996) p.28ff.

114 TNA, *1851 Census of England and Wales*: HO 107/1711 f.8 p.8.

115 Coward (1988) p.6.

116 Norma Landau, 'Who Was Subjected to the Laws of Settlement? Procedure under the Settlement Laws in Eighteenth-Century England', *The Agricultural History Review*, Vol. 43, No. 2, 1995.

117 M.F. Pickles, 'Labour Migration: Yorkshire c. 1670 to 1743', in *Local Population Studies,* 57 (1996) 30.49.

118 Moira H. Long, 'A Study of Occupations in Yorkshire Parish Registers in the Eighteenth and Early Nineteenth Centuries' in *Local Population Studies,* 71 (autumn, 2003).

119 Andrew Todd, *Family History Nuts and Bolts, Problem Solving through Family Reconstitution Techniques* (3rd edition, Allen & Todd, 2015).

120 Todd (2015), p.25.

121 Armstrong (1988), p.110.

122 Armstrong (1988), p.25/6.

123 TNA, *1851 Census of England and Wales*: HO 107/1618/72 p.3 and 1861 Census Ref: RG9/504/55 p.3.

124 London Metropolitan Archives; p92/pet1/006, Ancestry.com. *London, England, Church of England Births and Baptisms, 1813–1917* (database online, accessed 28 September 2020).

125 *The Readers Digest*: https://www.sabre-roads.org.uk (accessed 24 August 2020).

126 Francis T. Evans, 'Roads Railways and Canals, Technical Choices in 19th Century Britain' in *Technology and Culture* Vol. 22, 1981.

127 David Hey, *Oxford Companion to Family and Local History* (2nd ed., 2008), p.371.

128 Purvis, Thomas L. 'The European Ancestry of the United States Population, 1790: A Symposium' *The William and Mary Quarterly* 41, no. 1 (1984): 85–101 (accessed 18 September 2020), doi:10.2307/1919209.

129 Hey (2008).

130 Amanda Bevan, *Tracing your Ancestors in the National Archives* (The National Archives, 7th edition, 2006) p.442.

131 Todd (2015).

Index